Professional Generalism in a Hyper-specialised World

Nektarios Karanikas

Professional Generalism in a Hyper-specialised World

Essential Concepts for Every Professional

Springer

Nektarios Karanikas
Queensland University of Technology
Brisbane, QLD, Australia

ISBN 978-981-96-4038-6   ISBN 978-981-96-4039-3 (eBook)
https://doi.org/10.1007/978-981-96-4039-3

This Springer imprint is published by the registered company Springer Nature Singapore Pte Ltd.
The registered company address is: 152 Beach Road, #21-01/04 Gateway East, Singapore 189721, Singapore

I dedicate this book, my first monograph, to my father and late mother. I owe my education, career, and achievements to the seeds they planted in me and to their unconditional love.

Preface

My inspiration for this book came from observations and experiences across various work environments, interactions with other professionals, and reflections on my practice. I worked with highly skilled and knowledgeable experts. Many wanted to expand their professional outlook and find a way to lead in their field. They sought wise investments for their career and how to identify, harness, and deploy their energy and the energy of others for better outcomes. I realised that one of the obstacles to the above was that several of those professionals could not connect their expertise area with other domains and place it in the bigger picture. While those experts deeply understood their disciplines, they struggled to see their relationships and reliance on other disciplines.

I have worked with engineers with a bright and inventive mind but a strong deductive and deterministic mindset who believed they would devise a technical solution for almost everything. It was not always clear to them that these solutions should work for nearly everyone. Some of those professionals could not easily accept that our world also has stochastic elements beyond Markov processes, and we cannot, or should not, control everything. Some thought we could control everything, yet we have not found the way or developed the technology.

I have met engineers who believe math and science alone explain everything, overlooking the role of other, less well-defined, more fluid disciplines. I came across sharp-minded engineering professionals who rarely reflected on their biases and often viewed the world as a smoothly running machine with occasional hiccups and secrets to discover.

I am lucky to have worked with great managers skilled in business cases, planning, design, and budgeting. However, many were uneasy about diversity and unprepared for the unexpected. Some selectively used expertise to confirm, not challenge, their opinions. I have seen professionals prioritise their own success at the expense of stability and sustainability of other areas around them and they are proud of it. I encountered managers who were obsessed with countable outputs and outcomes and only occasionally and reactively attending to inputs, and rarely looking deeper inside the processes.

My interactions have included collaborating with thought-provoking colleagues with a social science background. Some of them would confidently point the finger at imperfect decisions of engineers and managers and flawed systems without providing solid, tested, and actionable solutions. A few sounded like self-proclaimed judges of everything, some believed they could accurately read and interpret everyone because they had studied human behaviour in various contexts.

I have heard of end-user-focussed monovision approaches that disregard the needs of designers and manufacturers. I have come across academics and professionals from the humanities disciplines who are never satisfied and do not celebrate our constantly improving, still imperfect systems. I have had productive arguments with respected colleagues who cannot fully comprehend the real-world constraints we impose on each other and our systems because of diverse expectations and goals.

The more the expertise of the professionals I have met, the more intense and frequent my observations like the ones mentioned above have been. However, none of those are judgments of professions and disciplines. They could not be because my practice as an engineer, manager, safety and human factors professional, educator, and researcher has not always been inclusive or considerate of multi-, inter-, or trans-disciplinary approaches. Sometimes, my work was so defined that I needed someone else to shake me out of my professional bubble and help me see up and down, left and right, through the centre, and in and out. This realisation often sparked conversations with others and with myself.

The most interesting observation is that almost everyone is trying their best, doing their best, aiming for the best. However, specialised professionals representing diverse disciplines may not be exposed to foundational concepts that transcend disciplines and contributions of specific knowledge fields and can form a discipline-agnostic set of general professional principles. Over time, I also realised that some organisational approaches tend to be compartmentalised, poorly integrated, and inconsiderate of the opportunity to meld multidisciplinary specialities to achieve a functional organisational architecture and sustainably positive outcomes for everyone.

In response to all those pragmatic experiences and observations, at its core, in this book, I suggest an antidote to viewing extreme professional expertise as the sole solution. I argue that *Professional Generalism* is a quality, an approach, and a practice that should exist in parallel with and supplement technical expertise. In this book, while reconciling and blending approaches from different disciplines, I adopt a unique and carefully balanced approach that challenges several prevalent viewpoints in the professional context, introduces innovative and useful concepts for professional practice, and redefines and supplements commonly known principles.

The chapters of this book are products of my professional and inclusive exploration of concepts and frameworks not explicitly mentioned elsewhere in one place. Undoubtedly, you might have read or learned a few foundational concepts through scattered opportunities (e.g., school subjects, university units, industry courses, webinars, or conferences). Still, such concepts are primarily used as transitional to serve the comprehension of more specific topics. The benefits from an inclusive coverage of diverse but fundamental principles are rather reserved for a few highly experienced and multidisciplinary-educated professionals.

This book is for all professionals, regardless of background or experience, whether you are a recent university graduate, seasoned consultant and manager, or accomplished business leader. I aim to motivate you to uncover, consider, and connect with principles beyond your familiar disciplines and identify when and how you could supplement or complement your practice with concepts not appreciated previously. As David Epstein advocates, generalists might find their path later than others but often triumph in our specialised world.[1]

I have included topics that, regardless of specialisation, should consider. I cover fundamental principles that we should ideally be aware of from an early stage. Several of these principles refer to how we position ourselves in the world, and others can be deeply ontological. Indeed, several such concepts could have been shared during formal education. However, this presupposes educators of any role and across all levels (e.g., teachers, mentors, lecturers, coaches, trainers, senior figures), as professionals, would have an appreciation. Nevertheless, despite voices for non-linear thinking in education,[2,3] outdated single-facetted approaches to learning still exist and shape monolithic thinking, breeding generations of linear thinkers who perceive generalism as a weakness rather than a (rare) merit.

Brisbane, Australia Nektarios Karanikas

[1] Epstein, D. (2021). Range: Why Generalists Triumph in a Specialized World. Riverhead Books.

[2] Faul, M. V., & Savage, L. (2023). Systems Thinking in International Education and Development: Unlocking Learning for All? Edward Elgar Publishing.

[3] Lipman, M. (2003). Thinking in Education. (2nd ed.). Cambridge University Press.

Acknowledgements

I wholeheartedly thank and express my gratitude to the following colleagues, friends, and relatives who generously devoted their time to review a draft of this book and suggest improvements.

These professionals supported this book project in their individual capacities. Their engagement as reviewers of this work does not represent any of the organisations with which they have been affiliated.

Prof. Mikela Chatzimichailidou
Master of Engineering (Meng) in Mechanical and Manufacturing Engineering, Master of Science (MSc) in Systems Engineering Management for Civil Infrastructure, Doctor of Philosophy (PhD) in System Safety and Situational Awareness

Mr. Graham Easterby
Graduate of the Australian Federal Police College, Master of Arts (MA) (Justice Studies) in Criminology, Policy and Competing Concepts in the Justice System

Mrs. Foteini Karanika
Bachelor of Science (BSc) in Sociology, Master of Arts (MA) in Global Criminology

Dr. Sara Pazell
Bachelor of Applied Science (BAppSc) in Occupational Therapy, Master of Business Administration (MBA) in International Business, Doctor of Philosophy (PhD) in Work Design

Mrs. Selma Piric
Bachelor of Science (BSc) in Organisational Psychology, Master of Science (MSc) in Human Factors and Safety Assessment in Aeronautics

Dr. Anastasios Plioutsias
Bachelor of Science (BSc) in Aviation (Air Force Pilot), Bachelor of Business Administration and Management, Master of Science (MSc) in Project Management, Doctor of Philosophy (PhD) in Engineering and Ergonomics

About This Book

Why are the changes we design and pursue sometimes unsuccessful? How do random or systematic factors influence our decisions and actions? Who and what is part of our systems? Why and how do we tunnel our energy and for whose benefit? Why have we probably rejected persons who do not match with our ethics and beliefs? Why do we often trust concepts and practices that just reflect norms and not scrutinised truths? Why do we usually fixate on the material world and underestimate the power and effects of thoughts and emotions? Why do we sometimes apply double standards in our decisions and manifest selectivity when looking for scientific evidence?

Why do we occasionally find it hard to collaborate with others? Why do we perform well one day but not the next? Why do we form closed groups, clubs, communities, and other collectives? Is this form of 'guarded belonging' a distortion of the innate need to belong?[4] Could it be an outcome of fears of sharing with everyone around or a tendency to reject the different because it can influence us and threaten the status quo? How do we justify that a threat is indeed a threat? What are the solid criteria and reference points to judge this?

In this book, I explore these challenges and offer insights into how our energy can be invested for significant positive outcomes. I explore the intersections between different approaches and perspectives from various fields of knowledge without thoroughly delving into each one. Across the lines of this book, I have consolidated views and formulated well-intended propositions, most of them based on existing theories from management, engineering, humanities, and other fields.

Indeed, depending on your background, some of the book's content may remind you of concepts covered by various disciplines. However, the distinct value of this work is that I identify commonalities instead of rejecting concepts based on binary doctrines of 'this' or 'that'. My focus is on exploring 'this' alongside 'that'. In each chapter, I link the seemingly unrelated, connect the possibly unobvious, and discuss previously unthought associations and interdependencies.

---

[4] Allen, K.A. (2021). The Psychology of Belonging. London: Routledge, https://doi.org/10.4324/9780429327681

In this book, I show how you can break silos and connect dots from various domains to become a more inclusive and competent professional in any current and future role, whether this could be about a supervisor, an executive, C-Suite manager, or an educator. I demonstrate how you can adeptly connect, relate, blend, and cross-reference various approaches. However, togetherness does not always mean the middle path. Different professional situations require different paradigms and approaches from various areas; the 'average' and the 'middle' cannot match all contexts. By togetherness I mean the genuine consideration, and possible embracement, of the different, the opposite, and the seemingly awkward.

Importantly, this is not a dogmatic and normative piece of work. This book is not an encyclopaedia of all philosophical, scientific, professional, and best-practice approach expressed over the centuries of human civilisation. Importantly, under the narrow definition of science, this work is not scientific in the sense of experiments and studies. It is a scholarly and professional work, but this does not render it scientific. This is an important difference several professionals might forget. In academia, scientific work is scholarly work, but scholarly work is not always scientific.

Sources

This work uses ideas from the cited publications and two other sources. The first source is my accumulated knowledge in the professional arena and the amalgamation of cultures in my roles as an academic and industry employee; manager and worker; designer and end user; engineer and human factors and safety geek; author and reader; audience and speaker; customer and vendor; student and teacher; leader and follower; scientist and Orthodox Christian; Greek and Australian.

I have gained knowledge beyond my technical skills and degrees through diverse experiences. This knowledge is the joint product of thoughts and ideas of my interactions with or exposure to other professionals from various fields in several formal and informal settings, like conferences, social events, casual meetings, and classes. As such, this book authentically reflects my ongoing journey within and across various disciplines and natural observations after several years of interacting with everyone whom I met in-person or indirectly through their work.

Second, I tuned the content of this book based on the input from the reviewers mentioned in the Acknowledgements section above. Those professionals with diverse backgrounds offered their valuable comments when critically performing 'validity assessments'. Their primary role was not to accept or reject any content. I asked them to act as 'critical friends' and comment primarily on the structure, clarity, completeness, logic, and examples provided. The reviewers were also free to challenge the content of this work constructively. They were expected to object only when they could offer alternative perspectives or ideas.

Utilising professional peer-reviews did not mean to underestimate the value of collaboration in content creation, as Dave Snowden demonstrated in his CYNEFIN journey.[5] However, because of my professional roles, I have had limited opportunities to collaborate on the concept of Professional Generalism (e.g., through workshops and roundtables). For example, I have always tailored my teaching activities to the needs of the clients, whether it be students at universities or staff attending in-house company training. This left limited room for exploring broader and deeper topics and their intersections.

Contrary to academic expectations, in this book, I do not use tens of scholarly citations on each page. I only refer to indicative books and other documents to trigger you to search deeper, further, higher, and broader. These books are just suggestions about publications that deal with the topics I visit in this work. Any external reference to the work of others is indicative and not entirely exhaustive or wholly inclusive. As my academic supervisor, Stavros Drossos, once reassured me about my doctoral research, 'Nektarios, don't worry about that. In the literature, you can always find something that confirms or disconfirms your results'.

The above is another reason this work includes a relatively small number of bibliographic references regarding theories, positions, etc. I cite none of them to confirm positions and viewpoints expressed in the book. You can find sources that support or contest any perspectives and arguments, directly or indirectly, especially in our era of access to abundant (mis)information. Indeed, several writers often use external sources to make their words seem important and gain readers' approval. However, citing positions and theories of others to support arguments and results does not render both the former and the latter true.

Indeed, there have been plenty of instances in our human history when the masses passionately believed in widely promoted principles and doctrines, but, in hindsight, these proved catastrophic. Decades ago, if someone wanted to support racism and the shocking practice of human exhibitions of natives from colonies at circuses across the Western world, they could conveniently find perspectives to confirm such views. Scientific works from that era even asserted the superiority and inferiority of various human race clusters. Therefore, the popularity of a concept or theory should not render it acceptable by default. Thus, in this book, I refer to example publications elaborating on the areas covered when I wrote it. These references are not used to validate the content.

Content

The order I unfold several approaches in the following chapters aims to progressively introduce informed and professional views, moving from more abstract to more specific. In each of the six book parts and 21 chapters, I combine concepts, principles, approaches, and paradigms from science and professional practice. The book is neither about the details of micro-cosmos nor the vastness of macro-cosmos. It is

[5] Greenberg, R. & Bertsch, B. (2020). Cynefin—Weaving Sense-Making into the Fabric of Our World. Singapore: Cognitive Edge.

about the meso-cosmos of daily professional practice, offering a unique perspective that is useful, and in principle, correct but, at the same time, not detailed and context-specific.

Each chapter concludes with a section with key reflections and actions. These actions assume you have read the chapter and the key reflections so that you interpret them correctly and contextually. The concluding section does not mean to function as a checklist and the actions are not an exhaustive list. They are just starting points for testing and embedding each chapter's content in your professional practice. It lies on you to contextualise, endorse or question, test or accept those suggestions, and reject or modify the concepts, principles, and guidance I unfold in each chapter.

Importantly, apart from definitions I explicitly provide in several chapters, in the book, I use terms that can have different meanings across different disciplines. Therefore, when reading, I invite you to approach such words from the 'public' or 'common' viewpoint and not through a 'narrow' and 'technical' lens. For example, terms like 'observable', 'unobservable', or 'undetectable' I use in Chapter 1 when introducing classifications can refer to more specific and deep notions in several domains like physics and systems theory. Even between physics and systems and control theory, the same terms can have different meanings.

Part I—Foundational Concepts

The first part includes five chapters and establishes the core theoretical foundations of Professional Generalism, beginning with an examination of ethical frameworks and their reconciliation. It introduces essential definitions of 'unities' (physically perceivable entities) and 'constructs' (human-created concepts), exploring how the latter shape our understanding of reality while acknowledging their limitations. In the same book section, I also examine how constructs, both physically perceivable and unperceivable, serve as essential tools for professional communication and decision-making, while warning against their potential misuse. I conclude with a new framework distinguishing energy type (material, cognitive, affective) that underpins the book's concepts on professional practice and development.

Part II—Dialogue Concepts

Throughout its four chapters, this part explores the nature and evaluation of professional communication and scientific approaches. It establishes that all forms of information exchange are essentially storytelling and examines the gaps between reality, perception, and recall. In this specific part, I discuss the reliability and validity of stories used in professional settings, providing frameworks to evaluate sources and content. Then, I categorise sciences into four types: formal, exact, hybrid, and inexact, based on their relation to energy. This part concludes by examining the interplay and complementary nature of different scientific approaches, challenging misconceptions about their relative superiority while promoting an integrated approach.

Part III—Energy Flow Concepts

In the three chapters of this part, I examine the dynamics of how entities interact and exchange energy. I begin by establishing a framework for understanding different organisational arrangements through systems, networks, and groups, introducing the concepts of explicitly agreed, explicitly expected, and implicitly assumed objectives. The particular part then explores three fundamental activity types exhibited by all unities—Reaction, Self-Change, and Transformation of Others. It examines how these activity types manifest across different physical entities, emphasising human consciousness as a distinguishing factor. I conclude this part by presenting a comprehensive framework for understanding energy exchange patterns, introducing concepts like Energy State Tolerance Region and Energy State Motivational Envelope to explain how needs, desires, and motivations influence interactions between different energy actors.

Part IV—Management Concepts

This part reframes traditional management concepts through the lens of energy exchange and processing. Throughout three chapters, I introduce a broader conception of management as the orchestration of energy use through sensing, processing, and (in)acting, while challenging conventional terminology around what can be directly managed. This part then presents a typology of management types based on the alignment between sensing modes, processing approaches, and action options, introducing the concepts of 'consistent management' versus 'opportunistic' and 'presumptive' management. I conclude by examining the relationship between energy management, accountability, and responsibility, introducing the concept of 'energy custodianship' and exploring how mutual obligations emerge naturally from energy exchange patterns within systems.

Part V—Appraisal Concepts

This three-chapter part provides a comprehensive framework for understanding and evaluating differences and gaps (DaGs). It examines DaGs at both macro- and micro-levels, exploring how material, cognitive, and affective energies interact with environmental demands to influence performance. In this specific part, I challenge common perceptions about negative DaGs, demonstrating their essential role in driving adaptation, resilience, and evolution. The part concludes by presenting a consolidated framework of performance and evaluation principles. It establishes the interdependence of these constructs while emphasising the importance of context in making comparisons and judgments.

Part VI—Change Concepts

The last section (three chapters) explores complex organisational and systemic change using energy exchange as a framework. It challenges common change management assumptions, particularly the Good Individual—Bad System concept perspective, while exploring the artificial distinction between systematic and random factors in change processes. The section stresses focussing on change where you have the most control (your immediate surroundings), while recognising the wider effects. It concludes by presenting a comprehensive framework for change implementation, introducing typologies of intervention, suitability, and optimisation that can help professionals navigate the complexities of organisational transformation while balancing diverse stakeholder interests.

Representations

Notably, in this work, I include graphs, tables, mathematical symbols, and equations in different sections. The graphs and tables help summarise key areas covered in the text. The equations illustrate relationships, not precise mathematical functions. They are conceptual tools designed to summarise and convey ideas in a symbolic format. There is no scientific testing validating any of the equations, nor are they connected with any experiments or studies. They might be valid, or they might not. There might have been empirical research relevant to some equations. They may inspire you and newer generations of professionals and researchers to consider, specify, change, test, etc. them. Most importantly, you can surely skip them and still understand fully the positions I express in this book.

The main reasons for formulating equations in some sections are because they can be easily copied and transferred elsewhere and be used as a reminder to recite the respective content. These equations are just alternative representations to satisfy any reader who particularly appreciates symbols besides text or can comprehend concepts better when presented symbolically. Rather than presenting rigid functions, the equations symbolise conceptual relationships, where operations like addition '+', subtraction '−', multiplication '*', and division '/' represent complementary, counteracting, interactive, and moderating relationships, respectively. These are not strict mathematical functions but serve to reflect how different factors may relate to one another in professional practice.

For instance, a generic equation:

$$Outcome \propto f(parameter_1,\ parameter_2, \ldots.,\ parameter_n)$$

Represents not a scientific model but a conceptual framework to summarise complex ideas.

As such, if you use elsewhere any graphs, tables, equations, or any other material from this script, you must acknowledge that they comprise professional and scholarly prepositions and perspectives and not scientific positions. Similarly, when mentioning any of the content of this book, using verbs such as supported, claimed, suggested, thought, believed, argued, etc. would be appropriate, but verbs such as proved, found, etc. should be avoided. You must also refrain from measuring and making calculations just because the book contains some symbolic formulas. Many of the variables within the equations I present in the book are not directly measured. As eloquently Carsten Busch noted, if you cannot measure it, maybe you should not.[6]

[6] Busch, C. (2019). If You Can't Measure It... Maybe You Shouldn't: Reflections on Measuring Safety, Indicators, and Goals. Mind the Risk.

Contents

Part VI Change Concepts

About the Author

Nektarios Karanikas With over 28 years of experience spanning academia and industry while writing this book, I have observed first-hand the challenges and limitations of hyper-specialisation in professional environments, and I bring a unique, multidisciplinary perspective to the concept of Professional Generalism.

My career began with 18 years as an Aeronautical Engineering Officer in the Hellenic Air Force, where I held various leadership positions. This experience provided me with invaluable insights into the complexities of integrating diverse professional disciplines within high-stakes environments. Currently an Associate Professor in Health, Safety & Environment at the Queensland University of Technology (QUT), Australia, I have a diverse educational background. I hold a BSc in Aviation Science, an MSc in Human Factors and Safety Assessment in Aeronautics, and a Doctorate in Safety and Quality Management. This interdisciplinary foundation has shaped my holistic approach to professional practice and education.

In academia, I have spearheaded innovative teaching approaches that bridge theory and practice. My work in curriculum development and course coordination at QUT and my previous appointment at the Amsterdam University of Applied Sciences (Netherlands) reflects my commitment to fostering a more integrated understanding of professional disciplines amongst students. As a researcher, I have published extensively in top-tier journals across multiple fields, demonstrating my ability to synthesise knowledge from various domains.

My expertise is recognised both nationally and internationally. I am a Fellow of the Royal Aeronautical Society, the Australian Institute of Health and Safety, and the Higher Education Academy; I also serve as an Associate Editor for Safety Science. These roles have allowed me to advocate for more holistic approaches to professional development and organisational management.

Throughout my career, I have consistently worked to break down silos between disciplines, encouraging professionals to look beyond their specialisations. This book represents the culmination of my experiences and observations, offering a compelling case for the importance of Professional Generalism in our increasingly complex and interconnected world.

Part I
Foundational Concepts

Chapter 1
Ethics

1.1 General

Throughout history, there has been a vast amount of literature on ethics and related schools of thinking.[1,2,3,4,5] Ethics, plainly put, concern our standpoints towards humanity and the world. Perspectives about everything around can be deeply rooted in our human history and societies but also emerging and influence how we interact with the world, within and outside work, and how we classify those interactions, their results and their role: bad or good, beneficial or detrimental, malevolent or benevolent, professional or unprofessional, amongst others. At the same time, the outputs of our interactions with the surrounding world become outcomes and shape or tweak our perspectives.

Professional ethics source from all the above and regard specific occupations, organisations, etc. Bodies, agencies and management traditionally formulate ethics as professional conduct expectations, and these are endorsed and accepted as principles of ethical behaviour. If someone does not adhere to those conduct rules, they can get banned from the professional body or club, or even from the profession by losing their licence.

Nevertheless, in this chapter, I do not specifically explore professional ethics. Rather, I primarily present principles from generic schools of ethics that can translate into codes of professional behaviours and conduct. Such codes can combine several principles from various schools depending on the particulars of each profession,

---

[1] Donlevy, J. K., & Walker K. D. (2011). Ethical schools of thought. In *Working through ethics in education and leadership*. Sense Publishers. https://doi.org/10.1007/978-94-6091-376-1_3.

[2] Benn, P. (1998). *Ethics*. UCL Press.

[3] Angier, T. (2012). *Ethics*. Bloomsbury.

[4] Anderson, R. (2012). *Ethics*. Hodder Education.

[5] Satyanarayana, Y. V. (2009). *Ethics*. Pearson India.

N. Karanikas, *Professional Generalism in a Hyper-specialised World*,
https://doi.org/10.1007/978-981-96-4039-3_1

the social and other expectations at the location of the organisation, and any other contextual parameters. Although a single, unified, and global professional ethics code does not exist, Sect. 1.4 can serve as a reference for an inclusive professional ethics code regardless of discipline, location, or other parameters.

1.2 Indicative Schools of Ethics

The schools of ethics summarised below are the ones I came across at different points in time. Of note, the brief presentation of each school below aims to provide a high-level overview and not explain the respective ethics and their implications. Several of the ideas and beliefs underpinning these ethics schools have ancient roots, evolved through branching and societal responses, and continue to change.

The ethics of *Natural Law*[6] suggest that everything around occurs and functions in a predetermined and inherent manner based on universal and objective laws, including how we reason and behave. Scientists apply mathematics to find laws for different natural phenomena, which could result in a single universal law. This ethics approach implies that we operate within a predefined envelope. Everything ultimately obeys natural laws, regardless of personal interpretations or desires. Terms like fate and destiny relate to this school of thinking.

The *Behaviourist* approach,[7] as originally formed, views living beings as stimuli-response mechanisms. This view borrows from cause–effects concepts in physics and other fields dealing with observable phenomena, such as mechanics. Traditional behaviourism approaches humans like programmable technical entities. It aims to predict and change behaviour by analysing responses to things. Methods such as rewards and punishment fall under this ethical perspective.

Pragmatic ethics[8] are grounded in the rationality of performing long and iterative inquiries about testing the practical usefulness of whatever we accept as true knowledge with the goal to correct the errors of previous inquiries. Scientific findings, societal norms, and anything that exists today can disappear, change, or be replaced based on the results of future inquiries. This line of thinking implicitly rejects intuition as a reliable driver and questions our capability to formulate eternally valid truths and knowledge.

Deontological ethics[9] focusses on the imperative to follow rules and procedures. They assume normative standards define what is right and wrong to do, regardless of the outcomes of actions. The morality of actions, as per this school, is more important

[6] Angier, T. (2019). *The Cambridge companion to natural law ethics.* Cambridge University Press. https://doi.org/10.1017/9781108525077.

[7] Biasucci, C., & Prentice, R. (2020). *Behavioral ethics in practice: Why we sometimes make the wrong decisions.* Routledge. https://doi.org/10.4324/9780429324246.

[8] Liszka, J. J. (2021). *Pragmatist ethics: A problem-based approach to what matters.* Suny Press.

[9] McNaughton, D., & Rawling, P. (2011). *Deontological ethics.* Routledge Encyclopedia of Philosophy. Taylor and Francis. https://doi.org/10.4324/9780415249126-L015-2.

than the results. The latter can take a positive or negative sign because of other factors lying outside our control. Disregarding established laws, regulations, and directives signals disrespect to fellow citizens and previous generations.

Normative constructivism[10] in ethics focusses on judging actions by their results, not abstract ideas of right and wrong. This approach suggests that someone can always predict outcomes, there is a clear boundary between right and wrong, and there are tools to facilitate rationality in every situation and condition.

Utilitarian ethics[11] contend the ends justify the means if it brings maximum happiness and well-being to the majority. This perspective excuses discomforting or even harming the minority for the sake of satisfying the majority.

The *Existential Dialectic* philosophy[12] emphasises the individuality of humans as conscious beings. The specific school poses that we give our own meaning to matters while experiencing the world and ourselves. This viewpoint believes that subjectivity is universal and achieving objective rationality is unrealistic.

Situational ethics[13] deny the applicability of objective and universal laws. They support that any judgment must consider the contextual factors through the lens of what is good for the majority at a specific time-point and within a specific environment. The notion of local rationality underpins the specific line of thinking that emphasises what makes sense within a particular context and unfolding situation. Under this perspective, science is limited; it offers no absolute answers due to subjective viewpoints.

Virtue ethics[14] maintains that moral identity originates from our internal and unobservable characteristics that shape our mindset towards the world. We may not express those characteristics as observable behaviours because of external influences from various factors. One of the consequential standpoints of this school is that we are not defined by what we do, but by what we believe and think.

The *Care Feminist* movement[15] examines power dynamics and the strengths and vulnerabilities of people in relationships. It advocates that care should be a normative reality where the more powerful care about the weaker. This school accepts that absolute equality does not exist, but rejects the use of relative power to magnify current gaps. Instead, inequality must be the driver towards sharing and not an excuse to control and manipulate.

---

[10] Bagnoli, C. (Ed.). (2013). *Constructivism in ethics*. Cambridge University Press. https://doi.org/10.1017/CBO9781139094221.

[11] Quinton, A. (1973). *Utilitarian ethics*. Palgrave Macmillan. https://doi.org/10.1007/978-1-349-00248-1.

[12] Wolk, B. J. (2016). *Being and dialectic: Core tenets of existential dialectical materialism*. iUniverse.

[13] Fletcher, J. (1998). *Situation ethics: The new morality*. Westminster John Knox Press.

[14] van Hooft, S. (2006). *Understanding virtue ethics*. Routledge. https://doi.org/10.4324/9781315712130.

[15] Held, V. (1995). *Justice and care: Essential readings in feminist ethics*. Routledge. https://doi.org/10.4324/9780429499463.

1.3 Absolutism Versus Reconciliation

Indeed, all schools of ethics outlined above view the world from a different angle. The question, however, is whether all the above could coexist and apply together. Could you implement them as complementary instead of being viewed as opposites? The former is possible only if you are prepared to leave behind any absolutism and focus on reconciliation. Opposition and rejection without prior attempts to explore common grounds and acknowledge possible positives in other approaches could mainly serve indoctrination and commercialisation goals.

For instance, we have not yet discovered a unified and single universal law. However, it is a common experience that there are limits to physical existence. Such limits are not subject to intentions, desires, and ethical morality. If we do not consume physical energy of sufficient quantity and quality, we will starve and become significantly weaker. We will then be more vulnerable to attacks from external environmental agents like viruses, and after some time, our bodies will cease to function. Thus, we might not have natural laws for everything, but there are laws for plenty of physical phenomena.

Also, we indeed observe causes–effects all around and use them to adapt our behaviours and formulate natural laws. However, our observations are limited to phenomena we can sense, and they mainly describe them. Observations cannot fully explain phenomena and cannot predict everything because of the constant changes and variability in the world. Each time we make a discovery and claim we can now explain a phenomenon, we might then discover something else we did not know. Thus, any explanation today becomes a mere description tomorrow.

Science through experiments has significantly contributed to helping us understand the world over time by constantly questioning our knowledge and by testing ways to use, combine, and change the elements of the environment. Indeed, this is how we have developed technology, medicine, and other products of civilisation. This is also how we have revised various laws and specified how different versions of natural laws apply to different phenomena. However, can science measure and explain everything? No, not right now. Maybe it even seems unimaginable that science could achieve this at any time.

Have collective stimuli-response experiences from the past formed best practices as (un)written norms, legislation, codes, and standards which we use with trust in the knowledge of previous generations? It unquestionably seems so as we initially follow the rules of families, schools, communities, professions, organisations, nations, and cultures. This occurs until the point that our own knowledge and experience of the world, possibly together with science, might suggest the inapplicability of some rules across contexts and time, giving birth to doubts about their validity.

This knowledge develops through the outcomes of our actions, which are based on sensing cause–effect relationships. How do we evaluate these results and their impacts without considering who, what, and how benefits? Will we perceive those benefits the same? The answer is no because personal feelings and logic do not always agree with scientific facts and normative practices.

Do we always have a biased opinion when dealing with others in our professional lives? Yes, as different professionals can assign various meanings to different matters. Is it acceptable to use diverse opinions as a reason for not agreeing on what needs to be done and define expected outputs and outcomes? Indeed, we cannot satisfy everyone's views on what is good or bad or accommodate the rights of different groups. We usually attempt to reach an agreement and anticipate the future together.

Such agreement does not necessarily mean we do not yet hold a different professional or personal standpoint that differentiates us from others. We cannot deny the absence of a diversity of mindsets simply because professionals agree. These mindsets, although not completely capitalised on today, might shape the future and bring changes if the previously agreed actions do not deliver the expected outputs or outcomes.

Also, diversity can mean, for example, that some have more physical strength than others. You have your own unique knowledge and experiences, and some individuals are emotionally vulnerable. Does this mean you are relatively more advantaged than others? Although we all have our advantages in different areas, no one possesses a complete professional advantage over everyone else. The highly educated scientist in the lab relies on the physically strong farmer to produce goods. Conversely, the farmer needs the scientist to improve farming via scientific understanding and invention.

Actually, there is neither rationale nor requirement to subscribe piously to a particular ethics framework. All schools of ethics have their value if you realise their principles do not apply to everyone, everything, and always. Extremes of the positions of any ethical school can serve nothing but separation and discrimination. I belong here; you belong there; she belongs to this; he belongs to that. The need to belong should not automatically mean the right to reject and inability or prohibition to change the areas we belong. In Table 1.1, I illustrate how absolutism towards any ethical approach could manifest.

1.4 Reconciled Ethical Principles

The reconciliation of various ethical principles can form a unified framework that recognises and values the strengths of different schools of thought. By blending aspects like Deontology's logic, Situational Ethics' context awareness, and Feminist Ethics' compassion, such principles can achieve a balance between rigidity and adaptability. Such a synthesis not only acknowledges the complexity and diversity of professional challenges but also provides a flexible yet principled foundation for ethical decision-making across varying contexts. By harmonising seemingly opposing viewpoints, reconciled principles empower professionals to navigate ethical dilemmas with clarity and inclusiveness.

In Table 1.2, I demonstrate how we can reconcile and possibly inform professional ethics using the ethical principles discussed in Sect. 1.2. The principles I present in Table 1.2 can be seen as a standpoint and philosophy about the world and humans, under the disclaimer that in this chapter I do not cover all schools of ethics and their

Table 1.1 Extremes of schools of ethics

School of ethics	Absolute rejection	Absolute acceptance
Natural Law-ism	Everything is random	Everything is predetermined
Behaviourism	We can anticipate nothing	We can predict everything
Pragmatism	We know everything we need to know	We know nothing
Deontology	We are completely free to do whatever we wish	We must unquestioningly follow written and unwritten norms and rule
Normative constructivism	Personal reasoning is always right	Personal reasoning is always wrong
Utilitarianism	We must pursue the best for ourselves	We must pursue the best for the majority
Existential Dialectic-ism	We must hold the same understanding	We can never achieve a shared understanding
Situational-ism	There is only a single and universal reality	All individual interpretations of reality are right
Virtue-ism	Only actions matter	Only intentions matter
Care feminism	Only the strongest may survive	We must provide care unconditionally and without discretion

variations. Also, the list below might change. This is a natural expectation as we all get exposed to more theories of ethics and realise more about the position and role of ourselves as professionals.

The *reconciled ethical principles* above underline the supra-disciplinary and reconciling approach I unfold in the rest of this book. They can serve as a reference point for creating a unified professional ethical conduct code. Still, under specific contexts, there can be potential conflicts between the 55 reconciled principles recommended, as different principles could suggest different courses of action.

For instance, imagine a pharmaceutical company developing a potentially life-saving drug. The company's research team could face a situation where they need to decide between releasing the drug faster with current test results, which show good efficacy but have some gaps in long-term safety data, or conducting additional years of testing to gather more comprehensive safety data. This creates tension between several of the reconciled ethical principles:

- Principle 40: 'No specific individual, minority or majority group is given precedence by default for any benefits to be harvested': There are currently patients urgently needing the drug (minority) versus the broader future patient population (majority).
- Principle 42: 'Equity must be the primary criterion for choosing between possible actions and their outputs and anticipated outcomes, considering that everyone

Table 1.2 Reconciled ethical principles

Ethical principle	Example
Part 1: Laws of the observable	
EP-1 Laws[16] are human constructs made to model and describe to varying degrees and provisionally explain relationships between specific observable events involving specific observable agents under particular conditions	In economics, the law of supply and demand is a human construct that models the relationship between the price of a product and its availability in the market. While it generally holds true, it does not account for all factors that might influence pricing or consumer behaviour in every situation.
EP-2 Laws always contain errors because of the variability and constant change of everything	In meteorology, weather prediction models are based on laws of physics and historical data. However, these models are never 100% accurate because of the chaotic nature of environmental systems and the constant changes in their factors.
EP-3 Laws for the unobservable cannot be formulated	In quantum physics, scientists cannot directly observe subatomic particles in the traditional sense. While the theories and models developed are based on observable effects, they do not yield absolute laws governing the behaviour of these particles.
EP-4 Laws carry the subjective interpretations of their maker(s)	In psychology, different schools of thought (e.g., behaviourism, psychoanalysis, and cognitive psychology) have proposed different 'laws' or principles of human behaviour. These laws often reflect the subjective interpretations and philosophical leanings of their creators.
EP-5 The world does not exist because of laws and does not function precisely and always according to the laws the humanity constructs	In biology, while the theory of evolution explains the diversity of life, it does not mean that every single mutation or adaptation will follow a predictable pattern. Genes can change unexpectedly, defying current evolutionary theories.

(continued)

[16] Natural, scientific, etc. laws. Not to be confused with legislation.

Table 1.2 (continued)

Ethical principle	Example
EP-6 Modelled relationships between events and their agents do not comprise global and eternal truths	In business, economic models like the Product Life Cycle are useful for understanding market dynamics, but they do not always apply universally to all products in all markets. Some products may skip stages or behave differently than the model predicts.
EP-7 Any determinism about modelled relationships cannot withstand scrutiny across time and different contexts	In psychology, Freud's psychosexual stages of development were once widely accepted. However, as research methods improved and cultural contexts changed, many of Freud's deterministic ideas have been challenged or discarded.
EP-8 Connections between observable events can be established based on human-made criteria	A marketing analyst working for an e-commerce company observes that whenever there is a sale in a specific product category, there is a corresponding increase in website traffic. Based on these observable events, the analyst can establish a connection: 'Sales promotions associate with increased website traffic'. This connection is based on analyst-made criteria: the analyst has defined 'sales promotion' and 'increased website traffic' as relevant events and claimed a relationship between the two.
EP-9 Despite the subjectivity of their makers, the criteria devised for specific events can constitute an agreeably rational basis to examine relationships between other similar events	In medicine, the criteria for diagnosing a specific disease, while initially developed based on subjective observations, can provide a rational basis for diagnosing similar conditions or for developing diagnostic criteria for related diseases. For instance, understanding the metabolic disorders of diabetes mellitus helped diagnose similar conditions like gestational and type 2 diabetes.
EP-10 Repetitive observations of the same independent events in the same contexts can inform preliminary modelled relationships	In manufacturing, quality control processes often involve repetitive observations of product defects. These observations can inform preliminary models of where errors are likely to occur in the production process.
EP-11 Repetitive observations of the same independent events in the same contexts cannot be used to establish laws without first determining mechanisms, paths, and connections between these events according to an agreed rational basis	Climate science needs more than temperature increases to establish climate change laws. Scientists must determine mechanisms (e.g., the greenhouse effect), pathways (e.g., carbon cycles), and connections (e.g., human activities and greenhouse gas emissions) to formulate laws or principles of climate change.

(continued)

Table 1.2 (continued)

Ethical principle	Example
Part 2: The unobservable	
EP-12 Assumed or presumed relationships amongst unobservable agents/events and between unobservable and observable agents/events can function as plausible explanations but cannot constitute laws	In theoretical physics, string theory plausibly explains how gravity might work at the quantum level. However, the inability to observe strings means string theory remains hypothetical currently.
EP-13 The unobservable of the past can become the observable of the future	In astronomy, Einstein's theory predicted gravitational waves, which were initially undetectable. New detectors have made gravitational waves visible, confirming a key part of Einstein's theory and creating a new field of astronomy.
Part 3: Norms	
EP-14 Repetitive events and their perceived connections give birth to norms, which could constitute initial guidance when respective laws do not yet exist	In exoplanet astronomy, repetitive observations of certain types of stars wobbling led to the norm of assuming the presence of orbiting planets. Early exoplanet detection lacked formal laws; astronomers relied on normative methods such as observing star velocity changes for potential discoveries. These norms, born from repetitive observations and perceived connections, served as initial guidance for exoplanet hunters before formal detection methods and statistical confidence levels were established.
EP-15 Norms are shaped through voluntary or random interactions amongst individuals who exchange theoretical perspectives about observable events or endorse and adopt the responses of others to such events	In the tech industry, the norm of 'move fast and break things' emerged through interactions amongst startup founders and was adopted widely before being critically examined. This norm shaped how many tech companies approached product development and innovation.
EP-16 Legislation, standards, directives, procedures, rules, and code based on norms are weaker and more questionable than the ones sourcing from laws	In corporate governance, many companies adopt 'best practices' based on industry norms (e.g., having a certain number of independent directors). These practices, while broadly accepted, may be less robust than governance rules based on empirical studies of effective board structures for specific organisational sizes and profiles.

(continued)

Table 1.2 (continued)

Ethical principle	Example
Part 4: Applicability of laws and norms	
EP-17 Current laws and norms are the starting points for anyone who deals with a specific context for the first time	When a physicist studies quantum mechanics for the first time, they start with the current understanding of quantum laws. These laws are a good starting point for understanding quantum phenomena, though they have limitations.
EP-18 Laws are not readily transferable to contexts other than the ones for which they were originally formulated	Newton's laws accurately describe the motion of objects, from everyday things to spacecraft. However, they do not accurately describe the motion of subatomic particles or objects moving at speeds approaching the speed of light.
EP-19 What applies to a specific level of observation does not necessarily apply to more detailed or abstract levels than the original version of the law targets	In economics, the law of diminishing returns applies at a macro-level to factors of production. However, the rule may not work for small-scale, micro-level processes or abstract concepts such as intellectual property.
EP-20 As knowledge and experience in a specific context increase, current laws may seem irrelevant, and existing norms may appear invalid	In artificial intelligence (AI), as our understanding of machine learning algorithms grows, some early norms about AI safety and ethics may seem inadequate or irrelevant, necessitating the development of new, more sophisticated guidelines.
EP-21 All laws have exceptions	In biology, Mendel's laws of inheritance describe how genetic traits are passed from parents to offspring. However, there are many exceptions to these laws, such as genetic linkage, gene interactions, and epigenetic inheritance.
EP-22 Established norms are not legitimate reasons for rejecting deviations from those norms	In the automotive industry, the norm has been to produce cars with internal-combustion engines. This norm is not a legitimate reason to reject the development and adoption of electric vehicles, which deviate from this established practice.
EP-23 Exceptions and deviations cannot justify the complete rejection of laws and norms	In physics, the discovery of quantum mechanics revealed many phenomena that classical physics could not explain, such as wave-particle duality and quantum tunnelling. However, this did not lead to a complete rejection of classical physics. Instead, classical physics is now understood as a limiting case of quantum mechanics, still valid and extremely useful for describing macroscopic objects in typical everyday environments.

(continued)

Table 1.2 (continued)

Ethical principle	Example
Part 5: Changes to laws and norms	
EP-24 A new or revised law is necessary for modelling and describing events and relationships deeper or broader than the original law addresses	In physics, Einstein's theory of general relativity was necessary to model and describe gravitational phenomena that Newton's law of universal gravitation could not fully explain, such as the precession of Mercury's orbit and the bending of light by massive objects.
EP-25 Intuition and curiosity can trigger enquiries to introduce, cancel, or amend laws	Biologists in the 1950s believed genetic information only moved from DNA to RNA to proteins. This was considered a universal, unidirectional process. However, in 1970, Howard Temin and David Baltimore independently discovered reverse transcriptase, an enzyme that could copy RNA into DNA. This discovery was initially met with scepticism as it contradicted the accepted 'law' of information flow in biology. Temin's initial intuition and curiosity about retroviruses led him to hypothesise and then show that genetic information could flow 'backwards' from RNA to DNA. This discovery ultimately amended our understanding of the central dogma and revolutionised our comprehension of viral replication and gene regulation.
EP-26 Recognition of unacceptable flaws in previous laws can trigger enquiries to introduce, cancel, or amend laws	In the early twentieth century, the 'law' of peptic ulcer aetiology stated that stress and diet primarily caused these ulcers. This was a widely accepted medical principle that guided treatment for decades. The standard treatment involved lifestyle changes, antacids, and, in severe cases, surgery. This accepted medical belief was questioned by Australian researchers Marshall and Warren during the 1980s. They observed that many peptic ulcer patients had a specific type of bacteria in their stomachs, which did not align with the stress and diet theory. Their recognition of these unacceptable flaws in the previous understanding triggered an enquiry that would ultimately amend the 'law' of peptic ulcer aetiology. Despite initial scepticism from the medical community, Marshall and Warren persisted in their research and discovered that a large percentage of peptic ulcers were actually caused by H. pylori infection, not primarily by stress or diet, as previously thought. This amended 'law' revolutionised the treatment of peptic ulcers.

(continued)

Table 1.2 (continued)

Ethical principle	Example
EP-27 A will to transfer laws from one context to another can trigger enquiries to introduce, cancel, or amend laws	In astrobiology, the will to transfer laws from Earth-based biology to potential extraterrestrial life has triggered many enquiries to introduce, amend, or cancel existing biological laws.
EP-28 Changed or new needs or desires of individuals, minorities, or majorities can trigger enquiries to introduce, cancel, or amend laws	In medicine and epidemiology, the HIV/Aids crisis of the 1980s triggered significant enquiries to introduce, amend, and potentially cancel existing laws of infectious disease transmission and immune system function. This was driven by the urgent need to understand and combat a new, deadly disease affecting individuals and communities worldwide.
EP-29 Inapplicability of laws and invalidity of norms in some conditions do not unequivocally mean the uselessness and rejection of those laws and norms in their entirety	In chemistry, while the Bohr Model of the atom is not applicable to multi-electron atoms and is invalid for explaining many atomic phenomena, it is not entirely useless. It is still used as a simplified model to introduce students to atomic structure and to explain some basic concepts in spectroscopy.
EP-30 Inapplicability of laws and invalidity of norms in some conditions should warrant their re-examination for the conditions of observed inapplicability and invalidity	In physics, the inapplicability of Newton's laws of motion at very high speeds warranted a re-examination of these laws. This prompted Einstein to create the theory of special relativity; this theory is similar to Newton's at slower speeds but more accurate at speeds close to light speed.
EP-31 Norms must be replaced by laws when the latter can be established with an agreed margin of error, certainty, confidence level, and any other human-made and agreed criterion	Instead of assuming extreme weather is just natural, climate science now uses more precise attribution studies. These studies quantify human-induced climate change's impact on extreme weather events using statistical methods and climate models.
EP-32 Norms do not change through enquiries	In corporate culture, norms around work attire rarely change through formal enquiries or studies. Instead, they evolve gradually through changing social attitudes and practices.
EP-33 Enforced changes of norms are not sustainable	Mandated cultural changes in organisations are often unsuccessful. Sustainable changes in organisational culture typically require buy-in and gradual adoption at all levels of the organisation.

(continued)

Table 1.2 (continued)

Ethical principle	Example
Part 6: General principles	
EP-34 Objectivity is not an absolute and directly measurable entity	In journalism, while reporters strive for objectivity, it is recognised that complete objectivity is impossible. Every story requires choices about what to include or emphasise, which are inherently subjective decisions.
EP-35 Objectivity is the product of overlapping of various subjectivities, which cannot be measured	Academic peer review gets its objectivity from combining many reviewers' subjective viewpoints. The degree of this objectivity cannot be directly measured but is assumed to increase with the involvement of more diverse reviewers.
EP-36 The fewer the subjectivities consulted and the more they overlap, the higher the delusion of absolute objectivity	In the early to mid-twentieth century, much of psychological research was conducted primarily by Western-educated researchers studying Western-educated subjects—often college students from their own universities. This narrow demographic was used to formulate theories about human behaviour, cognition, and development that were assumed to be universal. The 'law' that emerged from this research was that these findings were representative of human psychology in general. Researchers, peer reviewers, and the academic community largely shared similar backgrounds and perspectives, reinforcing the belief in the universality of their findings. However, in the 1960s and 1970s, cross-cultural psychologists recognised the flaws in this approach. They noted that by consulting a limited, overlapping set of subjectivities (Western, educated, industrialized, rich, and democratic—or *WEIRD*—societies), psychologists had developed a skewed and often inaccurate view of human psychology. This recognition led to broader, more inclusive psychological research with diverse participants and new culturally sensitive methods.
EP-37 Same actions will not always lead to same outputs and outcomes	In digital marketing, running the exact same advertising campaign twice, even with the same budget and targeting, may yield different results because of changes in the market, competition, or audience behaviour.

(continued)

Table 1.2 (continued)

Ethical principle	Example
EP-38 Same outputs or outcomes are not always the result of identical actions	Two salespeople can hit the same targets in different ways: many small sales or a few big ones.
EP-39 Each living being might not perform the same actions in the same manner forever, even under seemingly identical circumstances	An employee who has always been punctual may suddenly start coming in late, even though their circumstances seem unchanged. This could be because of unseen factors like health issues or changes in motivation.
EP-40 No specific individual, minority, or majority group is given precedence by default for any benefits to be harvested	In public policy, when designing a city's public transportation system, planners should consider the needs of all groups—majority commuters, minority communities, elderly, disabled, etc.—without automatically prioritising any one group.
EP-41 No relatively stronger or more vulnerable agent of the environment is given precedence by default for any benefits to be harvested	In environmental conservation, when managing an ecosystem, neither the apex predators (i.e., stronger agents) nor the smaller, more populous species (i.e., more vulnerable agents) should be given automatic precedence. The entire ecosystem's balance should be considered.
EP-42 Equity must be the primary criterion for choosing between possible actions and their outputs and anticipated outcomes, considering that everyone can belong to different minorities and majorities simultaneously	In education policy, when allocating resources, decision-makers should consider that students might belong to multiple categories simultaneously (e.g., racial minority, high academic achiever, low-income family) and strive for equitable outcomes across all dimensions.
EP-43 Equity must be the primary criterion for choosing between possible actions and their outputs and anticipated outcomes, considering that everyone can be relatively advantaged or disadvantaged in different contexts	In workplace diversity initiatives, it is important to recognise that an individual might be in a position of privilege in one context (e.g., a senior executive) but face disadvantages in another (e.g., being a woman in a male-dominated industry).
EP-44 Establishing equity involves giving everyone the opportunity to raise their physical, cognitive, and emotional capabilities at the same level as others dealing with similar contexts	Equity in professional development means giving extra support to employees from disadvantaged backgrounds for equal advancement.
EP-45 Nobody can uniformly define the physical, cognitive, and emotional capabilities necessary for each individual to survive and perform in specific contexts	Firefighting is a profession that requires a complex mix of physical, cognitive, and emotional capabilities. However, it is challenging to define uniformly these capabilities across all fire fighters due to the diverse nature of their work, the varying contexts they operate in, and their individual traits.

(continued)

Table 1.2 (continued)

Ethical principle	Example
EP-46 One can relatively express necessary capabilities when considering the expectations sourcing from norms and the probable cause–effect relationships described by laws	In project management, while it is difficult to define all necessary capabilities for a project manager, one can express relative necessary capabilities based on industry norms (e.g., communication skills) and known cause–effect relationships (e.g., the impact of risk management on project outcomes).
EP-47 Deficits in capabilities reflect unmet needs in specific contexts	In customer service, if employees consistently struggle with handling difficult customers, this deficit might reflect an unmet need for training in conflict resolution or emotional competence, rather than an inherent lack of capability in the employees.
EP-48 Increasing capabilities at the expense of equity represents greediness	If a company invests heavily in advanced leadership training for its top executives while neglecting basic skill development for lower-level employees, the organisation could be seen as increasing capabilities of some at the expense of equity.
EP-49 Denial to support deficient individuals to develop capabilities corresponds to selfishness	In a software development team, experienced developers refusing to mentor or share knowledge with junior team members because of time constraints or job security concerns could represent a selfish denial support junior staff to develop their capabilities.
EP-50 The larger the gaps in the capabilities between individuals, the more the energy must be directed from the ones with higher capabilities to others with relatively lower capabilities	In a multinational corporation, if there is a significant gap in digital literacy between employees in different countries, the company should allocate more resources and training efforts to bring the less digitally literate employees up to speed, rather than focussing on advanced training for those already proficient.
EP-51 Anyone who has not used timely, maximally, and effectively the energy provided to build their capabilities and minimise capability gaps must be further supported and not be deprived of this opportunity	Students who need extra help beyond tutoring should not be abandoned by their school. The focus should shift to identifying the reasons for the initial support's ineffectiveness and exploring alternative strategies, including different learning techniques and addressing potential learning disabilities or personal obstacles.

(continued)

Table 1.2 (continued)

Ethical principle	Example
EP-52 Available energy should be provided in agreeable proportions to the ones in need, the persons who use energy effectively for the benefit of others and individuals who present potential for effective energy use	In a startup incubator, resources (e.g., mentoring time, funding, or office space) should be allocated considering startups in critical need of support to survive, those who have demonstrated they can effectively use resources to grow and create jobs, and promising new entrants who show potential for high impact.
EP-53 Physical, cognitive, and emotional capabilities of individuals cannot be separated from each other and approached as self-standing entities	Doctors consider a patient's emotional and mental state, as well as their physical health. A holistic approach that addresses all these interconnected aspects often leads to better health outcomes.
EP-54 Each capability type (i.e., physical, cognitive, and emotional) affects the others and is influenced by others	Professional sports training is not just physical; it also covers mental strategies and emotional control. Improvement in any one area often leads to enhancements in the others
EP-55 The consideration of intentions, feelings, actions, and any observable and unobservable characteristic in isolation from one another and from the context of each living being is likely invalid	In performance management, evaluating an employee's actions (e.g., missed deadlines) without considering their intentions (e.g., taking on extra work to help the team), feelings (e.g., negative mood because of personal issues), and context (e.g., understaffed department) would likely lead to an invalid assessment of their performance and potential.

can belong to different minorities and majorities simultaneously': Is it more equitable to provide immediate access to those in urgent need, or ensure equal safety standards for all current and future patients?
- Principle 47: 'Deficits in capabilities reflect unmet needs in specific contexts': The deficit in current treatment options represents an unmet need.
- Principle 52: 'Available energy should be provided in agreeable proportions to the ones in need, the persons who use energy effectively for the benefit of others and individuals who present potential for effective energy use': Should resources be directed towards helping current patients or ensuring long-term safety?

In the case above, the principles could support different courses of action. Principles 47 and 52 might favour faster release to address immediate unmet needs, whereas Principles 40 and 42 might favour more testing to ensure equitable protection for all potential future patients. However, this type of conflict does not invalidate the principles but rather highlights the complexity of applying them in real-world situations where multiple ethical considerations must be balanced. The resolution might require careful weighing of context-specific factors and possibly finding creative solutions that address multiple principles simultaneously (e.g., a controlled release program with enhanced monitoring).

Ethics: Key Reflections and Actions

Reflections
- Ethics in professional practice cannot be confined to a single framework. A reconciliatory approach that blends principles from diverse ethical schools can provide flexibility and inclusiveness.
- Both laws and norms are human constructs with limitations. They must be critically examined, refined, and adapted as contexts and understanding evolve.
- Objectivity is not an absolute truth, but the convergence of subjective perspectives. Recognising this can help avoid the trap of false objectivity often rooted in limited viewpoints.
- Equity is central to ethical decision-making, acknowledging that individuals occupy multiple, overlapping identities as parts of majorities and minorities.
- Capability-building is a dynamic interplay of physical, cognitive, and emotional dimensions, and deficits should be seen as unmet needs, not inherent limitations.

Actions
1. Explore Ethical Diversity: Review the principles of various ethical schools such as Deontology, Utilitarianism, and Virtue Ethics. Identify instances in your professional life where these principles may complement each other rather than conflict.
2. Practice Reconciliation: When faced with ethical dilemmas, look for commonalities between opposing viewpoints. Use these shared principles as a foundation for building consensus.

3. Apply Critical Examination: When encountering established norms or laws, question their relevance and applicability to your context. Consider how evolving societal or professional needs might warrant their adaptation or refinement.
4. Champion Equity: Strive to recognise and address inequities in your professional environment. Allocate resources and opportunities proportionally, focussing on both immediate needs and long-term capacity building.
5. Foster Holistic Growth: Evaluate your own capabilities across physical, cognitive, and emotional dimensions. Seek development opportunities in areas where you identify gaps and support others in doing the same.

By synthesizing ethical perspectives and taking thoughtful, context-sensitive actions, you can navigate complex professional challenges with integrity, adaptability, and inclusivity.

Chapter 2
Definitions

2.1 General

To ensure everyone is on the same page, regardless of discipline and topic, it is crucial that we pursue utmost clarity and accuracy in requirements, specifications, measures, and any other concept we use. It is important that we insist on commonly acceptable and understandable definitions. We should make any effort to convey clearly what we mean to the extent possible.

Otherwise, we let our interlocutors speculate and imagine, and often rely on metaphors. If this happens, the message might be misinterpreted. Conversing about different things or concepts, whereas we believe we discuss the same, is an unfavourable scenario at work and beyond, according to communication theories.[1]

Professional writing and communication differ from writing novels or fairy tales, which focus on triggering imagination for entertainment. It also differs from day-to-day language, where we use metaphors very often to explain and highlight concepts. One skill you must master is to translate metaphors into accurate definitions to the extent possible, work with these definitions to design, produce, and offer something tangible and then possibly support its implementation, distribution, and acceptance through metaphors. Translating concepts and metaphors successfully also requires understanding cultural differences.

For instance, a software development team is tasked with creating a new customer relationship management (CRM) system for a large retail company. The Chief Executive Officer (CEO) uses a metaphor, saying, 'We need a CRM that acts like a Swiss Army knife for our sales team'. The software needs to break down this metaphor into specific, tangible requirements (e.g., multi-functional tool, adaptable to various scenarios, integration of multiple features such as contact management, sales tracking) and verify those with the CEO.

[1] Littlejohn, S. W., Littlejohn, S. W., & Foss, K. A. (2009). *Encyclopedia of communication theory*. Sage.

N. Karanikas, *Professional Generalism in a Hyper-specialised World*,
https://doi.org/10.1007/978-981-96-4039-3_2

Then, the development team can use clearly defined requirements to design and develop the CRM software. Yet, when introducing the software to the sales team, the developers might reintroduce metaphors to explain functionality, like 'Think of the dashboard as your cockpit, giving you a bird's-eye view of all customer interactions'. Importantly, if the software is to be used internationally, the team must be mindful of cultural differences. For instance, the 'Swiss Army knife' metaphor might not resonate in all cultures, so they may need to adapt their explanations for different regions.

2.2 Fluidity and Impact

Whoever does not define to the detail possible assumes no responsibility for and accountability of their words. This is because meanings can float across a smaller or larger spectrum of possibilities. Here, the messenger always has an exit gate available such as 'I did not mean exactly that', 'you misunderstood my messages', or anything similar. Professional debates will continue until an explicit and understandable definition is agreed-upon.

Debates about definitions can be very productive if the actors involved try to define the term of interest clearly, even if they cannot always reach an absolute agreement. Such professional debates are excellent vehicles towards agreeably new, cancelled, or revised definitions, a journey of positions and oppositions as important as the destination. Indeed, definitions are human-made constructs and subject to changes over time; these changes often require efforts and sacrifices.

What the society had defined as punishable and intolerable decades ago, today might be acceptable and rewarded. What physics defines as dark matter today might radically differ or be replaced by something entirely new tomorrow. The definition of time has also changed over the years. The concept of privacy has evolved dramatically over the years, significantly influenced by societal, technological, and cultural changes.

In the early twentieth century, privacy was largely understood in the context of physical spaces, such as the sanctity of one's home. The famous 1890 legal article by Warren and Brandeis, The Right to Privacy, described it as 'the right to be let alone'. This definition sufficed in an era when personal information was not easily accessible, and technology played a minimal role in daily life. Nowadays, with the advent of the internet and social media, the definition of privacy has expanded to include the protection of personal data and online interactions.

Data privacy laws like the General Data Protection Regulation (GDPR) in the European Union introduced terms like 'data minimisation' and 'the right to be forgotten', redefining privacy to address digital vulnerabilities. In our age of artificial intelligence and surveillance technologies, privacy also intersects with concepts like consent, transparency, and algorithmic accountability. For instance, the use of facial recognition software has raised questions about what constitutes 'informed consent' and whether privacy applies to biometric data collected in public spaces.

For professionals in fields like cybersecurity, law, or healthcare, the evolving definition of privacy affects decision-making, compliance, and ethical considerations. For example, the healthcare industry's shift to electronic medical records required rethinking how patient privacy is maintained, leading to new standards like the Health Insurance Portability and Accountability Act (HIPAA) in the United States.

Importantly, anyone could critique others' definitions in a professional discussion if the ones criticising are clear and consistent in their own definitions. Judging others' definitions without offering specific alternatives and reasonable arguments contributes nothing valuable. Rather, as a professional, you should not rather enter the discussion or use the ill-defined concept. Exchanging a vague concept for another or replacing it within metaphors will not add much value.

For instance, imagine that during a quarterly architecture review meeting at a mid-sized software company, there is a heated discussion arose about the concept of 'technical debt' and how to measure it for reporting purposes. The senior developer could challenge the team's use of the term to label every quick fix and workaround as 'technical debt' without distinguishing between intentional design compromises and actual maintenance issues.

The developer can then define technical debt as 'architectural or implementation decisions that trade future maintainability for immediate delivery, where the cost of future changes is quantifiable and tracked'. Although admittedly quite longer, this is a more workable and accurate definition. The team would now need to document decisions at the time they are made, estimate the future cost of revisions, set a timeline for addressing them and track these metrics separately from general maintenance needs.

2.3 Unities and Constructs

The term *unity*, as I use it in this book, encompasses anything that has physically perceivable boundaries and can be observed either macroscopically or microscopically (e.g., humans, plants, animals, heart, lungs, trees, fruits, atoms, electrons). Any other perceivable entity without clear physical boundaries (e.g., clouds and waves; justice and truth; school or professional club) is not classified as a unity and belongs to one of the construct types I present below.

The scientific community is still discussing what constitutes life and how to categorise the world's unities, both known and unknown. However, for the sake of simplicity, we can logically categorise unities into two families: raw material and living organisms. The former have no biological processes, whereas the latter have such processes. There are three categories of living organisms: microorganisms (e.g., bacteria, fungi, archaea, protists), plants, and animals.

According to several biologists, humans fall under the animals' group. It is important to note, however, that the very concept of 'groups' is a human invention, a system of categorisation that we impose upon the world rather than a naturally occurring phenomenon. These constructs deserve respect yet embracing them is not mandatory despite widespread acceptance.

For instance, I prefer seeing us as a unique species, while others view us as extraordinarily intelligent animals. We do not yet know whether any animal species contemplate about the world, but, currently, theorising seems to be an enormous difference between us and the rest of the surrounding unities. Maybe animals engage in some forms of abstract thinking, and we are yet to discover it.

However, it is unnecessary at this point to decide about the classification of humans as animals or not. This work examines humans as unified beings; however, its topics are relevant to other organisms and unities. This book largely concerns humans, despite including some general, non-human examples.

A *construct* is anything we have created to make sense of the world, interact with it, survive, and, frequently, influence or control our world. Everything we have conceived, articulated, designed, developed, manufactured, used, transformed, decommissioned, and discarded brings the characteristics of a construct. Each construct serves or served a specific need or desire of individuals or collections of individuals for a short or long period.

The definition of construct above does not imply that unities and their collections and other phenomena do not ontologically exist. It is about their perceptual existence. Constructs define unities, and unities are needed to create constructs. Anything becomes only 'true' for those who observe it (i.e., perceivable) or experience it first-hand or through its makings (i.e., perceptible) or trust the accounts of others who have interacted with it.

Also, it means that whatever labels we place on another person might differ from the labels some others assign to this person. They could also differ from the physical and unobservable characteristics this person carries and assigns to themselves. Considering the above, the question then becomes: who exactly is this individual?

It is whoever each other individual decides. Some may agree with these individuals in defining the professional traits of the person of interest, while others may not. We all exist in different versions at each time-point, including the version we have adopted for ourselves.

Although there are various ways to classify constructs, and several authors have reviewed and criticised such taxonomies,[2,3] in Tables 2.1 and 2.2 I recommend a more unified and inclusive *typology of constructs*. The particular classification presents three interrelated groups of constructs: elementary, primary, and supportive/interpretative. It will facilitate the understanding of other topics I discuss later in the book.

Everything around perceptually 'exists' for us when:

- It is physically sensed or defined (i.e., *perceptible AND physically perceivable construct*). These constructs rely on the physical human senses (i.e., sight, touch, taste, smell, and hearing) and are categorised into:

---

[2] Foucault, M. (1970). *The order of things* (2nd ed.). Routledge. https://doi.org/10.4324/9781315660301.

[3] Brown, B. (2004). *Things*. The University of Chicago Press.

Table 2.1 Perceptible and physically perceivable constructs

Types	Sub-type(s)	Examples
Elementary/foundational		
Media constructs	Symbols and signs	Letters, numbers, lines, etc.
	Collections of symbols and signs	Words, phrases, shapes, drawings, etc.
	Expanded collections of symbols and signs	Grammar, equations, syntax, rules, legislation, procedures, melodies, etc.
	Supplementary (collections of) symbols and signs	Sounds, idioms, gestures, postures, accents, etc.
Primary—aimed at 'who', 'how', 'what', 'when', and 'where'		
Assigned constructs	Unity (sub)categories	Molecules, atoms, planets, plants, animals, humans, etc.
	Unities or unity collections representing combinations and/or transformations of other smaller/individual unities	Family, community, team, company, galaxy, toolbox, building, device, cooked food, etc.
	Unity names	Nick, Peter, Earth, Uranus, etc.
	Unity collections' names	Names of cities, regions, associations, space constellations, etc.
Constitutional constructs	Established relative roles of unities	Employer-employee, relative-stranger, parent–child, teacher-student, technician-generalist, scientist-theorist, etc.
	Unity ranks within roles	Employee role: worker-supervisor-superintendent-line manager-senior manager, etc. Teacher role: instructor-lecturer-senior lecturer, etc. Military officer role: 2nd lieutenant-1st lieutenant-captain-major, etc.
Physical constructs	Physical features of unities	Height, width, gender, colour, tone, pitch, etc.
	Physical features of unity collections	Population, density, volume, etc.
	Physical states of unities or unity collections	Balance, motion, stability, etc.
Eventological constructs	Unrelated events: isolated activities of unities or unity collections without considering their environment	Moving, lifting, sitting, running, walking, talking, touching, etc.

(continued)

Table 2.1 (continued)

Types	Sub-type(s)	Examples
Elementary/foundational		
	Resultant events: outputs/effects of interactions between unities or unity collections within a specific environment and conditions	Flood, burn, drought, damage, injury, etc. Weather phenomena over a region and under specific atmospheric conditions Pressure (e.g., hydraulic or atmospheric), heat, waves, etc.
	Contextual events: interactions between unities or unity collections by considering their environment	Chemical reactions within specific conditions of temperature and pressure Friction between particular types of materials and under given conditions Human–human interactions within their physical, technical and social environment

- *Elementary or Foundational Constructs.* Those are the basis for building, interpreting, and communicating the meaning and other aspects of constructs.
- *Primary Constructs.* Those support exploring the 'who', 'how', 'what', 'when', and 'where' of matters.

- It is perceptible as a representation or meaning even though it cannot be physically sensed (i.e., *perceptible BUT physically unperceivable construct*). Such *supportive or interpretative constructs* are accepted by human societies or parts of them as existent and/or useful at different time-points. They complement elementary and primary constructs and supplement them with the 'why' of matters.

Elementary, primary, and supportive constructs are related in the way I propose in Fig. 2.1. Elementary/media constructs are the ones we employ to encode, send, receive, and decode everything that regards other constructs. They comprise the foundations of human civilisation. Animals use media constructs to communicate as well. Plants and microorganisms use external physical agents to transmit information, but they do not use innate media constructs.

Also, we rarely use the different constructs separately and in isolation from each other. For example, investigative constructs/sciences deal with structured explanations, interpretations, and discoveries of the physically perceivable (i.e., physical, assigned, constitutional, and eventological constructs) through calculative ones (e.g., calculated dimensions, characteristics). Scientific discoveries can create new abstract and inferential concepts (e.g., ideas, roles, judgements), and these concepts can, in turn, inspire more scientific research.

Abstract constructs and various sub-types of inferential constructs mentioned in Table 2.2 typically use words with the same roots to derive states and results, ideas, values, and concepts/properties. For instance, you can feel professionally fulfilled (i.e., fulfilment as a state or result), embrace the concept of professional

Table 2.2 Perceptible but physically unperceivable constructs

Supportive or interpretative—interested in or representing 'why'		
Type(s)	Sub-type(s)	Examples
Investigative constructs	All scientific fields	Mathematics, statistics, logic, linguistics, physics, chemistry, biology, neuroscience, engineering, medicine, sociology, behavioural psychology, criminology, anthropology, management, law, etc.
Calculative constructs	Concepts and properties within and/ or outside unities or unity collections	Time, space, entropy, temperature, weight, past, future, speed, age, reliability, efficiency, productivity, etc.
Abstract constructs	Relative ideas	Diversity-uniformity, philanthropy-misanthropy, inclusion–exclusion, love-hate, hope-despair, belonging-isolation, etc.
Inferential constructs	Emerging relative roles of unities or unity collections	Leader–follower, giver-taker, hero-villain, holding-subsidiary, etc.
	Relative judgments on unities or unity collections	Useful-useless, important-meaningless, good- bad, credible-incredible, safe-unsafe, etc.
	Intangible features of unities or unity collections	Knowledge, decisions, emotions, beliefs, ideas, etc.
	Intangible relative states of unities/ collections	Happiness-sadness, satisfaction-dissatisfaction, comfort-discomfort, safety-accident, etc.
	Intangible resultant events from interactions between unities or unity collections	

fulfilment (i.e., fulfilment as an idea), and judge something as fulfilling or valueless (i.e., fulfilment and valuelessness as judgments).

2.4 Physically Unperceivable Constructs

Albeit in Sect. 8.4, I discuss the sciences dealing with physically unperceivable constructs, for the sake of coherence, in this section, I present briefly their important role and the traps when using those constructs. Sciences, as investigative constructs, use logic, experiments, and observations to investigate and evolve over time. These processes frequently result in standardised practices, methods, and other similar artefacts we use to describe, provisionally explain and manage ourselves and our interactions with the broader physical, social, and technical environments.

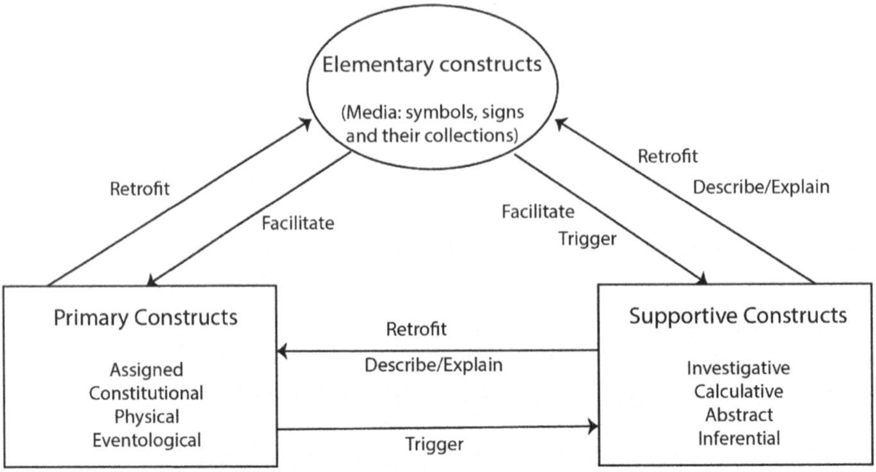

Fig. 2.1 Elementary, primary, and supportive constructs

Calculative constructs are tools that investigative constructs use to support explanations based on definitions against physically observable constructs. Calculative constructs are easier to define and use if there is an agreement on the physical aspects and observable events they represent. For example, weight is measured by standardised instruments that measure the gravitational force on an object free from other external forces. Scales that are properly calibrated will provide consistent measurements, although there may be slight variations due to varying gravity levels in different regions.

Abstract and inferential constructs represent high-level expressions that reflect groups, interactions, and effects of multiple primary constructs. The inferential and abstract constructs connect the unobservable and observable aspects of the world. They serve as the bridges between immaterial and material energy, which I discuss in Chapter 1.

However, the definitions of abstract and inferential constructs are complex and varied over time and across regions. We create such constructs socially, including workplaces, or scientifically. Social constructs carry meanings that develop over time along with humanity, making them difficult to trace to specific time-points and to conveniently decompose into constituents. Contrarily, scientific abstract and inferential constructs are typically created bottom-up and represent clearly defined sets of characteristics, including their interdependencies.

For instance, a common definition of situation awareness[4] includes these processes:

1. Perception of data and information from the environment through the physical senses and attention mechanisms.

[4] Endsley, M. R. (1995). Toward a theory of situation awareness in dynamic systems. *Human Factors, 37*(1), 32–64.

2. Comprehension of meaning and characteristics of the perceived environment. Stored knowledge and information are employed to judge the situation, determine if it is positive or negative, harmful or beneficial, and so on.
3. Projection of the outcomes and effects, depending on whether and how someone will intervene in the situation according to their knowledge and information.

The concept is that situation awareness informs the decision-making of whether and how to act. Someone can explore and break down each of the mentioned situation awareness processes in more detail. For example, senses receive and transmit signals through the nervous system as part of the perception process. Personal experiences and how this process works affect how, when, and if our brains filter information. However, regardless of how you can relate to Endsley's definition above, there are several other models and definitions, perhaps less known, including prescriptive and multi-agent approaches to situation awareness.[5]

Therefore, different when talking about weight where 80 kg means almost the same to everyone, always and everywhere from a definitional viewpoint (i.e., not its interpretation and meaning within professions and societies), when we converse about situational awareness, we might discuss different things depending on what each of us has read and adopted. This is often the case with several abstract and inferential constructs, both of social and scientific origins, within and outside workplaces and professions, when there is no single agreed definition.

For instance, in one region, a healthcare professional assisting a seriously ill individual to end their life might express the construct of philanthropy and the human right to dignity. Elsewhere, it might show unethical, even illegal, behaviour. You can think of plenty of similar examples. Nevertheless, it is not only about this first trap related to persons assuming they mean the same, while arguing about different constructs. There are more traps, possibly more dangerous, which I present in Chapter 3: the objectivisation and personalisation of physically unperceivable constructs and the (mis)use of classifications derived from them.

Definitions: Key Reflections and Actions

Reflections

- Clear and precise definitions are the cornerstone of effective professional communication and collaboration. Misinterpretation often arises when concepts are poorly defined or are reliant on metaphors without clarification.
- Definitions are dynamic constructs that evolve over time, reflecting changes in societal, technological, and professional contexts.
- Vague or inconsistent definitions undermine accountability and productive discourse. Professionals must strive for clarity and consistency in their terminology.

---

[5] National Research Council. (1998). *Modeling human and organizational behavior: Application to military simulations.* The National Academies Press. https://doi.org/10.17226/6173.

- Constructs, whether elementary, primary, or interpretative, are human-made tools designed to make sense of the world. Their categorisation and use must respect context and purpose.

Actions

1. Pursue Clarity: In your professional communications, ensure definitions are explicit and avoid assumptions. Translate metaphors into clear, tangible terms when setting expectations or explaining concepts.
2. Foster Productive Debates: Encourage discussions about definitions within your professional domain. Use these debates to refine shared understanding and adapt definitions to evolving contexts.
3. Evaluate Constructs Critically: Reflect on the constructs you rely on in your practice. Consider whether they adequately serve their intended purpose or if revisions are necessary to align with current realities.
4. Promote Inclusivity in Terminology: Recognise cultural and disciplinary differences in the interpretation of terms. Strive to use language that bridges gaps and invites participation from diverse perspectives.
5. Document Definitions: When working in teams or cross-disciplinary settings, collaboratively establish and document shared definitions to prevent miscommunication and ensure alignment.

By committing to precise, inclusive, and context-sensitive definitions, you can enhance mutual understanding, reduce miscommunication, and support collaborative success in your professional endeavours.

Chapter 3
Constructs and Simplifications

3.1 General

In professional and other communications, we often use metaphors to communicate analogies between physically perceivable (PHPE) constructs, and several of us might employ simplifications to convey meanings that can be complex. For instance, you can praise a professional work by naming it as the spearhead of advancing the respective discipline. Here, the work is not an actual spearhead; the term functions as a metaphor highlighting its significance. In a simplification example, instead of exactly explaining the complex geometry of our galaxy, we can simply state that it looks like a spiral. In this case, the galaxy's shape, which is a PHPE construct, is simplified through another physically perceivable construct, that is, the spiral.

Likewise, for the sake of brevity and efficiency, at work and elsewhere, physically unperceivable (PHUN) constructs often become subjects or objects of interest, although they are not material entities. However, when something takes the meaning of a subject or object, someone could instinctively treat it as PHPE, meaning as an entity that is possible to use, manage, or control directly.

For example, the statement 'Mathematics has helped to describe the world' could be misleading because mathematics, as a discipline, does not act independently and is nothing like a material tool that can help us. In reality, the statement above is a simplified way of saying, 'Mathematicians have provided investigative and calculative constructs which offer to humanity a commonly acceptable description of the physically perceivable world'. For instance, the use of imaginary and complex numbers in circuit theory is a PHUN construct used to describe the PHPE construct of power transmission.

Also, instead of genuinely appreciating the individuals and teams behind scientific developments, understanding their motives and aspirations, reading about the limitations and approximations of their work and findings, and listening to their struggles and their misses and imperfections while striving for success, venerating science can

N. Karanikas, *Professional Generalism in a Hyper-specialised World*,
https://doi.org/10.1007/978-981-96-4039-3_3

become a trap. This occurs when science is viewed as the only way to find truth, especially in professional settings.

In the name of scientific methods, we and all other elements of our world can become objects of mere rationalism. Metaphors about science like 'light in the darkness', 'bridge between known and unknown', 'ladder to new heights of knowledge' can shape false perceptions and mask the limitations and imperfections of science. In turn, intuition, along with whatever does not adhere to or is not subject to standardised techniques to decide and act, can become professionally unacceptable.[1] Obsession with science can make us ignore our professional truths and realities and that not all decisions can be based on science.

In general, in academia and industry, there are metaphorical expressions used to characterise disciplines and fields like health, safety, risk, security, quality, and their management (e.g., low safety, sufficient quality, high risk). There are many examples you can list. The crucial to note is that we cannot directly manage any physically unperceivable constructs. We could manage what these constructs represent, and what they consist of. From a pragmatic perspective, though, metaphorical and simplified expressions are not inherently problematic, and they have immense value in social and professional contexts.[2,3]

3.2 Oversimplification Traps

Several centuries ago, before science and its methods took their current form, people used to attribute unexplained and perceivably uncontrolled positives and negatives of life to metaphysical entities. Back then, there were gods and goddesses of sleep, time, music, wind, and sea. Over time, the inquisitive minds of a few pioneers, who deeply grasped the opportunities of their era and thoroughly considered the scripts and discoveries of previous generations, led to replacing gods and demons with logical connections between physical aspects and observable events.

Science has not explained everything since then, but there has been remarkable progress, and the discovery journey continues, as I further unfold in Chapters 8 and 9. However, sometimes professionals are regressing instead of progressing, despite the known scientific achievements. It seems like ancient demons, fairies, and muses have given their place to modern ones.

It is true almost nobody nowadays refers to Poseidon as the god of the seas, but it is also true that many of us use old and new physically unperceivable constructs as

---

[1] Fischer, E., & Collins, J. (2015). *Experimental philosophy, rationalism, and naturalism.* Routledge, https://doi.org/10.4324/9781315714196.

[2] Moon, B. L. (2007). *The role of metaphor in art therapy: Theory, method, and experience.* Charles C. Thomas.

[3] Beger, A. (2019). *The role of (deliberate) metaphor in communicating knowledge in academic discourse: An analysis of college lectures from different disciplines.* Peter Lang.

subjects and objects. Especially regarding abstract and inferential constructs, expressions such as 'immature culture' and 'increased morale', 'insufficient awareness' and 'focussed attention', 'poor communication' and 'adequate knowledge, 'uncontrolled complexity' and 'ineffective leadership' have become part of our daily professional vocabulary.

However, as mentioned in the section above, using such metaphors and simplifications is not an issue, by default. The problem arises when, instead of those constructs resulting from a bottom-up investigation of the elements they include, they often become verdicts and judgments easy to articulate without prior professional inquiry. Unfortunately, such judgments can hinder progress when used to label causes and effects instead of being used as vehicles and opportunities to move further down and up, right, and left, in and out by examining their constituents.[4]

The above occurs when we do not examine bottom-up any socially, professionally, and scientifically developed abstract and inferential constructs, we find shelter in metaphors, and we are fast in stating verdicts. In those cases, physically unperceivable constructs become the convenient scapegoats, instead of them being the starting points for or concluding arguments of professional debates, discussions, and enquiries.

It must have been the poor culture, the excellent awareness, or the unsuccessful communication that caused something or got affected by something. Sure, but these concepts should not be the starting and final points and destinations when explaining events without either a top-down deduction or bottom-up induction. Otherwise, we will miss every chance to learn, discover further, and improve ourselves, our professions, our clients, and our organisations. Those physically unperceivable constructs can become our modern fairies and demons.

Hence, one veritable trap is the overuse or mere use of subjectified or objectified physically unperceivable PHUN constructs through metaphors and oversimplifications, for they can divert us from what these constructs represent. There is a risk that such PHUN constructs could become the subject or object of interest instead of simple representations. Problems arise when abstract and inferential constructs are treated as physical objects. For instance, saying 'time management', where the PHUN construct of time becomes an objective, is technically inaccurate because we cannot manage time as it does not physically exist, it is not a material object. Actually, the phrase above means 'planning and running specific professional activities within a specific timeframe'.

Chronophobia[5] is another example of using the time construct unproductively as an object or a subject. Worrying about time management[6,7] can lead to an obsession with measuring time and judging ourselves and others by it. Instead, per unit of time or period, we could focus on what we do and how we do it, depending on our physical, mental, and emotional capabilities and the opportunities and obstacles present.

---

4 Dekker, S. (2014). *The field guide to understanding 'human error'*. Ashgate.

5 Lee, P. (2004). *Chronophobia: On time in the art of the 1960's*. MIT Press.

6 Bird, P. (2011). *Effective time management*. Hodder Education.

7 Forsyth, P. (2016). *Successful time management* (4th ed.). Kogan Page Limited.

Similarly, we could say 'Health promotion professionals need to support the public in controlling their weight to avoid long-term health implications'. However, someone does not directly control their weight, which is a physically unperceivable construct. They control their diet and activity that are linked to physically perceivable entities. As such, the expression above actually means something like 'The health promotion professional needs to inform the public about how much and what they could eat and drink to avoid harmful effects, and how they can maintain the balance between energy taken in and spent'.

To address unhealthy eating habits that lead to increasing body weight, it is crucial to understand and manage the underlying reasons. Unfortunately, many become fixated on the scale, connecting weight gain to societal stigma, low status, and poor self-image.[8,9] However, achieving the ideal and desired weight, which they have objectified, can put their overall mental and physical health at stake.[10] Some persons might even think that the ideal body weight means they are healthy, which is not always true.[11]

At the more professional level, such issues especially apply when there are ways to 'measure' the respective constructs. Instead of managing the constituent conditions, activities, and factors, which collectively represent physically unperceivable PHUN constructs like safety, quality, risk, and security, we often get overwhelmed with calculating and creating numerical dashboards to show trends of safety incidents and accidents, quality defects and complaints, security glitches and breachers, and so on. All those attempts link to obsessions with the metaphor of performance, missing to acknowledge that PHUN constructs cannot actually perform because they do not physically exist. Unities, like humans, and unity collections, such as organisations and engineering systems, can perform.

Interestingly, this practice comes with its side effects. For instance, when management overemphasises the reduction of occupational incidents as a reflection of good health and safety performance, workers might hide issues and not report them. That occurs because they do not aspire to be the reason for destroying the remarkably low incident rates an organisation achieved. Then, managers feel comfort because they do not have high incident rates, although they can be higher than what they believe.[12]

Add to cases like the above the diversity of definitions for several physically unperceivable PHUN constructs, especially bred by academics, which drives the development of various 'performance measurements' for exactly the same PHUN construct. This renders the situation even more perplexing. Company A measures quality

---

[8] Sullivan, K. (2004). *How to help your overweight child—Eat healthily and well, enjoy exercise, boost self-esteem & self-respect, achieve a healthier weight*. Rodale.

[9] Gailey, J. (2014). *The hyper(in)visible fat woman weight and gender discourse in contemporary society*. Palgrave Macmillan. https://doi.org/10.1057/9781137407177.

[10] Walker, S. (2015). *Dietland*. Schwartz Publishing Pty. Ltd.

[11] Bacon, L., & Aphramor, L. (2014). *Body respect: What conventional health books get wrong, leave out, and just plain fail to understand about weight*. BenBella Books, Incorporated.

[12] Dekker, S. (2014). *Safety differently: Human factors for a new era*. CRC Press.

performance differently from Company B. Journal article X presents a diametrically opposite quantification of security performance than article Z.

At the same time the definitions of quality in companies A and B and the definitions of security in papers X and Z can be different. This seems like an untold and underestimated chaos of definitions and measurements of PHUN constructs. This situation can be problematic if we are not aware of it, and we are not prepared to fully and transparently share the definitions and meanings we give to the constructs of interest.

3.3 Construct Relativeness

An interesting aspect of all human-made constructs is that we cannot validate them as categorically true or false, undeniably correct, or right. Even if we employ scientific validation, since everything is about constructs, it is not wise to believe that we can indisputably validate constructs based on other constructs. The very concept of validation is, in itself, a complex and multifaceted construct.

During validation, we just compare constructs based on criteria that are constructs themselves. This does not mean to downplay the practical utility and empirical importance of scientific validation methods. However, it is crucial to distinguish between absolute validity and practical, reliable validation methods that we use to test our understanding of the world.

For example, mathematics is a human-made construct developed and established over many centuries. Numbers, equations, calculations, etc. are constructs we decided they can describe the material world. This does not mean mathematics creates physical reality. Rather, it means that physical phenomena can be represented through mathematical models, sometimes with remarkable accuracy and predictive power.

The detection of mathematical patterns in the world reflects the fact that humanity devised mathematics as a language to describe better and possibly explain reality. Indeed, while our mathematical descriptions are indeed constructs, the underlying patterns they describe could exist independently of human observation. However, we cannot test this because we are the observers.

For instance, we accept axiomatically that if we have one apple and we receive one more, we will have two apples. However, we also know that this is a convention because these two apples are not precisely the same. We have two items, both of which we have named apples because we have observed them and decided that their commonalities across various characteristics (e.g., colour, shape, chemical composition, mass, volume, density, taste) outnumber their individual differences. We have accepted that these relative commonalities outweigh the respective dissimilarities.

Time itself presents another compelling example. Of note, in modern physics, the concept of time remains incompletely understood and is not universally accepted in all theoretical frameworks. Still, we use this construct to organise our professional and personal lives, plan, and refer to the past and the future, even though time does not tangibly exist. We calculate the time construct based on intervals of observable events, meaning once more that time is defined in relation to something. When reflecting on the utility of the time construct, some might realise that instead of using it to facilitate the organisation of their professional lives, time has overwhelmingly become a determinant and a performance measurement.

Thus, it is interesting how a non-physically existing entity has become an inextricable part of activities, although time is relevant and the comparisons against time-points is just a convention. Moving to physically perceivable constructs, technology is another example. We can devise criteria and measures to compare technological products between them. However, there is no way to reach any final and absolute conclusion whether any piece of technology is unquestionably good or bad, useful or useless, etc. or other similar attributes. This happens because there is no other non-human-made construct to render this assessment possible.

The central message is that any criteria and measures are constructs we have built to serve specific professional, scientific, societal, and other purposes. Despite their usefulness, they cannot represent the absolute truth. All professional judgments are based on constructs different from the construct under evaluation, which in turn, is compared with another construct, physically perceivable or not, and so on. This is our perpetual journey as humanity in our endeavour to get closer to an undeniable and ultimate truth. This is what partly mobilises our civilisation and, by extension, professions. Thus, it is paramount to acknowledge that everything is defined relatively to something else.

When understanding and interpretation fail against specific constructs, we amend or cancel those constructs, develop new ones, or change our beliefs to match existing constructs. Hence, it is also important to realise that our civilisation and professions rely on comparing constructs, not validating them against any external truth. Frankly, we cannot get out of our own professional truth, which is merely construct based. We cannot be wholly certain because the constructs that we accept or make bound us. Even when we believe we are thinking out of the box, we just build new constructs that replace or change other constructs.

To summarise, there is no absolute high or low, it is about higher and lower than something. There is no white and black, it is about different spectrums of the construct of light. Nothing exists independently; everything gains value through comparison with other things that share similarities and differences. Certainly, while everything is relative because we can only understand things relatively, fundamental physical constants and relationships could exist independently of our relative understanding of them. There is a difference between how we know things and what actually exists.

Someone is a teacher because there are students within the construct of school. I am an employee because there is an employer within the context of work. You are a professional in a specific area because there are other persons who do not possess the respective skills, knowledge, and experience. All the above constructed roles enjoy similarities (e.g., they refer to humans, they can regard persons with similar cultural background) and, at the same time, differ from each other (e.g., different job tasks, diverse anthropometric characteristics). The labels we all carry as human unities are constructs that serve other constructs within a constructed context.

3.4 Controversial Relativeness

Accidents can be controversial examples to illustrate the concept of relativeness. When an aircraft crashes and people die, it is classified as an accident. We assign to this event negative judgments and investigate it to avoid the recurrence of such an event in the future. We might build safer systems, but we can only compare them to older versions based on current knowledge and testing. We do not truly know if the new system is safer than another one if we do not monitor its behaviour over time, depending on the constructed definition of safety. Admittedly, the professionals involved are aware of all these presumptions.

Also, a fatal accident is a negative event because societies have decided that physical death equals to inexistence, and nobody and nothing should expedite this. Indeed, physical death is never welcome, but when people around us get older, we get more familiar with the possibility we will stop existing biologically at some point, eventually. However, why do many of us view 'expedited' death negatively when it is inevitable for everyone at some stage?

One reason is that we use the construct of age (i.e., time spent biologically alive as per the constructed definition of life) to compare current age with the construct of life expectancy. For instance, it is 'sad' for someone to die at 50 when the life expectancy is 85. Another reason is that nowadays people, mainly in the so-called Western culture, believe more in the construct of self-determination. Whatever age we have, we should have (full) control of our choices on how to live our lives, including whether we want to live longer.

Moreover, the belief that death is negative is based on the construct of existence and comparing the physical states of human bodies between different time-points. We have accepted that when there are no vital signs, which are constructs themselves, someone is dead. We confirm this as we see bodies unresponsive to external stimuli and decaying, which we have labelled as an undisputable sign of inexistence too. However, a completely rational person could claim that what we all observe is the transformation of physical material to other forms, the conversion of energy of specific states into others.

Thus, you would wonder why it is about inexistence and not just transformation. Why would we not label this phenomenon as just a change and prefer to name it as inexistence? Indeed, we believe we validate death by observing the effects of physical transformation. However, in reality, we just confirm that the death-related constructs are useful for the goal they were developed, that is, to decide what death is. We cannot know if death is really what we think it is if we have not gotten outside our boundaries of what we label as life.

Also, we often build memorials and hold remembrance events for the presumably inexistent. This is because some other constructs suggest we exist as long as the ones alive remember us. This can relate to the long-living debate about life after physical death, meaning the existence of non-material.[13,14] Maybe, the law of material energy conservation could extend to immaterial energy as well. The fact there is no scientific evidence about the 'survival' of immaterial energy means little, as science is mainly based on material energy constructs. Therefore, perhaps there might be immaterial energy that is not lost but transforms into something we have not yet understood or exists in a space we cannot physically sense.

Furthermore, the labelling of an air accident or death as irrefutably negative can be disputed from the viewpoint of the wider economy. The airline might suffer from direct and indirect business losses. Losing loved ones or having them seriously injured causes great emotional and practical hardship for the victims' families. For instance, there might be persons highly dependent on the ones harmed. Conversely, catastrophes generate income for others. Maybe they sympathise with others' losses but view the accident as a potential source of income, making it less negative for them.

Moreover, we often put aside our disagreements and differences and come together during adverse events like illness, pandemics, accidents, and natural catastrophes to help each other. Less often do we assemble to celebrate successes at the scale we convene to deal with adversities. Certainly, almost all cultures have birth, marriage, and death, and in between many other rites to celebrate events and get together, but not at the scale when calamities occur. Therefore, events sometimes generate favourable results and other times do not. It depends on the senders and receivers of their outcomes and our constructed criteria.

3.5 Inescapable Necessity

Who and what is absolutely A, B, or C will never be categorically proved because we cannot employ external validation. Whatever means of proof we employ, these means are just constructs. That we, as professionals, can agree on something does not mean that it is true and absolute. Despite this, an agreement remains a worthy goal.

This exact act of devising and mixing constructs is simultaneously the beauty, power, and curse of the humanity. Accepting that nobody can capture the absolute truth, and that we are bounded to our own versions of truths, is the cornerstone of defining us as humans and our societies. It is often the motive to find another truth, a better version of what is professionally accepted today.

Animals also use constructs (e.g., physical items such as nests, and media constructs to communicate). Nevertheless, it seems that only humans wonder about their own existence and the whys behind the world, even far back in time. We try to

---

[13] Davis, S. T. (2015). *After we die: Theology, philosophy, and the question of life after death.* Baylor University Press.

[14] Martin, M., & Augustine, K. (2015). *The myth of an afterlife: The case against life after death.* Rowman & Littlefield.

make sense of our environment and the world by devising physically unperceivable constructs. Although the real meaning of these constructs can vary across individuals and can carry positive or negative connotations, collectively are catalysts pushing us to discuss, debate, cooperate, conflict, build and destroy, accept and reject, change and resist.

Civilisation would not possibly exist without the diversity of stories and truths, without gaps and differences in meanings and explanations based on perceivable and unperceivable constructs. Our civilisation and professions would not probably grow and change without physically unperceivable constructs. If everyone was completely certain of the whole truth, conversations would be unnecessary.

Gathering around a table would be pointless if we did not acknowledge our biases and somehow realise our limitations. There would be no need to maintain social systems based on values, beliefs, ideas, and other constructs. We could just join our physical powers like animal flocks to ensure survival in nature.

How grateful we must be when we can socialise and, especially, when we professionally disagree. It is evidence that we admit our imperfection to capture the truth and acknowledge our imprisonment in our understanding of the constructs that we have made or adopted. This is the reason we choose to relate to others professionally regardless of whether we express verbally these acknowledgements while other times we keep them internally.

Otherwise, there would be no need for professional associations, groups, and bodies, there would be no reason to commune professionally. At the community level, we could just hunt and kill together, build nests, share food (or not!), and, generally, try to survive as most of the creatures on earth. We would only need to create constructs essential for our survival, like shelters and tools, and communicate through basic sounds, symbols, and language.

Therefore, the professional challenge is not only to define the roles relative to others, provided there is an agreement on the respective constructs-nouns (e.g., skilled-novice, employer-employee, teacher-student). The two other key challenges you will always have to address depending on the ever-changing context and societal and professional landscapes are:

- when it is proper to discard old and embrace newly born or modified constructs-nous, and
- establishing the basis and criteria for comparing construct–adjectives such as good and bad, trustworthy and doubtful, responsible and irresponsible.

Constructs and Simplifications: Key Reflections and Actions

Reflections

- Constructs are essential tools for understanding and navigating the world, but they are inherently subjective and shaped by context. Recognising their relativity is key to avoiding rigid or overly simplistic interpretations.

- Oversimplification can lead to misjudgements and flawed decisions, especially when nuances are disregarded, or complexities are underestimated.
- The relativeness of constructs requires professionals to critically evaluate their use and implications, ensuring they align with the specific context and purpose.
- Controversial or conflicting constructs should not be dismissed outright but understood as opportunities for dialogue and exploration.
- Simplifications, while necessary for communication and decision-making, must always be treated as provisional frameworks rather than absolute truths.

Actions

1. Critically Assess Constructs: Reflect on the constructs you rely on in your professional practice. Are they overly simplistic? Do they accurately represent the complexities of the issues you address?
2. Avoid Oversimplification Traps: When presenting ideas or making decisions, ensure that simplifications are appropriately qualified. Highlight their limitations and avoid presenting them as definitive answers.
3. Engage with Diverse Perspectives: Encourage dialogue with professionals from different disciplines or backgrounds to uncover potential biases or blind spots in your constructs and interpretations.
4. Challenge and Refine Constructs: Periodically revisit the constructs you use to ensure they remain relevant and accurate in light of new information, evolving contexts, or emerging challenges.
5. Communicate Nuance: In professional settings, articulate the assumptions and limitations of the constructs you use. This transparency fosters trust and promotes a shared understanding amongst colleagues and stakeholders.

By embracing the fluidity of constructs and balancing simplifications with critical reflection, you can navigate complexity more effectively and contribute to a more nuanced and informed professional practice.

Chapter 4
Classifications

4.1 General

Professional practice and science extensively use classifications. We cannot escape classifications because this is the way we understand the world and communicate with ourselves and others. In this book, I present several classifications and groupings of constructs in my effort to introduce structure in the content and facilitate understanding. For the same reason, I present complex concepts in simplified forms, like graphs and symbolic equations.

Driven by innate laws of survival and efficiency, it seems the human brain is wired to categorise everything with the aim of minimising the amount of effort necessary to make sense of the environment. Mental shortcuts simplify complex decision-making processes, meaning that we do not have to analyse everything constantly and thoroughly. When such simplifications generate favourable outcomes, most analysts focus on the underlying processes, called heuristics. When those mechanisms retrospectively lead to anything undesired, often under the influence of external factors, most scholars use the term biases. These two terms have opposite connotations (i.e., heuristics—positive; biases—negative), but they have their roots in the same natural trait.[1,2] All heuristics can lead to biases and many biases source from heuristics.

Classifications represent capabilities (syntactics—what something can do) and meanings (semantics—what something is about) of unities and constructs and are used to inform decisions and (in)actions. For example, when somebody encounters a snake, they will probably avoid close contact with it as it might attack and poison them. We cannot know if the latter is always true, but most likely the person above does not want to test it. This is what their brain informs them because they have classified snakes as a potential threat to their life. This classification resulted from seeing humans attacked by snakes and similar reptiles in documentaries and stories.

---

[1] Kahneman, D., Slovic, P., & Tversky, A. (1982). *Judgment under uncertainty: Heuristics and biases*. Cambridge University Press.

[2] Caverni, J.-P., Fabre, J.-M., & Gonzalez, M. (1990). *Cognitive biases*. North-Holland.

N. Karanikas, *Professional Generalism in a Hyper-specialised World*,
https://doi.org/10.1007/978-981-96-4039-3_4

Besides, the particular person might not be a biologist or professionally skilled at classifying a snake as venomous or not. As such, they better not cross paths with the snake or whatever resembles a snake.

Of course, someone unfamiliar with negative snake stories or who has rejected them as untrue or exaggerating might classify snakes as wondrous and approach them closely. Will they be attacked? We cannot know as it does not depend only on the individual. Does the fact that someone is afraid of snakes mean that those exquisitely shaped and coloured animals are useless, and we must annihilate them? Of course, not. This would be a misuse of the classification of snakes as threats for somebody's life under specific circumstances. Apart from the fact many snakes are not venomous, we also need to recognise the importance of biodiversity and the role each unity plays in stabilising the world and contributing to its fine balance.[3]

Beyond classifications of physical agents, there are also role classifications. The utility of roles relates to particular expectations and responsibilities as per various social, professional, legislative, and other similar types of constructs. Medical professionals must improve the health of their patients, and the latter are expected to follow medical advice. Teachers need to teach students current information, and students need to show they learned it. Employers must offer a suitable work environment and compensate workers fairly, and workers must perform their tasks as agreed with the employer.

Another interesting point regards classifications that do not emerge 'naturally'. Those are the ones suggested, sometimes vigorously advertised through intense promotion. Social sciences are an example of a domain introducing tens of classification schemes to categorise persons and groups. Personality types (e.g., extravert and introvert), learning styles (e.g., converger and diverger), leadership styles (e.g., transactional, transformative, and servant), and other less and more popular classifications are abundant in the publication landscape and professional arena. They are spreading through online and in-person events, becoming common in education, management, and professional fields. There are also variations of those categories across demographics (e.g., age, work experience, geographical location, gender, and others), leading to a blend of many subcategories.

Nonetheless, an understanding of my personality type can be of value if you and I use this information for some good cause. The latter for me could be the identification of channels to render my personality traits more useful for the society and my profession. For you, a good cause should be the accommodation of who I am and what I need to perform, as per my personality type, to the extent that my preferences do not clash profoundly with the ones of yours and others.

[3] Leveque, C., & Mounolou, J. (2003). *Biodiversity*. Wiley.

4.2 Classification Perils

Despite the necessity and value of classifications, things seem different from ideal. First, the connotations some classifications carry, mainly because of broader social and professional stereotypes, render people who fall mainly into one category automatically 'worse' than others. Thus, inadvertently perhaps, such classifications introduce divisions. Somebody is extremely proud of themselves for being a 'personality type A' predominantly. They are also sorry about others being a 'personality type B' mainly, just because this is what the classification implies or directly claims. Some persons go so far as to label people as 'toxic' and suggest avoiding them like harmful substances and excluding them from work activities and social initiatives.

There is an abundance of popular self-management books that people read in their genuine endeavour to understand themselves and their surroundings. Unfortunately, these publications often simplify too much, leading to unhelpful divisions instead of solutions. After reading a considerable number of such books, which can be far from scientifically sound, some individuals start feeling confident in decoding others, grouping them, and, inadvertently, discriminate. Some best-selling books sometimes create blindly devoted fans we have to manage.

Unfortunately, the situation above sometimes extends to professional and other role and ranking constructs (e.g., worker, supervisor, line manager, middle manager, senior manager). Although their utility should be the facilitation of connecting levels of knowledge, skills, and experience with expectations and responsibilities, such constructs are used to assign authority, privilege, and other powers over others. The situation gets more intriguing with inferential constructs, especially judgements towards humans and various emerging roles.

If you are 'a good team player', you can join the group, but if you are 'a bad team player', you do not belong here. If you fall somewhere in between, you do not still belong to the professional community. However, you can become eligible if you successfully complete a probation period, the length and form of which the specific community has decided based on their constructed criteria. If you dislike or challenge these criteria, then you should look somewhere else. Also, if you are 'professionally friendly', the group will share with you, but if you look 'professionally unfriendly', you are not worthy of receiving from the group. If you are 'professionally semi-friendly, semi-unfriendly', you must prove you can become consistently 'professionally friendly' as per the constructed criteria. If you do not endorse these criteria, you should look elsewhere.

Indeed, we can refine classifications to prevent discrimination based on individual traits. However, substituting group names does not solve the problem if any new wording still carries similar connotations. For example, many societies discourage any form of racism by banning the use of skin colour to distinguish between humans. Thus, instead of talking about black, brown, and other skin colours different from white, they devised the term 'people of colour'. They believe this is less insulting and discriminatory.

The real meaning of the new classification above is 'people who do not have the same skin colour as ours, which is white'. After all, white, being a colour also, encompasses white people as individuals of colour. Also, it is interesting to observe how many use the particular classification. They use it mostly to describe disadvantaged communities, but they do not use it the same often to praise them. But is it really the 'people of colour' who really suffer? Is it perhaps the 'people whom others have treated unfairly because of (un)conscious biases and stereotypes related to their different skin colour'? A vast difference exists between those two expressions.

It is also true that several societies have made significant steps to accommodate the 'disabled', which is another grouping variable frequently used. In some regions, laypersons and professionals prefer using the term 'persons with special abilities'. This sounds indeed better than the term 'disabled' as it removes the 'dis-' part, which carries negative connotations most of the time (e.g., disorganised, dissonance). The new term tries to convey a more positive perspective. However, this change is inadequate; we all possess diverse abilities (e.g., skills, talents) in different areas, a reality that does not make us 'disabled' in the narrow sense the term targets.

We are all 'persons with special abilities' and, from a broader perspective, we are all 'disabled' to perform professional and other activities across any context. This is because we lack the experience and skills needed for every situation. However, this is not what the particular classifications targets; it is not about 'disability'. It is actually about 'difficulties of some fellow citizens to live in the world the majority has constructed to accommodate the average human'. If we would all be 'disabled' under the current definition of the term, what we today call 'disability' would become the 'regular' reality. Societies would have discovered ways to convert what we today classify 'disability' into normative 'ability'. Again, the message here is that the use of the blanket construct 'disabled' might not allow to think that it represents the people whom the majority has marginalised through their choices to focus on the needs of the 'regular'.

The above apply similarly when performing studies and generating results for worker groups of different demographics (e.g., young, mature, and older workers). For instance, some might know the ergonomic principle of 'design the work environment to match the people'. Yet, many organisations do the opposite. They mainly design tasks and processes, and purchase equipment solely based on efficiency and productivity criteria, and then select workers that match best the 'given' work environment. In other cases, instead of empowering everyone to mobilise their abilities for the collective benefit, management discourages recruiting people who are less experienced, older than an age threshold, trained at a low-ranking university, and so on.

Hence, instead of using classifications to accommodate diversity and get prepared for changing ourselves and the environment to fulfil the needs of as many as possible, several employ screening tests to classify others as acceptable or not. For instance, they want to attract and retain only persons with personalities that match the work environment, which they often perceive as fixed and unchangeable. I might have the technical skills and proper education, but the selection panel cannot accept my job application because I am more vocal and less agreeable than others in the particular organisation. Their definition of diversity is limited to the demographics (e.g., gender, age, nationality) and not personality types.

Indeed, we cannot constantly change things just because someone new joins. However, presuming you have professionally done your best on the system design side, and you are keen to 'classify' to understand and accommodate differences amongst groups, there is another challenge, as explained below. Given a specific environment and system capability (e.g., time, equipment, workforce composition), the groups that seem 'more advantaged' might not want to spare resources to become 'averagely advantaged' and elevate the 'less advantaged'. Here, any grouping has no real value.

Hence, such classifications should be about the concurrent and mutually beneficial adaptation of one to another. It should not be about comparing skills and talents between professionals. It must be about actively contemplating the efforts and opportunities to develop those skills and talents and discovering avenues to share them openly with everyone. What you are missing could be found in the professional peers at the next desk, and what the latter are missing can be offered by you or someone else. The currently 'less advantaged' must be also determined to use those resources provided by the 'more advantaged' to lift their level. Failing such conditions, groups become divisive and stigmatising.

This point is vitally important as sometimes the groups and classifications become excuse platforms for the ones who lie at the edges of the distributions. Certain 'highly disadvantaged' outsiders might purposefully not grab the opportunities shared by others and choose to remain 'marginalised' for various reasons. On the other hand, some 'highly advantaged' outsiders might feel they unquestionably and fully deserve their status and choose to maintain their relatively prominent position instead of sharing with others.

Do examples such as the ones above suggest that those classifications and judgements are used correctly or misused? The answer is tricky and depends on who responds. Is it about the ones who decide the acceptance or rejection or the ones who are classified? Also, what criteria does each of these two sides apply? Admittedly, there is no sign of any malevolent intentions of the creators of classifications. Thus, we should approach the utility and misuse of such categorisations based on the presumption of innocence. Perhaps the classifiers wanted to help our society and its professions somehow, despite the side effects of their efforts.

Still, it is crucial to note that classifications often carry implicit assumptions that reflect the perspectives of dominant groups, shaping what is considered 'normal' or 'regular'. Any term that implies a deviation from a socially constructed norm of ability often privileges the perspectives of those who fit that norm. This framing can marginalise individuals by defining them primarily in terms of their differences rather than their contributions. Exploring the power dynamics inherent in such classifications can reveal how they often perpetuate systemic inequalities. By examining who defines these norms and why, we must critically assess classifications and seek more inclusive, context-sensitive alternatives.

4.3 Comparisons and Exclusivity

Two additional points of attention regarding some classifications are *false comparisons* and the *delusion of mutually exclusive values*. Both points relate primarily to the misuse and not the original intentions behind introducing classifications. The discipline of leadership and management are good examples to illustrate those issues. First, in some professional circles, there have been several arguments based on comparisons between managers/bosses and leaders. Those positions suggest the former comprise the 'bad' guys (i.e., something that we should never pursue becoming), and the latter are the 'good' guys, the ones whom we would like to resemble. This is a tangible example of a false dichotomy as managers are appointed roles and leaders emerge, and those two groups have distinctly different but complementary functions.[4]

At the abstract level, the role of a manager is to ensure a systematic way to run an organisation (structure, targets, processes, measurements, etc.). The leader's role is to recognise, respect, and mobilise all active and dormant organisational capabilities and assets. A leader should capitalise on human and other unity interactions to achieve organisational objectives. Hence, there is no conflict, and many professionals execute both functions in parallel, although with varying intensity.[5] Given the time and space to prioritise organisational development, they can emerge as a 'leading manager'. They can be a 'managing leader' when there are pressures, emergencies, and critical situations to confront, where they harvest the results of the 'leading manager' role previously. The new normal involves combining the roles of entrepreneur, leader, and manager instead of keeping them separate.[6]

Regarding the delusion of mutually exclusive values, a cursory search online or elsewhere will return mainly three leadership types amongst other classifications[7]: transactional, transformational, and servant. The first one corresponds to the 'bad' manager/boss mentioned above, and the second type closely reflects the 'good' leader role discussed above. The last type, the servant, is the evolution of the 'good' leader type. Servant leadership inverts the leader–follower dynamic, utilising organisational capacity to serve members instead of organisational goals. Frankly speaking, the servant leader type cancels and opposes diametrically the transactional leader role. Those two types seem to lie at the extremes of leadership paradigms and allegedly cannot coexist in the same individual. Despite initial impressions, a closer look reveals that this assertion is incorrect.

First, if we blindly accept that all leaders must be servants to deliver outcomes, it could create the false impression the organisational mission is not to produce and offer services and goods for its clients, customers, and the public. Staff could form the view that their sole goal is to serve the needs of each other within the organisation

[4] Murphy, R., & Murphy, K. (2017). *Manager vs. leader: Untying the Gordian Knot*. Routledge.

[5] Owen, J. (2018). *The mindset of success: Accelerate your career from good manager to great leader*. Kogan Page Limited.

[6] Bolton, B., & Thompson, J. (2015). *The entrepreneur: The all-in-one entrepreneur-leader-manager*. Routledge, Taylor & Francis Group.

[7] Kippenberger, T. (2002). *Leadership styles*. Capstone Pub.

despite the outcomes. This feels more like a family, guild, or social community, and less like a business. Structures like the former are primarily interested in meeting the needs of their members, although their role as a sub-system within a larger system also affects others around.

Second, contemporary management education always covers employee needs (often legally mandated). Modern management theory goes beyond just profits and production targets. These publications, amongst others, support the creation of common goals, both internally and externally. Therefore, why cannot one person use multiple leadership styles successfully, as, for example, the situational leadership model suggests?[8,9] System transformations require systematic transactions, and effective transactions require transformations. Transactions and transformations can together serve individuals, teams, departments, and the entire system based on a balanced and agreeable approach.

Genuinely accommodating the needs of others to the degree possible will also serve the acceptance and substantial implementation of transactions and transformations. Recognising that we do not manage people directly (e.g., the construct of human resources management) but the resources they possess, as I illustrate in Chapter 15, can bring greater clarity. Hence, classifications like the ones referring to leadership styles, although useful to trigger discussions and reflections, have no applicability to professional practice if presented as mutually exclusive categories.

The bottom line is that you must use classifications with caution. Classifications are helpful, but we should remember their limits. For instance, organisations now use the concepts of 'inclusion' and 'diversity' to address inequality in jobs and other opportunities. Indeed, in cases like this, classifications are valuable if honestly consulted to improve and not discriminate.

Unfortunately, some individuals often use them to produce stereotypes and accept and embrace or reject and despise. In our era of inclusivity, it is rather ironic to still use classifications as grounds to screen, profile, or reject humans based on their characteristics, demographics, and so on. The message is not that classifications are useless. However, they might be catastrophic in the 'wrong' hands.

Classifications: Key Reflections and Actions

Reflections

- Classifications are powerful tools for organising and understanding information, but they are human constructs that carry inherent biases and limitations.
- Over-reliance on rigid classifications can lead to exclusionary practices and a failure to recognise overlaps, nuances, and evolving dynamics.
- Classifications often reflect the perspectives and priorities of their creators. Awareness of this subjectivity is critical for their responsible use.

---

[8] Blanchard, K. H., Zigarmi, P., & Zigarmi, D. (1985). *Leadership and the one minute manager: Increasing effectiveness through situational leadership*. Morrow.

[9] Blanchard, K. H. (2007). *Leading at a higher level: Blanchard on leadership and creating high performing organizations*. Prentice Hall.

- Comparisons based on classifications can unintentionally foster exclusivity or competition, rather than collaboration or mutual understanding.
- Effective use of classifications requires an understanding of their context, purpose, and limitations, as well as a willingness to adapt them as needed.

Actions

1. Examine Classification Biases: Reflect on the classifications you use in your professional work. Identify any inherent biases or limitations and consider their potential impact on decisions or outcomes.
2. Embrace Flexibility: Avoid treating classifications as absolute or immutable. Be open to revising or expanding them to account for new insights, perspectives, or changes in context.
3. Foster Inclusivity: When using classifications, ensure they do not exclude or disadvantage individuals or groups. Aim for frameworks that accommodate diversity and complexity.
4. Contextualise Comparisons: Use classifications as a basis for comparisons but always contextualise their application. Highlight the specific factors and assumptions underlying your analyses.
5. Promote Critical Dialogue: Encourage discussions within your team or organisation about the classifications you rely on. This can help uncover blind spots and lead to more comprehensive and equitable frameworks.

By recognising the fluid and subjective nature of classifications and using them thoughtfully, you can avoid the pitfalls of rigidity and contribute to more nuanced and inclusive professional practices.

Chapter 5
Energy

5.1 General

There have been several definitions of *energy*. Depending on the discipline (e.g., physics, biology), energy can be defined as a capacity, ability, power, vitality, and other constructs. These definitions of energy all share a common denominator: they reflect the potential within a single unit. Energy can enable changes, physically observable or not, internally or externally to unities.

A unity, depending on its type and its constituent sub-unities, can receive, store, use, and transmit energy at different time-points, consecutively or in parallel. As no unity exists in an absolute vacuum and every unit is in a constant exposure to and interaction with other unities, each unity can affect and be affected concurrently by the energy of itself and other unities. No exposure or interaction can occur without the presence of energy, and, reciprocally, where energy exists, exposures and interactions occur. More specifically:

- A *nonreciprocally exposed unity* (hereafter commonly referred to as *exposed unity*) only receives energy from one or more unities and does not send any energy back to these unities (i.e., unidirectional energy flow). For example, when someone is exposed to radiation or to the behaviours of a group of individuals, they are the exposed unity.
- A *nonreciprocally emitting unity* (hereafter commonly referred to as *emitting unity*) radiates energy to other unities that do not send energy back to the specific unity, at least noticeably (i.e., unidirectional energy flow). For instance, a radio transmitter emits energy waves that are received by radios, televisions, and other devices. Such devices do not send any significant amount of energy back to the transmitter.
- A *reciprocally interacting unity* (hereafter commonly referred to as *interacting unity*) engages in energy exchange with one or more unities (i.e., bidirectional and multidirectional energy flow). This occurs, for example, during conversations involving multiple individuals.

N. Karanikas, *Professional Generalism in a Hyper-specialised World*,
https://doi.org/10.1007/978-981-96-4039-3_5

The definitions above suggest that interaction is a broad concept that encompasses energy exposures and emissions between the unities involved. Nevertheless, single exposures and emissions can also trigger interactions. This occurs when the unities want to influence the intensity, effects, and other characteristics of exposures or emissions at the time they occur, or want to avoid or minimise those in the future.

For example, when you are under the sunlight, you cannot interact with the sun and influence the energy coming from it. Therefore, you can say you are the exposed unity, and the sun is the emitting unity. However, your internal body elements (i.e., smaller unities within you) interact with each other because of the sun exposure (e.g., produce sweat and alter the heartbeat). Hence, although as a larger unity you do not interact directly with the sun, your exposure to the sun triggers internal interactions amongst your sub-unities.

You can also protect your skin and gain thermal comfort through interactions with other unities that you engage while under the sun. For instance, putting a hat on and applying sun protection means you interact with the hat and sun cream. Those items are now more directly exposed to the sun because they are placed between you and the sun.

Another example is when someone witnesses a person misbehaving towards another person. If for any reason the witness does not intervene in this situation, they are exposed to the energy emitted by each of these persons and exchanged between them. However, this does not mean that the energy of the observer remains unaffected. Their thoughts and emotions regarding the event may persist beyond its conclusion. They can also report this unacceptable behaviour. This means the exposure to the event led them to interact with available reporting channels (e.g., calling the police). Also, they can directly intervene when witnessing the event and attempt to protect the victim, meaning they will interact with the persons involved.

Hence, the differentiation between interactions, exposures, and emissions depends on the unities of focus and whether the energy flows unidirectionally or bidirectionally (Fig. 5.1). Of note, in Fig. 5.1, I have not included multidirectional flows as those in reality comprise multiple bidirectional flows.

5.2 Energy and the Brain

All living organisms, by their very nature, are fundamentally driven by the imperative of survival, an instinct that shapes their behaviours and adaptations. Their priority is to meet the needs of their own and close environment with the goal of living longer and ensuring the conservation of their species. In energy terms, living beings aim to efficiently use and replenish their energy to prolong their physical existence. Conceptually, this extends to everyone, from individuals to large organisations and nations.

Naturally, the above assumes living organisms know the 'how', 'who', 'when', 'where', and 'what' of matters related to themselves and the other unities with which they interact. Scientists are not sure yet how plants and microorganisms without

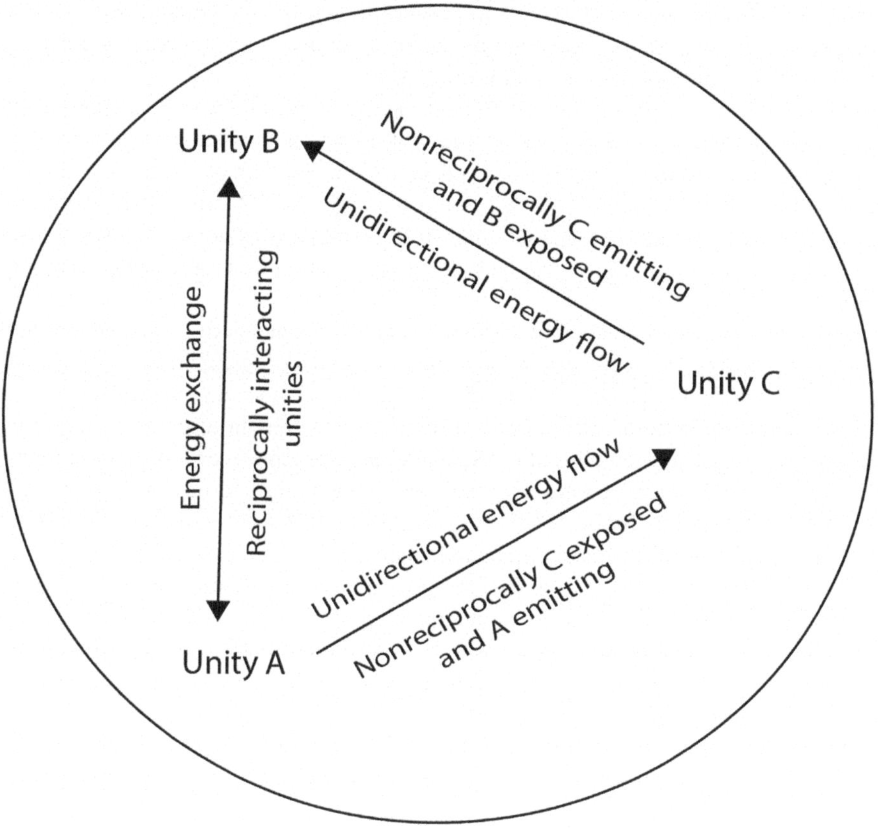

Fig. 5.1 Unidirectional and bidirectional energy flows

a (fully developed) brain 'know', as per our constructed definitions of brain and knowledge. Nevertheless, those unities 'know' at least some of the interrogative aspects above.

Viruses know how to inhabit other organisms, reproduce within the latter, and try to take control of them. There are indications that plants can sense their environment and use material energy to communicate,[1,2] a process which humans perform with the employment of both material (e.g., the functioning of our senses) and immaterial means (e.g., knowledge and decisions).

Undoubtedly, the fields of biology and genetics have advanced incredibly and acknowledge the effects of interactions between living organisms and their environment. Scientists have discovered the tremendous role of Deoxyribonucleic acid

---

[1] Karban, R. (2015). *Plant sensing and communication*. University of Chicago Press.

[2] Becard, G. (2017). *How plants communicate with their biotic environment*. Academic Press.

(DNA) and Ribonucleic acid (RNA) and other tiny unities and collections in development and physical traits. However, these observations have not provided answers about how all these smaller physical unities 'know'.

Plants somehow know how to use solar energy to grow, where to expand their roots, and where to turn when seeking sunlight. Research now shows plants may be intelligent, social, and sensitive to sleep deprivation. You can choose to say a virus mutates because of random flaws while reproducing itself. Many avoid attributing this to the virus's agency or external control. It would be convenient, indeed, to hold the former belief, but it could also be a flawed perception that intelligence is solely a human privilege.

Therefore, it is not wise to apply double standards when dealing with humans and other living beings. While not overlooking fundamental biological differences, immaterial elements might exist in all living things. Nonetheless, science is more confident in how biological systems like animals develop knowledge through observing them and analysing signs from their bodies. Scientists are even more certain about humans. Neuroscience has developed exponentially and amazingly and has offered insights into the functioning of brains. Still, there are no universal references to how basic human brain functions develop, grow, and change.

For example, in linguistics, although there are various theories about language acquisition, we still lack a solid understanding of how we acquire such knowledge. There is the behaviourist approach (i.e., children imitate adults), innate ability perspective (i.e., language learning mechanisms in the brain), cognitive theory (i.e., language learning as a mental process), and interactionism (i.e., language as a means of communication within a context of interaction). Of course, there are a few more approaches, but all those apply here and fail elsewhere, as they do not offer explanations that apply universally.

The development of our beliefs and knowledge about the brain over time suggests that humanity is not far away from the point when it started exploring answers to the 'big' questions, mainly about the nature of cognition, emotions, and consciousness.[3,4] However, scientists now know much more about the brain in physical and chemical terms. In one of his books,[3] Andrew Wickens explains the beliefs in ancient times about the duality of body and spirit. Then he continues with the discoveries about the nervous system over time, and he concludes with the interesting observation '*However, it should also not be forgotten that the human brain is incredibly complex with many mysteries, including its capacity for consciousness and free will, which in theory should not exist in a predetermined material world*' (p. 345).

Indeed, Andrew, in his work, unfolds the stages of discovery and understanding of our brains. Roman physician Galen revealed the cranial nerves and charted our peripheral nervous system. Herman von Helmholtz measured how fast the electrical impulse of nerves travel and laid the grounds for later explanations of the several biophysical and biochemical properties of our bodies. The emergence of the

---

[3] Wickens, A. P. (2015). *A history of the brain: From Stone Age surgery to modern neuroscience*. Psychology Press.

[4] Wickens, A. P. (2019). *Key thinkers in neuroscience*. Routledge.

neuron doctrine and the observations of synapses gave birth to neuroscience with astonishingly beneficial results since then.

John Newport Langley discovered the sympathetic and parasympathetic nervous systems. Scientists realised that learning and memory involve networks of reflexive neural activity. Cortical localisation has helped to target and support specific regions of brain activities. Nathaniel Kleitman understood the sleep mechanisms and the role of circadian rhythms, and he discovered the rapid eye movement phase of sleep.

Brenda Milner revealed the importance of the hippocampus in long-term memory. James Oldsand identified the brain parts hosting our pleasure and reward centres. Various experiments confirmed chemical transmissions occur in the central nervous system. Roger Sperry showed that the two cerebral hemispheres of our brains correspond to diverse psychological abilities and personalities. These discoveries about the brain have enhanced life through advancements in psychology, psychiatry, and medicine.

Nonetheless, the eighteenth-century debate between Haller (brain mechanics) and Whytt (soul-like principle) is still unresolved.[3] Paul MacLean attempted to explain human behaviour and emotions by introducing the limbic system, which, in simple terms, is a layer which mammals supposedly inherit through evolution. It allegedly mediates our affective behaviour and primary social emotion. The limbic system is something like a programmatic mechanism that predisposes us.

However, the limbic system remains vastly an inferential construct as there has been no universal acceptance of what constitutes it, whereas some scientists have also assigned to it mental functions.[4] Besides, Benjamin Libetsky's research suggests a time gap between intending an action and performing it, allowing consciousness to intervene. In his latest work,[5] Benjamin claimed we cannot describe consciousness in terms of any observable constituents. Thus, although scholars and others have transformed the mind-soul dipole debates into discussions about consciousness and unconsciousness, humanity still lacks definite answers.

Andrew[4] also outlines the work of Michael Gazzaniga '*... decision-making, judgement, perception and almost every other cognitive and emotional actions in the brain are unconscious—and what we recognise as consciousness arises after in the left hemisphere, through a process which Gazzaniga calls post-hoc rationalisation*' (p. 252). Andrew finishes his book with a reference to the works of Joseph Edward LeDoux and Patricia and Paul Churchland. The former insists that emotions fall under the concept of mental information processing. Joseph Edward LeDoux denies any attribution of phenomenological experiences to emotions. Patricia and Paul recommend a collaborative neuroscience and philosophy approach to understanding the brain. Such debates in neuroscience and philosophy can be far more complex than I have summarised above.

---

[5] Libet, B. (2004). *Perspectives in cognitive neuroscience. Mind time: The temporal factor in consciousness*. Harvard University Press.

Table 5.1 Basic differences in energy types

Energy type	Used	Sensed	Felt
Material (physical potential)	X	X	–
Cognitive (mental potential)	X	–	–
Affective (emotional potential)	–	–	X

5.3 Energy Types and States

Developments and positions like the ones I reviewed in the section above suggest that our inability to measure directly immaterial aspects has led to scientific and philosophical debates about their existence. There have been continuous and rich discussions about the materialism-immaterialism dipole since ancient times.[6,7,8,9] Nevertheless, the fact we cannot physically sense something should not reject it exists.

Therefore, subject to future developments and based on what science (does not) know at the time of writing this book, we can safely support that energy comes in two major forms, namely material energy and immaterial energy. Material energy corresponds to the physical potential in unities. Immaterial energy can be classified into cognitive energy (mental potential) and affective energy (emotional potential) of unities.[10] As a first distinction between the three energy types (Table 5.1):

- material energy can be sensed and used but cannot be felt.
- cognitive energy can be used but cannot be sensed or felt.
- affective energy can be felt but cannot be sensed or used.

Of note, the use of the terms 'sense' and 'feel' above represents different categories of 'experience', depending on the context. Simply put, sensing relates to experiencing external unities, whereas feeling relates to experiencing internal responses to whatever we sense externally. Often, it is challenging to discern between those two categories of experience because they emerge simultaneously. For example, you can sense a desk office (e.g., see, touch), which contains material energy, and feel glee while working on it. Also, you can feel overwhelmingly happy for winning a contract, but you cannot directly use your happiness. You can use your knowledge to solve a problem, but you cannot touch or feel your knowledge.

More specifically, *physical or material energy* is contained in all unities. It can be sensed and used, and it is the only energy type that is directly measurable through investigative and calculative constructs. Conventionally, *joule* is the unit of measuring material energy. Measurement constructs for material energy focus on the properties

---

[6] Brown, R., & Ladyman, J. (2019). *Materialism: A historical and philosophical inquiry*. Routledge.

[7] Wolfe, C. (2016). *Materialism: A historico-philosophical introduction*. Springer. https://doi.org/10.1007/978-3-319-24820-2.

[8] Harman, G. (2016). *Immaterialism: objects and social theory*. Polity.

[9] Tipton, I. (2019). *Berkeley: The philosophy of immaterialism*. Routledge.

[10] Blackman, L., & Rojek, C. (2012). *Immaterial bodies affect, embodiment, mediation*. Sage.

of unities and the degree to which empirically sensed interactions and changes, which are usually named physical processes, occur within and between unities.

For instance, most can sense cold and hot through thermal energy and sour and sweet tastes through chemical energy. Most can see objects in the environment through radiated light energy, hear sounds because of atmospheric pressure changes, and so on. Also, the chemical energy we all receive through food is physical energy that represents reactions of tiny unities and the structures they form. When we want to move an object, we apply a force that is physical energy originating from chemical reactions in our bodies. Specialists can measure many of those interactions and changes through different instruments and devices scientists have developed.

Cognitive energy is dimensionless. It is the type of immaterial energy no unity can sense or feel but which all unities use to control their physical energy. Cognitive energy associates with mental features (e.g., memories, knowledge, thoughts, mental models) and processes such as recalling, decision-making, storage, and thinking. Although we cannot sense the features of cognitive energy (e.g., we cannot see or touch our knowledge or memories), we use those as necessary parts of cognitive processes. We employ these processes when accepting or creating constructs based on our own experiences or as shared by others. Examples include classifications (e.g., employer and employee, professional and practitioner) and values attached to the material energy (e.g., acceptable and unacceptable, critical and unimportant, ethical and unethical).

Notably, cognitive processes can be indirectly observable and physically traceable when physical energy changes occur. For example, we can infer cognitive energy when we observe a unity externally (e.g., specific face gestures and body postures denoting someone is thinking) or use special equipment that scans and monitors internal parts of a unity (e.g., electroencephalographs in brain-type unities). In this book, I use the construct of *cognitive associations* to refer to foundational elements of cognitive energy.

Different from cognitive and material energy, *affective energy* does not include processes. It is the dimensionless type of energy that a unity can feel but cannot use or sense. Affective energy is the type of immaterial energy born through the interactions between and combinations of:

- each unity's experiences of material energy,
- the attachment of values by cognitive energy to (a) own material energy experiences or (b) information from the experiences of other unities, and
- internalised ethical principles (Sect. 1.4).

Affective energy drives cognitive energy and its processes to deal with material energy. It can also drive material energy directly without the (substantial) engagement of cognition, as I elaborate on further in Sect. 11.3. In the rest of the book, I use the concept of *affective references* to refer to the foundational elements of affective energy.

For instance, when seeing a building on fire, we can feel worried and scared. Our feelings will depend on whether we have experienced fire and its effects on us, witnessed its impacts on others, or been informed that this is an unwanted event, and unacceptable if intentionally caused. These feelings (i.e., affective energy) can drive us to help the building occupants to fight the fire, call the fire brigade, start calling others to help, and report the persons who caused it. This means that our affective energy would lead us to use our cognitive energy to mobilise our physical energy. It can also happen that we instinctively run away without even thinking. This denotes the direct mobilisation of our physical energy with the minimum use of cognitive energy, which we predominantly use to navigate in the environment when running away.

Material and cognitive energy work in tandem, and because they can be used, together represent the *Usable Energy State (UES)*. The collaborations between cognitive and material channels can also transmit information about the state of the affective energy of a unity. You could tell a colleague is upset if their project went over budget by watching their body language and listening to their tone.

However, translating and interpreting what we sense in other unities cannot ensure we authentically reconstruct their originally experienced feelings and emotions. An individual or unity can use their cognitive and material energy to communicate with others about what they feel. However, although we can all mutually share with others how we feel, we can never feel what the ones sharing exactly feel.

Material and cognitive energy can also be characterised by three basic constructs, which together shape the construct of *energy state* in each time-point:

Quantity	how much/many,
Quality	how good, and
Accessibility	how available/ready.

Consequently, the energy state construct encompasses more than just the amount of material and cognitive energies. Admittedly, in our era, some overvalue quantity and undervalue the significance of quality and accessibility. For example, somebody might have a lot of material energy but cannot use it. When someone is obese, they have large material energy quantities. However, if they cannot move around easily and perform necessary manual tasks within a reasonable timeframe, their material energy might not be of adequate quality and accessibility for the specific context. Therefore, this case does not represent an overall 'good' energy state from a holistic viewpoint or for the particular context.

Because affective energy can only be experienced and cannot be physically observed or used, it reflects a space shaped by multiple and multidirectional exposures, interactions, and their combined effects. Hence, we could not attribute to it distinct quantity, quality, and accessibility dimensions. Therefore, the construct of *Affective Energy Balance (AEB)* can correspond to the state of this energy type. The term balance here is not used to mean equilibrium, but the cumulative state of affective energy. AEB can take positive or negative signs in correspondence with positive and negative emotions and feelings. It is like the balance of a bank account that represents the difference between credits and debits.

5.4 Usable and Overall Energy

In this section, I discuss the interactions of the three energy types from the overall energy state perspective. Of note, the perspectives I discuss when referring to energy regard a single unity. However, the concepts I cover, along with the examples I provide, also apply to cases of sub-unities, inter-unity interactions, and unity systems, networks, and groups with defined boundaries.

As mentioned earlier, per time-point, the collaboration between material and cognitive energy of each unity, as symbolised in Eq. (5.1), represents its *Usable Energy State (UES)*.

$$\begin{aligned}&\textit{Usable Energy State}\ (\textit{UES})\\&\qquad\propto \textit{Material Energy State}\ (\textit{MES}) + \textit{Cognitive Energy State}\ (\textit{CES})\end{aligned} \tag{5.1}$$

In each moment, useable energy UES can be:

- stored and be later available for use/exchange (*reserved energy*), or
- currently used (*activated energy*), or
- purposefully invested in protecting the reserved and active energies (*passive energy*).

It is necessary to highlight that any type of energy is always 'active' regardless of whether we can sense energy activity (i.e., activated energy) or we know it is 'actively protecting' but we cannot always sense it (i.e., passive energy) or it is 'actively standby' in the background, but we cannot sense it at all (i.e., reserved energy). The difference between passive and reserved energy lies in the fact that passive energy has been already assigned a protective role. When passive energy actions this role, it becomes activated energy.

The three energy categories above have an interrelationship. Activated and passive energies source from reserved energy. The latter can also increase by suspending activated energy consumption and passive energy allocation. Similarly, as mentioned above, passive energy can still become activated and contribute to the functioning of the unity or any decision and actions of it by protecting the unity's activated and reserved energies. This energy investment in protection corresponds to the constructs of safety and security.[11,12]

For example, our bodies have material and cognitive energy stored in the brains, muscles, organs, tissues, and other body parts and organs. When this energy is not actively used or assigned a protective role, it represents reserved energy. However, at each time-point, some of this energy is converted so that our bodies can physically survive, and we can perform our activities, meaning it becomes activated energy. In parallel, our immune system comprises elements looking for threats to fight (i.e.,

[11] Bieder, C., & Pettersen Gould, K. (2020). *The coupling of safety and security: Exploring interrelations in theory and practice*. Springer. https://doi.org/10.1007/978-3-030-47229-0.

[12] Griffor, E., & Griffor, E. (2016). *Handbook of system safety and security*. Syngress.

activated energy) or patiently waiting to intervene when needed (i.e., passive energy). Thus, our immune system represents a blend of activated and passive energies that together aim to protect the bodies from external threats, such as viruses. However, our immune system does not directly contribute to performing any activities.

The same concept applies to unity collections, such as organisations. For instance, a business uses personnel and material sources (i.e., activated energy) from the pool of resources it has (i.e., reserved energy). This pool can include knowledgeable and skilled workers, warehouse components and other necessary unities. At the same time, the business allocates energy to protect its cyber and physical integrity. Such energy can be passive (e.g., water tanks and sprinklers to be used only in the case of fire) or activated (e.g., software constantly scanning incoming internet traffic for threats).

Therefore, the more detailed energy groups mentioned above can expand the expression of *Usable Energy State (UES)* per time-point Eq. (5.2).

$$\begin{aligned} \mathit{Usable\ Energy\ State}\ (\mathit{UES}) &= \mathit{Activated\ UES} + \mathit{Passive\ UES} + \mathit{Reserved\ UES} \\ &= (\mathit{Activated\ material\ MES} + \mathit{Activated\ cognitive\ CES}) \\ &\quad + (\mathit{Passive\ material\ MES} + \mathit{Passive\ cognitive\ CES}) \\ &\quad + (\mathit{Reserved\ material\ MES} + \mathit{Reserved\ cognitive\ CES}) \end{aligned} \tag{5.2}$$

Activated physical and cognitive energies constantly interact with each other and with affective energy. Consequently, they can shape and trigger one another and be influenced by each other. For instance, when a person suffers from physical illness (i.e., physical energy effects), they might think about what the cause is (i.e., cognitive energy employment). They might take medication to mitigate the symptoms (i.e., intake of physical energy) and could feel internal discomfort because they cannot attend a meeting (i.e., affective energy expression).

As another example, professional satisfaction can source from your exposure to good news. This is physical energy of sound and light received by your senses, which you process cognitively and compare it with your beliefs and values, as per your affective energy. Satisfaction can trigger you and manifest through physical changes such as changes in your facial gestures, body postures, and heart rate. It can also stimulate your thinking further through cognitive energy. Why am I feeling satisfied? What more can I do to feel similar in the future? Then, you can take actions (i.e., physical energy of body mobilised through cognitive energy) to find more information (i.e., receive physical energy from the environment which you process cognitively). This information may help you reconsider your career goals (i.e., use of cognitive energy) and how achieving them would make you feel (i.e., affective energy manifestation).

You can think of such interplays and come up with millions of examples of interactions between physical, cognitive, and affective energy, or simply put, material and immaterial energy. We could confidently accept that affective energy is the only form that uses and drives both other energies. Indeed, there is growing consensus

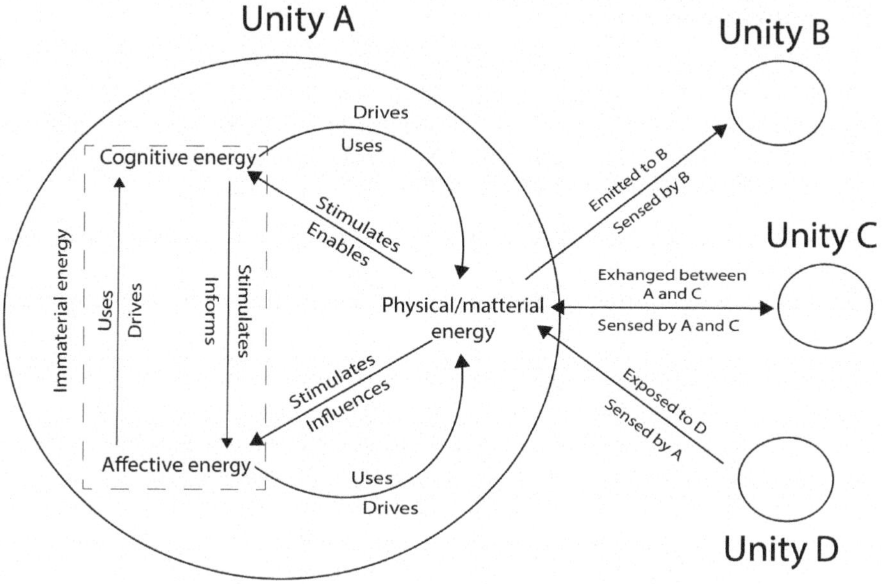

Fig. 5.2 Energy types and interactions

that affection functions as the primary driver of how unities employ their physical and cognitive energies and deploy their material energy in their environment, while physical and cognitive energies also influence affective energy.[13,14,15]

Therefore, we could reasonably accept that the *Overall Energy State (OES)* is shaped by the interaction between usable energy and affective energy (5.3).

$$\begin{aligned} &\mathit{Overall\ Energy\ State\ (OES)} \\ &\quad \propto \mathit{Affective\ Energy\ Balance\ AEB} * \mathit{Useable\ Energy\ State\ UES} \\ &\quad \propto \mathit{AEB} * [(\mathit{Activated\ material\ MES} + \mathit{Activated\ cognitive\ CES}) \\ &\quad + (\mathit{Passive\ material\ MES} + \mathit{Passive\ cognitive\ CES}) \\ &\quad + (\mathit{Reserved\ material\ MES} + \mathit{Reserved\ cognitive\ CES})] \end{aligned} \tag{5.3}$$

In Fig. 5.2, I present the interactions of energy types within each unity and with external unities. The most essential to contemplate is that within the same living unity, the three energy types interact, support, and affect each other. Hence, any approach that isolates one or two energy types from the rest could be flagged as limited and inadequate to offer a holistic understanding of the living unities of interest.

---

[13] Sellers, M. (2017). *Law, reason, and emotion*. Cambridge University Press.

[14] Morag, T. (2016). *Emotion, imagination, and the limits of reason*. Routledge.

[15] Chaudhuri, A. (2006). *Emotion and reason in consumer behavior*. Routledge. https://doi.org/10.4324/9780080461762.

5.5 Anticipated Energy

Besides the current levels of usable energy UES, there is the construct of *Anticipated Energy Exchange (ANEE)*, which, if realised, could lower, increase, or not affect UES per time-point. More specifically, ANEE includes the material and cognitive energy assumed to be gained (+ANEE) or lost (−ANEE) through:

- *Trusted Energy-Representing Exchange Units (TEREU)*, such as money and other currencies, and/or
- exposures and interactions within the physical, social, and technical environments without or not the use of TEREUs.

Considering the basic definitions about energy I provided in Sect. 5.3, although material energy is the only form physically sensed, through cognitive processes we assign to material energy and sensed events various connotations and characteristics (e.g., high and low sound, local or foreign worker). We can also apply to material energy various judgements and values (e.g., good or bad attitude, trusted or not group of persons) and can feel positively or negatively towards them.

Exchange units TEREUs (e.g., cash notes or monetary digits on the display) hold no energy value apart from the inherent energy they carry as materials (e.g., paper, metal, light). They only represent energy we can gain directly (e.g., raw material, consumables) or get exposed to or interact with (e.g., attend a conference). They reflect a medium and an indirect path of getting exposed to and interacting with energy. Thus, although TEREUs and interactions/exposures, strictly speaking, relate only to material energy, they can also mean changes in cognitive energy and trigger emotional experiences. Similarly, any expected combination of material and cognitive changes is 'translated' by affective energy and can generate positive or negative affective balances.

Consequently, any perceived need to possess or gain exchange units TEREUs, aversion to losing TEREUs, and potential to use them for securing or getting exposed to more energy depends on current cognitive associations and the expected affective balance. For example, if a professional has more money, they can enrol in a course and upskill; if they upskill, they will feel more confident. Thus, we can develop plans to earn more TEREUs (i.e., use of current energy to increase future energy) or lower the expenditure of existing ones (i.e., decrease the rate of current energy usage to increase future energy).

For instance, you could decide to work more hours, meaning to consume more of your current physical and cognitive energy, with the expectation to gain more physical and cognitive energy in the future and boost your affective balance (e.g., feeling of achievement). Also, an organisation could decide to reduce its warehouse stock, meaning to decrease the physical energy it possesses, in anticipation of increasing its useable energy UES in the future (e.g., saving money now and using them for better opportunities later). The book by Kuroda is an enlightening reading about the history of money, which is the dominant exchange unit TEREU of our era.[16]

[16] Kuroda, A. (2020). *A global history of money*. Routledge.

The value of exchange units TEREUs varies over time and across areas. For example, 20 TEREUs in one region might reflect the potential to buy 1 tonne of iron. The same amount in other areas can correspond to a different quantity of iron, with any of the above correspondences being subject to changes with time. Also, TEREUs can be classified similarly to the concepts of activated, reserved and passive energy (Sect. 5.4). Per time-point, activated TEREUs could be the money a business is spending or actively investing (e.g., shares), reserved TEREUs could be the business capital in savings, and passive TEREUs could be the capital invested in insurance (e.g., workers' compensation insurance and business assets).

Besides exchange units TEREUs, contact with other unities will also lead to exposure to or exchange of material energy and affect unity's current and future energies. For instance, someone with livestock can harvest milk, meat, and wool as material energy. They can exchange their livestock or materials above for TEREUs or other materials. They can also build cognitive associations to manage the livestock and develop respective affections (e.g., how much is enough, how to manage the livestock in the best way possible, and how emotionally attached they feel to the livestock).

A worker who might interact with a hazardous substance (e.g., asbestos) will get exposed to material energy, but in this case, this exposure might affect this person's energy state negatively. The realisation through material and cognitive means of this harmful exposure (e.g., using instruments and interpreting their readings) and volition or mandate to avoid this exposure could lead to the business investing current energy and exchange units TEREUs in protective measures. These would secure that the future energy states of its staff will not be lower than the current ones.

From a social viewpoint, the interactions between colleagues can lead to generating and exchanging information about new ideas, relations, and feelings or building collaborations to manage material energy more effectively and efficiently or gain more exchange units TEREUs. As an example from the technical environment, the possession of an advanced equipment can offer the potential to save material energy by processing it more efficiently, produce more materials per unit of time, and gain more TEREUs with time.

You can think of plenty of cases where interactions and exposures are linked to anticipated energy exchange ANEE, which, if realised as expected, leads to modifications of the overall energy OES, and can generate further expectations about future OES or useable energy UES. Also, from a broader viewpoint, ANEE relates to the construct of risk that has been studied across many disciplines and debated for a long time.[17,18,19] There are several qualitative and quantitative methods being used to estimate risk levels for different unity types and their interactions. In its core, the risk construct is indeed about predicting or evaluating the effects of ANEE on the OES and UES of individuals, teams, organisations, and other unities and collections.

[17] Adams, J. (1995). *Risk*. UCL Press.

[18] Skinns, L., Scott, M., & Cox, T. (2011). *Risk*. Cambridge University Press.

[19] Engemann. K. J. (2018). *The Routledge companion to risk, crisis and security in business*. Routledge.

In its most abstract symbolic form, anticipated energy ANEEU for a unity would be the sum of anticipated energy exchange through direct energy exchange with other unities (Sect. 12.1)—energy sponsors or antagonists (Sect. 12.3)—and through exchange units TEREUs (5.4). By extension, Anticipated Useable Energy State of the Unity (ANUES) would be the sum of its Current Usable Energy (CUES) and Anticipated Energy Exchange (ANEE) (5.5).

$$\textit{Anticipated Energy Exchange } (\textit{ANEE}) \propto \textit{Direct energy exchange} + \textit{TEREUs} \tag{5.4}$$

$$\begin{aligned} &\textit{Anticipated Usable Energy } (\textit{ANUES}) \\ &\quad \propto \textit{Current Useable Energy CUES} \\ &\quad + \textit{Anticipated Energy Exchange ANEE} \end{aligned} \tag{5.5}$$

Energy: Key Reflections and Actions

Reflections

- Energy, in its material, cognitive, and emotional forms, is a central concept for understanding professional practice and decision-making. It shapes interactions, motivations, and outcomes.
- Human energy dynamics are unique, influenced by consciousness, needs, desires, and complex interdependencies between energy types.
- Usable energy is finite and context-dependent, requiring careful management to avoid depletion and ensure sustainable performance.
- Anticipating energy needs and understanding energy states can enhance decision-making and support effective collaboration in professional contexts.
- Acknowledging the variability in energy states across individuals and contexts is essential for fostering equitable and empathetic professional environments.

Actions

1. Understand Energy Dynamics: Reflect on how material, cognitive, and emotional energy manifest in your work and interactions. Identify areas where energy is well-utilised and areas where it might be wasted or underutilised.
2. Prioritise Energy Management: Implement practices to monitor and manage energy levels effectively. This could include scheduling tasks based on energy requirements or incorporating breaks to recharge.
3. Foster Awareness in Teams: Encourage discussions about energy dynamics within your team or organisation. Recognise that individuals may have different energy states and needs, and adapt workflows accordingly.
4. Anticipate Energy Demands: Develop strategies for anticipating energy requirements in professional projects. This includes planning for contingencies to address unexpected challenges without overburdening resources.

5. Promote Equity in Energy Allocation: Advocate for equitable distribution of tasks and responsibilities, considering the material, cognitive, and emotional capabilities of team members.

By appreciating the multifaceted nature of energy and managing it thoughtfully, you can optimise individual and collective performance while fostering a more equitable and sustainable professional environment.

Part II
Dialogue Concepts

Chapter 6
Story Sharing

6.1 General

We constantly receive information from a variety of unities (e.g., other persons, animals) through verbal (e.g., written and oral) and non-verbal (e.g., gestures and postures) communication. Cognitive energy allows us to develop some understanding of the area, event, or topic of interest and create new or alter current cognitive associations. Communication also contributes to the development and cultivation of affections towards other unities and situations. We show our feelings by accepting or rejecting, respecting or disrespecting, sympathising or ignoring, and more.

Literature presents communication as a process and construct with its own elements and mechanisms.[1] However, literature does not always acknowledge that communication is all about sharing stories. The communication processes and their outputs ultimately aim to share with others some stories. Those can take several forms, less or more structured, and be conveyed through various media constructs (e.g., symbols, figures, colours, and letters).

Story sharing is an age-old concept ingrained in humanity. Admittedly, there is literature focussing on the power of storytelling and its harnessing to achieve effective communication and success in various contexts.[2,3] Those publications' storytelling regards the way we could communicate with using, for instance, narratives and plain language and avoid technical jargon.

However, whether it is a narrative storytelling format or a formal business presentation, regardless of the words, techniques, or manners, when we communicate at professional and personal levels, we always share a story. Many professionals might not have realised that communication is and will always be about sharing stories. Per

[1] Mortensen, D. (2017). *Communication theory*. (2nd ed.). Taylor and Francis.

[2] Rabiger, M. (2017). *Developing story ideas: The power and purpose and storytelling* (3rd ed.). Routledge.

[3] Nossel, M. (2018). *Powered by storytelling: Excavate, craft, and present stories to transform business communication* (1st ed.). McGraw-Hill.

N. Karanikas, *Professional Generalism in a Hyper-specialised World*,
https://doi.org/10.1007/978-981-96-4039-3_6

time-point, through communication, we all transmit pieces of data and information which together form a short or long story.[4]

Communication revolves around stories, which in turn are the main outcome of every communication. Whether it is pure mathematical equations or proofs, direct imperative commands in emergency situations or raw data transmission between machines, communications share stories with varying structures, formats, and other characteristics. We and any other unity that communicates in any way are story sharers.

Although, normatively, stories are associated with the past (e.g., sharing something that has happened), stories can have elements referring to the past, present, or future. For instance, when discussing a problem with a project, we share a story that could include elements of the past (e.g., our understanding of the issue experienced), elements of the present (e.g., opinions about how the issue affects the project, us and others) and elements of the future (e.g., evaluation about which measures could help).

Every time we communicate, we share our story, and we are all exposed to the stories of others. Even when we do not have an interlocutor to converse, we make stories in our minds. This happens when we communicate with ourselves or observe other people, technology, animals, plants, the sky, the rain, or whatever around us. Biological bodies share stories too through postures and gestures that carry connotations and messages.

Medical professionals examine bodies and use their knowledge to share with somebody the 'story' of their illness. The medical experts explain causes (past/present story elements), options (present/future story elements) and expected outputs and outcomes (future story elements). Explanations of phenomena and recommended remedies for problems are stories as well. The former say a story about mechanisms and the latter share a story about solutions. The answers of others to questions about experiences at work are stories. Any ideas about organisational improvements are stories.

The instruction manual accompanying any technological artefact is a story each designer and producer share with the end user. It includes what the device can do and not, what could go wrong and how it can be fixed, and how the device will help the user and meet their needs. The posters and other graphics used to inform others are stories. Every communication through symbols, graphics, and colours about products, services, upcoming events and other unities is a story.

---

[4] Vora, S. (2019). *The power of data storytelling* (1st ed.). Sage Publications.

6.2 Truth Versions

It is important to acknowledge that each story shared through various means is a version of one's truth, not the truth itself.[5] We can never impart absolutely true information about events and other constructs. Not always because we do not want, but because we all are natural story makers. Any information or data shared is mixed with our own understanding of the events and their context. They carry visible or invisible traces of our decisions and thoughts and embed our ideas and emotions. We express all these via symbols, voice pitch and tone, body gestures, and postures that collectively shape our story.

Different individuals looking at a piece of art can each form their own understanding of the truth, distinct from that of others and separate from the artist's intended message. Does it matter in this case? Perhaps not if the artist as a story-sharer aimed at triggering imagination alone. When someone views a painting, especially when the painter is not physically present, they build their own story by imagining the messages the artist wanted to share. Even when the painter is ready to answer questions, it does not imply that the conversation will centre around exchanging identical story versions. Whatever the artist conveys might not be complete, and whatever we perceive, process and store as a truth in our minds might be different, too.

However, life is not only about art. Communications can be significant in several aspects of interactions within smaller and larger groups, teams, and communities. Stories shared about the present and the past can drive the actions of others, shape the future, and influence decisions, meaning that they should ideally represent one, single, indisputable truth.

It is crucial that a patient shares a true story about what they did, ate, and touched yesterday so that the doctor can form a first opinion of what causes them fever. It is paramount that someone shares with the police staff the true story of where, when, how and why they met a person yesterday who has been reported missing today. It is vital that witnesses and interviewees share a true story about what and how happened yesterday and in the past at the workplace so that investigators can understand the causes that led to a fatality and recommend preventative measures for protecting others now and in the future.

Stories carry limitations and imperfections. Inevitably, each story is characterised by gaps between what happens and what we perceive, what we perceive and what we store in our minds, what we store and what we recall. We cannot measure these gaps accurately and exhaustively and, based on this measurement, compile the original, primordial truth. Indeed, we can compare observable events and detect differences and gaps of material nature. However, this is not enough.

The inability to capture all gaps starts from the ones generated within each unity and lies in the foundational fact that we cannot directly observe and measure immaterial energy. We can only speculate about immaterial energy or believe the accounts of those who claim to have experienced it. There will always be a black box with

[5] Chouraqui, F. (2014). *Ambiguity and the absolute: Nietzsche and Merleau-Ponty on the question of truth*. Fordham University Press.

unknowns to us as external observers, regardless of how much we will materially decompose a living unity of interest or try to dig deeper into the stories shared.

We cannot precisely measure any gaps between and within senders and receivers of energy, and we cannot accurately reconstruct any stories and compile the truth. We cannot even unequivocally validate our current versions of truth because there is no solid and indisputable reference point to examine and compare them against. We just compare the various story versions against constructed criteria, which are stories themselves as well.

Acknowledging that absolute truth may be unattainable, we construct and use degrees of verification that employ multiple, adequately independent lines of evidence to increase our confidence in claims about truth. This is how we achieve *practical truth.* This happens because we can only observe material changes driven by the unobservable immaterial energy and, in turn, use immaterial energy to interpret gaps and differences sensed in and through material energy.

It is a vicious cycle that deprives us of reconstructing the absolute truth, the ones with no gaps. Even more challenging, when the senders are not accessible (e.g., the designer of equipment or the authors of a legislative piece who passed away) there is no opportunity to interact with them physically and directly and get exposed to their immaterial energy. In these cases, we can only engage with the material energy others have left behind (e.g., equipment, legislation) and which reflects the immaterial energy of the transmitters. Still, various receivers perceive this energy differently.

For example, there have been investigations of catastrophic events. When the operators involved died (e.g., fatal aircraft accident) investigators infer what the operators were thinking or processing cognitively and what they felt. They do this based on manifestations of material energy, such as the sound from voice recorders and the actions of operators over switches, knobs, and levers. Experienced investigators know they cannot be utterly sure in these cases.

Although investigators know absolute truth is impossible, they work hard to find the most accurate version. Investigators know they always share a version of the truth based on the stories the data and information collected tell them. Investigators reconstruct a version of the story good enough, but they will never know how close they got to the truth. They miss an indisputable and unmovable reference point to validate.

Indeed, sometimes we deny accepting large story-type gaps. The awareness of such gaps drives us to minimise them further, even if their elimination is naturally unfeasible. We try to construct better practical truth versions as much as possible. Considering the existence of multiple truth versions, the identification of story-type gaps can spark discussions, debates and reflections driving us to collect, analyse, contrast and merge more information to develop an increasingly common understanding that could bring us closer to reality. For instance, when witnesses of a crime scene differ much in their stories, police collect more technology-type stories (e.g., camera footage) and collect more human-type stories (e.g., additional witnesses) to gain a more consistent picture of what happened.

It is also like in statistics, when analysts fit a predictive model to the data in hand. A good model fit does not mean absolute fit and still contains errors, meaning imperfect predictions. Based on constructed acceptable limits, researchers might choose to ignore those errors and believe that their model tells quite accurately the story of the data. If they are not satisfied with the accuracy-error gap, they collect more data and modify their model until they reduce the gap to a predetermined level. Of course, that level is defined through constructed criteria. This means that the only thing analysts know is whether they decreased the gap, not whether the remaining gap itself is big or small in absolute terms. That is, we cannot know what we do not know.

Last, the energy exchanged in a specific space and time (i.e., number of unities interacting and depending on each other) and familiarity with the specific conditions (i.e., how much sense the situation makes), affect the gaps between what we perceive is going on and what is really happening. Those gaps grow larger when unity interactions increase and intensify per unit of time. We could all confront instances of such gaps when energy exchange in the environment has a high tempo, meaning lots of unities interacting with a fast pace, or our mental models do not match the conditions satisfactorily.

For instance, when someone first drives in a busy urban area, they might feel lost until they develop an adequate understanding of the environment and connections with what they expected and what is unfolding around. When a worker first enters a business, they need time to comprehend the context, the interactions, and dependencies. The higher the energy exchange per unit of time and the lower the unity's familiarity, the more the time necessary to build practical truth versions that are good enough.

6.3 Knowledge and Information

In connection with the concepts which I discussed above, it is also important to cover the constructs of knowledge and information. From a pragmatic viewpoint, several professionals, and occasionally some literature,[6] use these constructs interchangeably. We tend to label information stored in our minds or devices as 'knowledge', regardless of its origin. This can lead to misperceptions that we all 'know', regardless of how we acquired the alleged knowledge.

Indeed, various dictionaries define knowledge as a product of educational activities and experiences. However, it seems many of us have correlated formal education with knowledge by default, which can be inaccurate. Learning can create knowledge,

[6] Managing Knowledge and Information: Building Your Intellectual Capital. (n.d.). LID Publishing.

but not always. Therefore, in this section, I aim to shed some light to complement some other published positions.[7,8]

During exposures and interactions, we all receive data from other unities through senses. We then process it in our brains and store it as cognitive energy, notwithstanding that these data can also influence our affective energy. However, although we know about those interactions and exposures with other unities (e.g., we witnessed they occurred, who took part, what happened), whatever data shared by other unities and received by us do not comprise knowledge for us.

I believe there is a huge misunderstanding when talking about knowledge, especially in formal training and education. That we read, study, and memorise something does not mean we really gain any knowledge of the topic. We only know that we read, studied, and memorised something. For example, you are aware of when and how often you have been reading this book. However, whatever you read in the book informs you about my views, positions, and arguments. None of this comprises knowledge of yours, at least not yet, even if you can recall some book content reliably.

Likewise, the theories, methods, experiences, and any other material a teacher communicates with students is part of the learning process, but do not directly comprise knowledge for the students. Indeed, the class interactions themselves constitute knowledge for the students and the teacher and can be stimulating and enjoyable. However, whatever content a teacher shares is stored in the cognitive energy space of students for longer or shorter periods as information; this is not knowledge.

This 'learned' information stems from the knowledge of the teacher or others, the transformation of this knowledge into information by the teacher and others, and the transmission of information data by the teacher and their reception by the students. Similarly, that you read about what an author of an article did, found or claimed, it does not mean you know anything about the content itself. The only thing you know is that you read the article. During reading, you just process the information any author has shared with you based on their knowledge. The authors do not directly share their knowledge, but information which represents their knowledge.

The above could read perplexing. Regardless, it is crucial to differentiate between information and knowledge in professional contexts and beyond. You can know where each piece of information comes from and that it might represent the knowledge of the sender. This does not mean that the information itself is knowledge for you. It remains information, and it is a story shared by others and stored in documents and devices or within your brain temporarily or for longer. As such, *information* (or, more precisely, *stored information*) is the entire set of semantic associations (meanings of constructs) and syntactic associations (capabilities of unities) present

[7] Nake, F. (2002). Data, information, and knowledge: A semiotic view of phenomena of organization. In K. Liu et al. (Eds.), *Organizational semiotics, IFIP International Federation for Information Processing* (pp. 41–50). SpringerLink.

[8] Braf, E. (2002). Knowledge or information—What makes the difference? In K. Liu et al. (Eds.), *Organizational semiotics, IFIP International Federation for Information Processing* (pp. 71–90). SpringerLink.

in the unity's cognitive energy. Such information is shaped by events, semantics, and syntactics shared by other unities but not experienced by the self-unity.

Real knowledge is built only through first-hand experiences. This entails the employment of the information stored internally (cognitive associations) or accessed externally (e.g., documentation) to drive interactions between material and immaterial energies. Thus, *knowledge* (or, more accurately, *experiential knowledge*) corresponds to episodic associations (events involving unities) in the cognitive energy space. Each of us perceives, translates, and stores those experiences as information in cognitive energy, put differently. The same events can result in uniquely different pieces of semantic and syntactic associations (information) and episodic associations (knowledge) for the actors involved.

Under this concept, education needs to provide opportunities for translating content-related information into context-relevant experiences to generate knowledge. Some scholars and professionals use the terms 'first-hand knowledge' for what I named as knowledge above and 'second-hand knowledge' for what I defined as information above. I believe the terms knowledge and information and their definitions above are clearer and can help to avoid misunderstandings. Knowing differs from being told or informed. Practised information shapes experience and becomes knowledge.

That you accept some information as true does not mean you have developed knowledge of the topics that information is about. Many accept that atoms exist, although they have never seen one, apart perhaps from photographs that they never checked for authenticity. Many accept oxygen's existence and vital role; they yet lack direct observation or experimentation. While they might feel the air, it is not the same as directly experiencing oxygen. They do not really know if what science names oxygen is what the air they breathe includes.

Interestingly, many accept their father is their biological parent, although they never tested this through a DNA test. They rely on second-hand accounts (e.g., birth certificates, and other relatives) and the father's role in the construct of the family to form their beliefs. Thus, the only thing they know is that the person named as their father conforms to what society expects from a parent. The person with the role of the father has also expectedly satisfied whatever criteria authorities have in place to verify their relation (e.g., formal declaration, birth in the frame of a marriage). There are several cases about persons who discovered their presumed parents were not the biological ones.

In Fig. 6.1, I present the concepts discussed above. In connection with Sect. 6.2 about truth versions, the specific figure can offer a more illustrative picture of how many gaps can exist across the paths shown. Of note, for the sake of brevity, in Fig. 6.1 I show in a simple and linear fashion the Data—Information—Knowledge path and vice versa between a sender and several receivers at a specific time-point. Indeed, during conversations and other interactions, we all act as senders and receivers simultaneously, meaning that in reality all arrows in Fig. 6.1 are bidirectional for each actor (e.g., Sender_X is also Receiver_X).

Besides, in Fig. 6.1 I do not mean to present a normative process description. For example, it can happen that persons experience something but never store the relevant

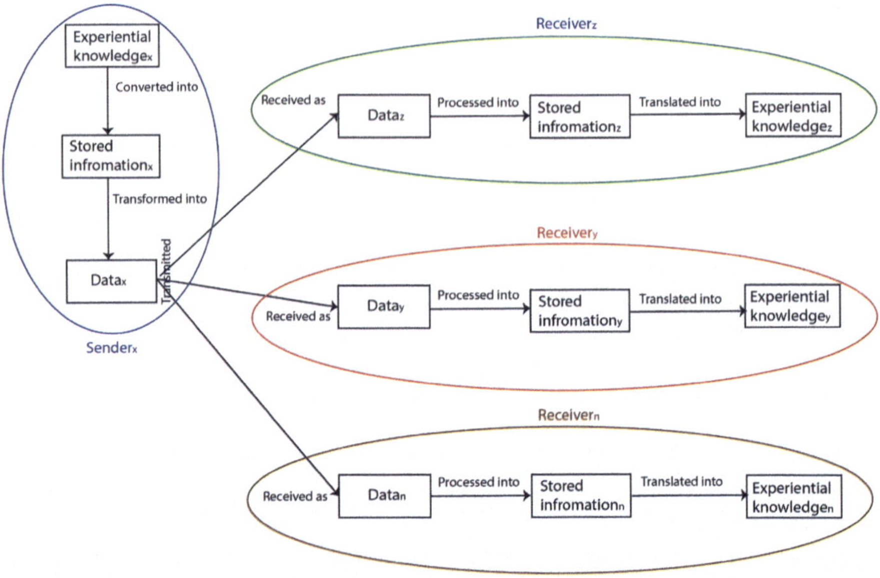

Fig. 6.1 Knowledge—Information—Data (unidirectional case)

information. Also, individuals can receive data without saving it or can remember things without understanding them experientially.

Story Sharing: Key Reflections and Actions

Reflections

- Story sharing is at the core of professional communication, shaping how information, knowledge and insights are exchanged and interpreted in professional contexts.
- The concept of 'truth' in stories is multifaceted and often reflects different versions shaped by individual perspectives, experiences and the contexts in which they are shared.
- The distinction between knowledge and information is critical: information is incoming data, while knowledge is refined, contextualised, and actionable understanding derived from that data.
- Stories that effectively convey knowledge require careful curation of the information transmitted, clarity of message, and a sensitivity to the audience's perspective and context.
- Misaligned stories or poorly shared information can lead to misunderstanding and ineffective decision-making.

Actions

1. Clarify Truth Versions: Reflect on the subjective nature of truth in the stories you share. Ensure that your narratives acknowledge varying perspectives and provide context to support their validity.
2. Distinguish Knowledge from Information: Evaluate whether the stories you share are merely transmitting information or genuinely fostering knowledge creation through practice and application. Aim to provide context, relevance, and actionable insights.
3. Ensure Story Coherence: When sharing stories, focus on clarity and structure. Use a logical flow to ensure your audience can easily follow the message and grasp its implications.
4. Adapt to Contexts: Tailor your stories to fit the professional and cultural context of your audience. Use language, examples, and analogies that resonate with their experiences and expectations.
5. Encourage Reflective Story Sharing: Promote an environment where team members feel encouraged to share their perspectives and experiences. Use story sharing as a way to build collective knowledge and foster mutual understanding.

By mastering the art of story sharing and focussing on the meaningful transformation of information into knowledge, you can enhance professional collaboration and decision-making.

Chapter 7
Story Elements

7.1 General

Most of the stories do not have a predetermined structure, detail, and evidence. Also, they do not have to be written. There were stories before the written word, and someone can share a story through art. For example, Indigenous Peoples in Australia never kept written records, only stories. Nevertheless, nowadays, many stories comply with predefined rules about the use of language and symbols. This is crucial as it enables to convey a message through widely and commonly comprehensible media constructs. As discussed in Chapter 2, we use constructs to talk about constructs.

Often, though, stories have a more formal structure. Analysts who share their studies and explain along a timeline the why, how, where, when, who and what of their activities, tell an organised story. The same applies to everyone, particularly professionals, who officially report a series of eventualities, decisions, actions, conditions, and outcomes based on a structure many accept and label as 'logical'.

Admittedly, story receivers, most of the times do not or cannot reproduce the analysis or follow all the steps the professional messenger employed. However, when a story is structured in an agreed and acceptable way (i.e., a constructed way) and the constructs used to explain the constructs under focus sound compliant with some predefined criteria, which are also constructs, often leads to label the story as true and credible and accept it.

Based on such criteria, for example, in academia, researchers typically trust and cite studies of others to support, complement, and compare the studies of theirs. However, most do not truly know if these other stories are accurate and how the beliefs and biases of analysts influenced them when writing about their studies. Almost everyone just trusts the system academics and other stakeholders constructed (e.g., journal editors, peer reviewers, accreditation of research institutions and universities) to verify the veracity of the stories received and published. This is inevitable and fair because no single person or small team could perform all the necessary checks and

N. Karanikas, *Professional Generalism in a Hyper-specialised World*,
https://doi.org/10.1007/978-981-96-4039-3_7

processes above. This widely accepted practice has brought us further, despite in the wrong directions occasionally and retrospectively.

The above applies equally to the industry and the wider community (e.g., industry and governmental reports). Interestingly, when a story is repeated across the industry becomes best practice and believable, regardless of whether science supports it. When a story is reproduced in social communities becomes a tradition and, often, a superstition worthless to consider. Frankly speaking, those two cases are identical from a scientific perspective. However, for some reasons, the concept of industry practice is more widely accepted than the concept of community practice.

We typically use the constructs of validity and reliability to determine the trustworthiness of stories, whether they are from everyday life, history, science, or work. More specifically:

- *Validity* is a judgement we make for a story that is believable based on comparisons to, at least, one different and accepted construct. Anything can be valid if it makes sense to some based on their existing beliefs or knowledge; the more the people who confirm that a story seems 'sensible', the higher the validity.
- *Reliability* is a judgement which regards the replication or reproduction of a particular story by others. Those third persons check if the same actions under the same conditions and with the same order generate similar outputs. This can regard multiple longitudinal reproductions (e.g., execution of the same experiment by different persons at various periods) or cases where a similar story is shared by more than one person who experienced it. The more the exact reproductions and the similarities of the stories shared, the higher the reliability.

If we accept a reliable story but cannot explain it based on current knowledge, we have *faith/belief* in the story. For instance, there can be several patients reporting identical symptoms that a medical professional cannot explain; if the medical experts accept these reports, it means they believe the patients' stories. If we accept a story that looks valid but has not been tested for reliability, we form a *hypothesis*. For example, a work intervention that seems effective to managers remains a hypothesis until it is pilot-tested on the field.

The achievement of both reliability and validity signals a *credible/trustworthy* story and leads to tag the story as true, correct, right, and any other similar term. Strangely, though, when a story lacks both satisfactory validity and reliability, we have constructed two different labels. The story can be *theoretical,* or you can name the story as *distrusted/untrustworthy*, and, subsequently, unreasonable, inconceivable, wrong, false, and so on. In Table 7.1 I summarise the concepts above.

Table 7.1 Story trustworthiness categories

Story validity	Story reliability	
	YES	NO
YES	Credible/Trustworthy	Hypothesis
NO	Faith/belief	Theory Or Distrust/Untrustworthy

The implications of the arguments above are crucial, as theories represent stories we cannot completely verify today, but we hope we can do so in the future. Contrary, distrust often means the rejection of the stories entirely and little or no opportunity for their verification in the future. However, once more, both theory and distrust regard the same situation: stories not fully satisfying the constructed validity and reliability criteria.

Here, indeed, is where the power of the organisation and structure of stories can become a trap. Because someone tells an organised story, they have more chances to be trusted. An academic working for an institution that has some processes to check methods-constructs and who has the skills-constructs to organise stories can be more believable than a messenger who does not know how to communicate a story in an organised manner (e.g., orderly, use of accurate terms, and application of recognised techniques).

Thus, when you do not have first-hand experience, the question is when and why you choose to scrutinise and investigate further some stories and apathetically embrace others. It is interesting why sometimes we point to the few differences between stories discussing the same topic to claim that they are untrustworthy, whereas, in other cases, we do not scrutinise stories with the same passion.

Broadly and pragmatically speaking, my experience across academic and industry settings suggests that science mainly gives precedence to validity with the hope to achieve reliability over time, whereas daily professional practice primarily assigns priority to reliability with the presumption of validity. This is where frictions sometimes emerge between academia and industry, feeding the so-called theory-practice gap in several domains.[1,2,3] Academics sometimes question the validity of what the industry repeatedly and consistently implements (i.e., industry best practice), especially when professionals intuitively connect repetitive practices directly with the achievement of desired outputs and outcomes.

More specifically, academia claims that the credible application of an accepted practice (e.g., consistent compliance with an industry standard that seems reasonable and relevant) does not directly guarantee the credibility of results (e.g., services that are consistently of acceptable quality). This is because the validity and reliability of any relationships between practices and their outputs must be first empirically established (i.e., credible cause-effect relationships).

For instance, in the safety management domain, there is a presumption in the industry that compliance with rules can ensure a basic level of safety. Academia has argued this claim is not adequately credible, although seemingly valid when acknowledging that the goal of such rules is to introduce a bare minimum of safety based on accumulated experience (i.e., good validity). Hence, the scientific position

[1] Auriol, E., Crampes, C., & Estache, A. (2021). *Regulating public services: Bridging the gap between theory and practice*. Cambridge University Press.

[2] Szwed, P. S. (2016). *Expert judgment in project management: narrowing the theory–practice gap*. Project Management Institute, Inc.

[3] Zonderland, M. E. (2021). *Handbook of healthcare logistics: bridging the gap between theory and practice*. Springer.

is that the industry needs rules to foster safety, but no set of rules can capture all combinations of conditions stemming from the dynamic operating environment and the various confounding factors.[4] Therefore, implementing rules cannot determine safety outputs or outcomes (i.e., poor reliability). Occasionally, being too focussed on enforcing and following rules can sometimes be risky, especially when unfamiliar situations require creative problem-solving.[5]

On the opposite side, the industry questions academic results' real-world applicability due to limitations in studies (e.g., small samples, low fidelity of the conditions, experiments in laboratories). Gratefully, recent initiatives show positive progress in this area; researchers work in industry environments (i.e., not just visiting to collect data) and practitioners grow their research skills in hybrid academic-industry settings. Yet, more efforts and commitment are necessary to create more *scientific practice* and more *practical science*. In Chapters 8 and 9, I provide more insights into how science can inform professional practice and vice versa.

7.2 Content and Sources

The concepts I introduced in the section above suggest that the overall story trustworthiness stems from two principal parts:

- the validity and reliability of the conveyed data, the 'content-stories', and
- the validity and reliability of the senders whose identity, in a broader sense, represents 'source-stories'.

For instance, the journey and achievements of a professional comprise a story attached to them (i.e., source-story) when sharing advice (i.e., content-stories) to their clients.

The reliability and validity of a source-story represent the construct of *reputation*. As such, someone can trust incoming data unquestioningly just because their immaterial energy has already flagged the source (e.g., a renowned media outlet) as trustworthy. On the other hands, some people decide if a story is true based on how believable it is, not who shared it. Also, another person can readily accept data that lacks validity (i.e., does not make direct sense to), possibly intending to examine those data later, just because they view the source as trustworthy.

When cross-referencing all possible cases, as in the examples above, in Table 7.2, I suggest what judgement a 'rational' human would make about the total trustworthiness of a story. In the specific table, the scale 0-4 represents the conceptual range of trustworthiness. Each number represents the sum of validity and reliability elements characterising the content/data received and their source/sender; the best case is when

[4] Dekker, S. (2017). *The safety anarchist: Relying on human expertise and innovation, reducing bureaucracy and compliance*. CRC Press LLC.

[5] Dekker, S. (2021). *Compliance capitalism: How free markets have led to unfree, overregulated workers*. Taylor & Francis Group.

both the content and source are credible, meaning they are valid and reliable. Of note, in Table 7.2, I do not mean to suggest a measurement scale. It is just a conceptual and qualitative description of what should 'logically' happen.

Importantly, the cases I present in Table 7.2 do not apply uniformly across all sources and content, are not constant over time for the same source and content, and may not regard the whole content we receive from the same source at each time-point. This variability means that trustworthiness can be assessed only within a specific context in time.

A biologist's credibility does not extend to their knowledge of mechanical engineering. Similarly, a credible scientist who conducts experiments in lab environments does not mean that generates results that can be blindly implemented in real-world settings. Notably, the above can be meaningless from a non-professional perspective. Attending a movie, comedy show, or any other enjoyable activity should simply be about having a good time. In such contexts, the trustworthiness potential does not matter, apart maybe only from verifying any expectations (e.g., actor's performance).

Validity and reliability judgements can apply only to specific conditions and could regard the whole or parts of the stories we get exposed. Also, any 'initial conditions' (e.g., one has faith in the abilities of somebody) can source first from data received from other means (e.g., a social media profile) and could be modified through personal experience or obtaining more information.

Therefore, regarding the sender, one could judge their validity from the experience and knowledge the sender carries to the extent these are known. For instance, somebody can believe a medical doctor is a valid source of information relevant to their specialisation. This belief means that the same person views the mechanisms and methods to test the knowledge and experience of the doctor as credible (e.g., university degrees, specialisation training and exams).

Table 7.2 Story trustworthiness potential

Source-story	Content-story			
	Credible (valid and reliable)	Hypothetical (valid only)	Faith/belief (reliable only)	Theoretical/ Distrusted (Neither valid nor reliable)
Credible (Valid and Reliable)	4	3	3	2
Hypothetical (Valid only)	3	2	2	1
Faith/belief (Reliable only)	3	2	2	1
Theoretical/ Distrusted (Neither Valid nor Reliable)	2	1	1	0

Sender reliability denotes whether the source has repeatedly delivered the same sensed events (e.g., services, outcomes) in terms of quantity, quality, and timeliness. As such, a medical doctor following the same practice and achieving identical outcomes in similar contexts is reliable. Of course, patients unhappy with results may seek a second opinion or sue the doctor for inadequate diagnosis or harmful surgery. This, however, does not negate the doctor's reliability. Somebody can be reliably beneficial or reliably harmful.

Regarding the content's validity and reliability, we can compare it with our stored information and knowledge or seek additional data from different sources. Thus, we can still label as invalid a piece of data coming from a source, which we have previously marked as credible. For instance, there have been plenty of debates about the validity of arguments in science and practice, all these stemming from credible mouths (e.g., the debate about the existence, magnitude, and causes of climate change). However, not all divergent arguments can be both valid and reliable simultaneously, unless we accept there can be parallel versions of the same world.

In such cases, though, the problem does not stem from the reliability of data, which can be tested, but a mismatch between what the data truly represents and what the analyst alleges it represents. For instance, in Sects. 14.2 to 14.4 about management, I discuss possible inconsistencies between what is monitored (i.e., data collected) and what is actions (i.e., data-informed changes). Using Table 7.2 could regard only conditions of having access to information about specific content and its sources, subject to adequate time and energy to process this information. This is what science systematically performs to resist excessive intuition and counteract its effects.

A profound example is when researchers execute tests and find impressive statistical correlations between variables that, however, cannot be associated rationally, namely spurious correlations. We can repeatedly analyse the same and similar datasets and get identical results (i.e., excellent reliability), but this does not render those results meaningful (i.e., poor validity). Hence, although an accredited researcher has been checked for credibility through constructed mechanisms and criteria (e.g., university exams and degrees, publication peer reviews, recruitment interviews), this does not guarantee that everything the specific researcher generates is inherently trustworthy by default. Therefore, cross-checked and repeated studies in science are standard practice to reproduce results and validate past findings and arguments.

However, it is not achievable in daily life to check systematically the credibility of sources and content to minimise the probability that any information is a product of intuition, luck, or randomness. In real-world settings, checking the reliability and validity of everything and everyone at each point in time is unfeasible. This is where automatic responses driven by affective energy can be useful, despite sometimes producing less-than-ideal outcomes (Sect. 11.3 and Chapter 16). During typical daily activities, we predominantly consult our built-in, previously shaped (dis)trust in human or technical sources, and we do not consistently check the credibility of the content we receive.

Hence, frequently, all cells of Table 7.2, regardless of their 'actual' score, might be assigned uniformly with the same score between 0-4 because of predispositions towards specific sources and content. For instance, if a professional has intuitively decided a particular strategy is useless for their practice, they will not invest much time in re-examining their position in the light of new data, unless something major occurs that forces them to do so (e.g., requirement from a client or a sponsor). A professional who blindly accepts specific content and/or its sources as credible (e.g., the studies published in a reputable and impactful scientific journal) might approach this content-source pair as always credible and might not question this stance if nothing important happens (e.g., a public outcry for a scandal with the peer-review process).

The above, of course, can be unfair. Just because a source has spread false information before does not mean that everything that they share is automatically untrustworthy. Similarly, that we trust a source because it proved useful in the past cannot guarantee that everything transmitted by the source is inherently credible. Despite the historical 'trustworthiness performance' or future potential of the source, the trustworthiness rates I show in Table 7.2 often depend on the potential or experienced energy impact of sources and content.

For example, we trust bus drivers, teachers, police officers, and colleagues, unless something happens that affects our useable and overall energy (Sect. 5.4). When we get the bus, we trust the driver holds a valid licence, has the permission to drive the bus, knows the way to the destination displayed, is fit for work and several other conditions. Thus, the starting point is full and unconditional trustworthiness. If we end up injured or at the wrong destination or unexpectedly very late, our trust in the 'failed' aspect might get a value of '0'. For instance, we can trust the safety of public transport, but not its punctuality. The trust we place in others daily and our mutual dependence on each other for credibility are immeasurable.

This is where the constructed societal structures like governments, agencies, regulators, councils, communities, and organisations take on the responsibility for ensuring trustworthiness for their members. Still, they must constantly compete with various information-spreaders (e.g., mainstream and social media and self-acclaimed educators). Under the right societal conditions (e.g., anxiety, fear, illiteracy), several channels can easily spread misinformation and conspiracy theories about secretive plans and deals between major players. The volume of conflicting information during the COVID-19 pandemic in 2020-2022 about its roots, spread, transmission, prevention, and treatment is an example of this. Such situations can mislead the ones with no first-hand knowledge about a specific topic and create mistrust in institutions in one area (e.g., new COVID-19 vaccines) where those same institutions are trusted in other similar areas (e.g., experimental cancer treatments).

The examples show that the 'rational trustworthiness' in Table 7.2 is only theoretical. In reality, trustworthiness is a binary YES/NO construct in each context. Simply put, we trust or not someone else in something at the specific time-point. It is rather more concrete if you state to me:

> 'I feel confident you are knowledgeable in this field *[i.e. I am a valid source]*, and I have observed what you deliver has been repeatedly coherent *[i.e. I am a reliable source]*. However, what you said in this case made little sense *[i.e. I shared invalid content]* although

you obviously achieved consistent results several times *[i.e. I shared reliable content]*' than stating something like: 'I trust you 2.5 out of 5'.

This score is unhelpful and does not allow for much improvement in trustworthiness.

Still, although Table 7.2 represents a merely qualitative, descriptive level of trustworthiness for each source-content pair at each time-point, the classification introduced in the particular table could be more practical and less abstract and vague to use than ranks and scales (e.g., Likert scales in psychological studies) that attempt to measure the inferential and immeasurable construct of trust.

7.3 Challenges

Regarding material energy, validity is grounded in senses through first-hand experiences. For example, we can all observe that a thermometer's indication increases when we feel that the temperature increases. This makes the story that a thermometer measures temperature valid. The more the observers we agree on this, the higher the validity of the argument about the function of the thermometer. If we get the same measurements from the thermometer repeatedly under same sensed temperatures, and if others experience and observe the same, then the story that the thermometer indications represent the respective temperature becomes also reliable. It does not matter if the increase of one unit in the scale of the thermometer represents really an increase of one unit in the temperature. We can never know, as it is about comparing two constructs. It does not matter as long as we all agree.

If several individuals accept and confirm the first-hand experiences of others by following the same protocol-constructs, they judge the stories as valid and reliable. When we do not have first-hand experience regarding material energy, we could believe those story sources. Most of us would label them as credible or trustworthy. The more organised the stories are and the more they comply with constructed criteria (methods for data collection, analysis, etc.), the more we name them as credible.

However, for immaterial energy, validity and reliability are not that easy to claim because these stories deal with the physically unperceivable. It is hard to be sure about the validity and reliability when comparing things that we cannot directly observe. Below and in several other sections of the book, I use 'culture' as an example of an unobservable, physically unperceivable construct. This does not negate the construct's usefulness. The choice to refer to it is because 'culture' has been one of the most used constructs in professional and organisational settings, especially in the last few decades. Hence, several professionals would be familiar with it.

For example, we cannot confidently quantitatively test the construct of organisational culture by comparing it with the construct of business risk appetite. This is because these two constructs can take any meaning and 'score' inside the mind of everyone. Also, such immaterial constructs can support each other, rather than independently verifying anything. Culture can affect risk appetite and risk appetite can shape the culture.

There are attempts to overcome the obstacles above by comparing or associating unobservable with observable constructs (e.g., asking people about culture and observing behaviours), but this still suffers. Everyone can declare the identical score X for a cultural aspect which somebody can link it to a behaviour. However, this does not mean that all X scores given have the same value across individuals and over time within individuals. Thus, even when behaviours are observable and measured through any human-made construct, their links to immaterial causes, factors, and effects are hard, if not impossible, to validate strongly and indisputably.

Yet, it is highly interesting how ill-defined and long-debated constructs have entered daily professional discussions. The use of such abstract concepts that are interpreted differently by everyone often displaces the desire for more precise knowledge. For instance, some publications and professionals personalise 'organisational culture', using it as a cause, reason, and explanation. As such, they refer to a culture that can trigger, inspire, suffer, grow, and so on, whereas there is still no agreed definition. It is paradoxical to name as a cause something with ambiguous meaning and physically inexistent.

Indeed, like material energy, we can use statistics to verify the reliability of immaterial energy measurements. However, if solid validity of the measurement is not secured, reliability does not really matter. By improving measurement instruments, scientists can achieve reliability over time and complete the model of truth for something that is valid. If a story is highly reliable but not highly valid, it lies far from a commonly acceptable truth in rational, professional and scientific terms. As I argued in Sect. 7.1, this case of good reliability but low validity is mostly about faith. To recap, a story's validity depends on agreement about its meaning, and its reliability depends on how easily its results can be repeated.

Story Elements: Key Reflections and Actions

Reflections

- Effective story sharing in professional settings depends on the clarity, reliability, and relevance of the content and sources that form the story.
- The accuracy and completeness of a story's content are critical. Misaligned or incomplete stories can lead to misinterpretation and poor decision-making.
- Evaluating the sources of a story involves assessing their credibility, expertise, and alignment with the context of the narrative.
- Stories often encounter challenges such as cognitive biases, emotional influences, and contextual misalignment, which can distort their meaning or impact.
- Recognising and addressing these challenges can enhance the integrity and effectiveness of storytelling in professional communication.

Actions

1. Evaluate Content Accuracy: Regularly assess whether the information within your stories is accurate, complete, and contextually appropriate. Address gaps or ambiguities proactively.
2. Assess Source Credibility: Critically examine the sources of your stories. Ensure they are reliable, well-informed, and relevant to the context of your message.
3. Address Cognitive Biases: Reflect on potential biases in your story sharing. Encourage open dialogue to uncover and mitigate biases that may distort the narrative or its interpretation.
4. Navigate Emotional Influences: Be mindful of the emotional undertones in your stories. Aim to strike a balance between emotional engagement and factual clarity to maintain credibility and professionalism.
5. Enhance Contextual Alignment: Tailor your stories to align with the audience's background, needs, and expectations. Use examples and analogies that resonate with their perspectives.
6. Foster Critical Story Analysis: Encourage your team or audience to question and critique the elements of stories they encounter. This builds a culture of thoughtful engagement and shared understanding.

By focusing on the integrity of story elements and addressing potential challenges, you can create narratives that are clear, credible, and impactful, fostering better communication and collaboration.

Chapter 8
Typology of Sciences

8.1 General

Professions typically relate to one or more scientific fields, which influence how we approach, inquire, analyse and synthesise data and information to facilitate decision-making and changes. Scientific methods, paradigms, and theories often transcend the academic and research environments. As professionals, we rely on scholarly publications and study findings to enhance systems, assess risks, gather requirements, develop products and services, and leverage operational feedback. As I mentioned in Chapter 2, sciences are investigative constructs we employ to describe, explain, interpret, and change the world.

The beauty and curse of science, and by extension of respective professions, is that each time someone claims there is an explanation, they later realise it might be imperfect or incomplete. Reasons usually include poor producibility (i.e., the explanation does not apply exactly to all similar cases) and low predictability (i.e., the explanation cannot be used to foresee accurately future states of the area of interest). Then, analysts and professionals decide to perfect current knowledge and start looking deeper and further. Therefore, yesterday's explanation becomes today just a description, and today's explanation becomes tomorrow's description. This opens a world of discovery to find more reproducible explanations and enhance predictability.

In this chapter, I present positions about various scientific fields, which can equally apply to professions using scientific methods and consulting with scientific findings to implement solutions. As a foundational and starting point, in Table 8.1, I present the typology of sciences. The particular typology relates scientific fields to specific energy types (Sect. 5.3) and respective constructs of focus (Sect. 2.3). Nonetheless, the correspondences in each row of Table 8.1 do not mean the absolute exclusion of other energy types and constructs. The boundaries between the types of sciences might not be as clear as I present them here for the sake of simplification.

N. Karanikas, *Professional Generalism in a Hyper-specialised World*,
https://doi.org/10.1007/978-981-96-4039-3_8

Table 8.1 Typology of sciences

Types of investigative constructs	Energy types of interest	Constructs of focus (Note: all sciences use media, assigned and constitutional constructs)	Examples
Formal sciences	(Not applicable—foundations of other sciences)	Media	Mathematics, statistics, logic, linguistics, etc
Exact sciences	Material energy	• Physical • Eventological • Calculative	Physics, chemistry, biology, neuroscience, engineering, medicine, meteorology, etc
Inexact sciences	Immaterial energy	• Inferential • Abstract	Theology, psychoanalysis, philosophy, cognitive psychology, etc
Hybrid sciences	Material and immaterial energy	Combinations of physical, eventological, calculative, inferential and abstract	Sociology, behavioural psychology, criminology, anthropology, management, law, etc

8.2 Formal Sciences

Formal sciences are energy- and construct-agnostic. They deal with the means to communicate about all other constructs. All formal sciences are abstract and provide the foundations for the rest of the scientific fields. Their role is to improvise, introduce, use, modify, and cancel media constructs. This includes communicating media constructs through other media constructs. For instance, linguistics uses mathematics and logic, and mathematics is a language itself. Formal sciences represent the conventions employed in personal, social, professional, academic, and any other context, and, as all constructs, they cannot be externally validated.

For example, as I mentioned in Sect. 3.1, scientists can describe many parts of the material world with mathematics, but this does not mean the world has been built with mathematics. Mathematics focusses on describing events, not explaining them, despite sometimes using the term 'explaining' for predictions. We do not always need to explain a phenomenon to predict. Reliable descriptions could suffice as, for example, in epidemiology. In our human history, there have been several instances where observational analyses through statistics led to preventive actions to protect public health even before the exact mechanisms of diseases were known.[1]

[1] Gordis, L. (2014). *Epidemiology* (5th ed.). Saunders.

Furthermore, although there are tens of equations to describe how material unities interact and behave, there still exist mathematical paradoxes,[2,3] meaning imperfect or impossible descriptions. Besides, mathematical equations can become extremely inaccurate for biological systems where complexity and dynamics do not always allow to describe with confidence. Indeed, we could not prove or disprove claims that mathematics is a discovery (i.e., something that exists regardless of humanity) and not a human invention. If we are the inventors of mathematics and observers of their value, it means we are part of the system we verify; hence, we cannot be objective verifiers.

Nonetheless, if we agree on what each construct of formal sciences represents, there is no problem. If we all agree that 1 + 1 equals 2, it suffices. If we all agree that the word pen corresponds to a specific type of unity, even with some variations, it is adequate. If we all agree a specific portion of a population denotes a particular standard deviation from the average, it is fine. If we all agree there are differences in the meaning of some terms across various geographical regions, but these terms hold the same meaning within each region, it could be sometimes enough. If we all agree that placing our letters, words and any item in a specific order signals logic, then there is no problem.

8.3 Exact Sciences

Exact sciences deal with the material energy of physical and eventological constructs (e.g., temperature, time, space, phenomena), and they generate and use calculative constructs. Exact sciences employ formal sciences (e.g., mathematics and statistics) and use human-constructed unities (e.g., devices and equipment) to deliver valid and reliable knowledge, subject to observer effects and some measurement uncertainties. For example, a mathematical formula defines the construct of average speed, which we can calculate with instruments measuring distance and time. In general, we expect that measurers are skilled and knowledgeable in using accurately the agreed-upon measurement instruments and techniques.

Exact sciences encompass *fundamental sciences* and some *applied sciences*. Fundamental fields study how material energy behaves, including the type, duration, area, effects and other traits of this energy type (e.g., physics and chemistry). Applied sciences (biology, engineering, neuroscience, etc.) relate to any activity based on observable and clearly defined events, such as the design, engineering and manufacturing of hardware, and the functions of supply chain and logistics. They describe and test these events while acknowledging confidence, accuracy, and other (un)certainty-related aspects that characterise science.

[2] Weber, Z. (2021). *Paradoxes and inconsistent mathematics*. Cambridge University Press.

[3] Křížek, M., & Somer, L. (2023). *Mathematical aspects of paradoxes in cosmology: Can mathematics explain the contemporary cosmological crisis?* Springer International Publishing AG.

From a broad perspective, though, all exact sciences are 'event' sciences focusing on different unity types. Physics and chemistry are fundamental sciences that examine the behaviours of raw material, particles, and their compounds. Biology is an applied science that observes behaviours of organic parts and elements and outputs and outcomes of their interactions. Medicine is another applied science that studies how body parts behave and interact with external agents (e.g., drugs and the environment).

Exact sciences observe, record, and analyse commotions and expressions of a unity and/or its observable sub-unities; all observable events relate to the actualisation and use of material energy. For instance, when you present your project progress, you use energy to move your leaps and adjacent facial areas. This is observable and measurable (e.g., the relative motion of your leaps). Biology and neuroscience are interested in the underlying behaviours of body parts, which make the leaps moving.

Exact sciences claim to uncover the essence of things by breaking them down into smaller components. In reality, these fields break down unities to study their smaller sub-unities. Every time scientists disintegrate a unity to discover its nature, they find other unities. Scientists track the smaller sub-unities' interactions and note their behaviours and results. Even when scientists think they reached the ultimate 'nature' of matter, they then get even more surprised, and the journey continues.

All exact science experiments are about causes-effects through event observations. Deduction (i.e., reasoning from general principles to specific cases) and decomposition and their denominations (e.g., backwards induction and counterfactual thinking) are fundamental to exact sciences for describing the world. Exact scientists use the products of their discoveries to combine, blend and merge various types of matter in new unities with new behaviours and leading to new events (e.g., technology, medicine, food supplements). Often, these new unities are the vehicles to continue the discovery journey (e.g., new technology is used to decompose unities further or reach other distant unities, such as stars and planets).

8.4 Hybrid and Inexact Sciences

Many times, the domain of exact sciences cannot fully understand observed events involving highly variable unities, such as humans, by employing only decomposition. Also, scientists cannot fully predict such events through analyses of observable cause-effect relationships and epidemiological criteria.[4] This happens because immaterial energy is immeasurable and unobservable while constantly interplaying with material energy. Something can be perceptible (e.g., you 'feel' it exists, or you understand its meaning) but not physically perceivable. For instance, you can feel safe and understand the meaning of safety, but you cannot see safety itself.

Indeed, neuroscience has explained many brain and body mechanisms of living beings' behaviours that were for long unknown. However, we have not yet discovered

[4] Hill, A. B. (1965). The environment and disease: Association or causation? *Proceedings of the Royal Society of Medicine, 58*(5), 295–300. https://doi.org/10.1177/003591576505800503.

mechanisms related uniquely to affective energy apart from its manifestation through cognitive and physical activities (Chapter 5). Also, we have not yet discovered the nature of immaterial energy. If scientists had done so, then this energy would not be labelled as immaterial. Therefore, to date, there is only partial information about the human nature, and several other living organisms.

We have filled the gap in our understanding of human nature and other organisms, especially animals, by coining abstract and inferential constructs. We use those to describe and explain immaterial energy, assign values to it, and connect it with material energy. For instance, following the rules (i.e., observable material energy) could mean knowledge, acceptance, motivation, fear, and other aspects of unobservable immaterial energy. To verify reliability, we can statistically test the methods analysts have devised to measure and analyse immaterial energy and its interactions with material energy. However, the validity is usually internally confined, and any results are typically limited to the subjects being measured.

As an example, the assessment of any type of culture (e.g., national, regional, organisational) through a reliable survey instrument can be internally valid only under a commonly agreed and comprehended definition adopted by the researchers and communicated to the participants. Other factors affecting validity include the way the respondents understood questions and concepts, the presence and effects of confounding factors and different initial conditions for each of the participants (e.g., prior information or knowledge). All these aspects vary across researchers and study subjects. They can also change after a few minutes, weeks, months, or years, depending on further exposure of study participants to material energy and its interactions with immaterial energy. This denotes that we cannot generalise the findings from cultural surveys to represent the 'whole' now and in the future.

Sciences studying immaterial energy confront the different interpretations of the abstract and inferential constructs addressed and the constant change of their meaning and definitions. Those variations mean that the findings of respective studies cannot be externally valid for different populations and over time. Hence, these sciences can fall under the category of:

- *Inexact Sciences* that study immaterial energy only (e.g., philosophy, theology, cognitive psychology),
- *Hybrid Sciences* that study the mutual effects of immaterial and material energies (e.g., behavioural psychology, neuropsychology, social sciences, human resources).

Differently from exact sciences, inexact and hybrid sciences, depending on their focus, prefer induction through a bottom-up journey (i.e., reasoning from specific observations to general principles) and are complemented by or include intuition and abduction (i.e., reasoning from an observation to a plausible explanation). Typically, lower-level abstract and inferential constructs are grouped into higher-level ones, the emerging constructs are blended and merged, definitions of these constructs change frequently, new constructs replace older ones, and so on.

The biggest challenge for scientists in these disciplines is when they study established social constructs that have not been built bottom-up. For instance, race is a social construct that has been established over centuries, not built bottom-up from scientific observations. The idea of distinct racial categories emerged from colonial and imperialist ideologies, not from rigorous scientific studies. Also, despite the widespread acceptance of the race construct, there is no clear genetic or biological basis for racial categories in the way these are commonly understood. Definitions of race can vary significantly across cultures and time periods, highlighting its constructed nature.

In such cases, scholars typically use deductive approaches to break down these constructs, like what exact sciences do with material constructs. However, we cannot decompose something that does not physically exist and has not been conceptually defined bottom-up. This is not inherently negative. However, the variety of approaches, perspectives, studies, and concepts about immaterial aspects can cause confusion and inconsistency amongst scientists and professionals. As such, researchers studying race-related topics must grapple with deeply ingrained societal beliefs and categories that may not align with biological reality. Even further, scientists could struggle to design studies that do not inadvertently reinforce existing racial categories, even when examining their validity.

Another problem, though, is when the decomposition of inferential and abstract constructs remains in the conceptual sphere and does not lead or become linked to observable behaviours and phenomena. Indeed, in this case, interlocutors can debate forever and exchange perspectives more than solid scientific results. A study investigating perceived ambition with perceived job satisfaction is mostly conceptual, regardless of the findings of statistical tests. This is because varied interpretations and importance levels of those concepts exist amongst study participants. Hence, if immaterial energy constructs are not linked to something observable, their power depends heavily on meanings.

Inexact and hybrid sciences frequently borrow from exact sciences and employ formal sciences to generate calculative constructs. However, their units, measurements, and products often remain conceptual in principle. Therefore, while observable phenomena and their derivatives have quantifiable units (e.g., seconds, kilograms), immaterial constructs (e.g., knowledge, motivation, trust) lack direct measurement units. Thus, because the unit of measurement is a fundamental scientific principle for calculations and estimations, inexact and hybrid sciences face additional challenges. As direct measurements are impossible, we use constructed proxy measurements and agreed operational definitions to quantify immaterial constructs.

Still, while ensuring reliability through mathematical and statistical processes to test conceptual measurement scales, validity might suffer if the constructs targeted do not hold the same meanings across the entire population and over time. Researchers studying immaterial energy cannot collect data like scientists studying physical things. Especially in surveys and interviews, what analysts record is information out of the data each person processes in their brain (Sect. 6.3). The human mind remains vastly a 'black box' not only because of its complex physiology but also the inability to trace immaterial energy through decomposition (Sect. 5.2).

Even further, using mathematics for immaterial energy could be misleading. As I mentioned in the section above, applied mathematics helps us understand and predict real-world events using cause and effect relationships; they were not constructed for describing immaterial energy. Also, as discussed above, calculative constructs are always defined with a unit of measurement, which is not the case with immaterial energy.

Surprisingly, ancient philosophers—leading scientists of their day—never recorded measurements of mental and emotional energy. They never devised scales of trust, happiness, anxiety, intelligence, knowledge and other constructs. Philosophers merely discussed immaterial energy and constructs, relating them to specific contexts, despite the existence of numbers and mathematics (e.g., currencies, calendars).

Hence, centuries ago, constructs were not measured with conceptual scales but there were rather viewed as present or absent within particular contexts. For instance, a professional knows how to use correctly a tool for a specific purpose and get a result with particular features. The same expert may lack knowledge in using different tools or using the same tool for different purposes.

In the past, there were no calculations comparing levels of knowledge between people. There was no mathematical operation to calculate the level of knowledge within individuals. Even further, incomplete knowledge, which again was never quantified, in ancient times was deemed as even worse than the lack of knowledge.

Conversation focussed solely on knowledge or not of a particular topic or specifics of it, not knowledge levels. This is what the term '-logy' at the end of several professions and academic disciplines reflects. It comes from the Greek word 'logos' which means 'talking about' with no measuring or calculating connotations. In its strict meaning and narrow translation, for instance, 'psychology' would mean to talk about the 'psych', with no perceived need to assess it quantitatively.

As such, it is interesting that scholars are so keen to analyse parts of immaterial energy stories mathematically and statistically to construct the 'overall truth'. Over time, the trend in academia and the industry is to quantify everything, believing numbers are more persuasive than words. This belief in the superiority of numbers has led to increased quantification. It follows a long tradition of what recent scholarly work names as the materiality of numbers.[5]

Typology of Sciences: Key Reflections and Actions

Reflections

- Sciences can be broadly categorised into formal, exact, hybrid, and inexact types, each with distinct methodologies and contributions to knowledge.
- Formal sciences, such as mathematics, provide foundational frameworks that underpin other scientific domains, offering structure and logical consistency.
- Exact sciences, like physics, aim to produce precise, predictable, and reproducible outcomes but are often limited to specific contexts and assumptions.
- Hybrid sciences bridge disciplines, integrating elements from both exact and inexact sciences to address complex, multifaceted challenges.

[5] Overmann, K. A. (2023). *The materiality of numbers: Emergence and elaboration from prehistory to present*. Cambridge University Press.

- Inexact sciences deal with variability, human behaviours, and contextual factors that resist absolute predictability but are crucial for understanding dynamic systems.
- Each type of science has unique strengths and limitations. An integrated approach that values their complementarity can lead to more holistic and effective professional practices.

Actions

1. Understand Science Typologies: Reflect on the types of sciences relevant to your professional domain. Identify which types underpin your knowledge base and how they interact with one another.
2. Appreciate Complementarity: Recognise the strengths and limitations of each scientific type. Use this understanding to integrate diverse methodologies and perspectives into your work.
3. Bridge Disciplines: Capitalise on opportunities to apply hybrid approaches by combining insights from exact and inexact sciences. This can foster innovative solutions to complex problems.
4. Adapt to Variability: When working with inexact sciences, embrace the challenges of variability and uncertainty. Use qualitative and contextual insights to complement quantitative analyses.
5. Promote Interdisciplinary Dialogue: Engage with professionals from diverse scientific backgrounds. Explore how their methodologies and frameworks can enrich your perspective and practice.

By understanding the typology of sciences and valuing their unique contributions, you can adopt a more inclusive and integrated approach to professional problem-solving and decision-making.

Chapter 9
Science Dialogues

9.1 General

The observations I expressed in Chapter 8 above do not mean that inexact and hybrid sciences are utterly inaccurate and that exact sciences are 100% accurate. Research in exact sciences still carries assumptions and limitations. Many physical sciences deal with uncertainty and probability (e.g., quantum mechanics), while many social sciences employ rigorous quantitative methods, even under the limitations of attaching numbers to immaterial energy. Thus, there is no dichotomy but a conceptual and relative exact-hybrid-inexact spectrum. It depends on whether the measured quantity is observable and unequivocally defined and understood across different unities and over time.

Admittedly though, different from immaterial energy sciences, exact scientists can monitor assumptions and variability more easily because their studies focus on physically observable constructs. Exact science findings usually extend previous results, offer opportunities for practical applications to mature products and services further, and, in general, grow and transform into tangible deliverables.

Certainly, inexact and hybrid sciences employ tests of variance to check for high variability across their samples. If they detect it, they can attribute high variability to systematic effects and confounding factors. However, reliable statistical test results could be misleading if validity is compromised (Chapter 7). A testimony to this is that the domains of hybrid and inexact sciences are the ones most often advocating

N. Karanikas, *Professional Generalism in a Hyper-specialised World*,
https://doi.org/10.1007/978-981-96-4039-3_9

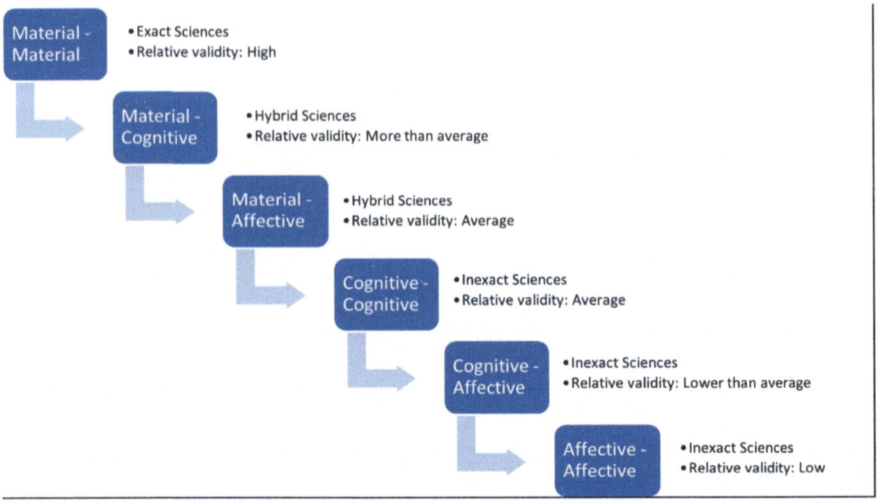

Fig. 9.1 Relative validity of sciences based on interactions between material, cognitive, and affective energies

the need to bridge theory and practice.[1,2,3,4] This happens because their results are not immediately transferable and generalised, as are most of the outputs of exact sciences. The theory–practice gap is an information-knowledge gap (Sect. 6.3).

In Fig. 9.1 I propose the relative validity strength of sciences depending on the pairs of interacting energy types under study: material, cognitive, and affective. In the specific figure, I assume that material energy is easier to measure and study compared to cognitive and affective energies, and cognitive energy is easier to evaluate than affective energy.

Of course, the validity of any study depends also on the instruments used, the subjects under study and the researchers. In principle, exact sciences perform experiments and analyses by collecting event-type data of material energy. This can be done through reliable instruments or reliable observers, including analysing documents and records. Of note, written artefacts are factual data since they are physically perceivable. However, not all exact sciences generate highly valid results by default. Good research designs should meticulously account for sample sizes and characteristics, confounding factors and other parameters, as it applies to all studies according to our constructed scientific criteria.

---

[1] Szwed, P. (2017). *Expert judgment in project management: Narrowing the theory–practice gap.* Project Management Institute, Inc.

[2] Khadka, S., & Lee, J. (2019). *Bridging the multimodal gap: From theory to practice.* Utah State University Press.

[3] Maliniak, D., Peterson, S., Powers, R., & Tierney, M. (2020). *Bridging the theory–practice divide in international relations.* Georgetown University Press.

[4] Hoffman, S., & Barrios, R. (2020). *Disaster upon disaster: Exploring the gap between knowledge, policy, and practice.* Berghahn Books.

Also, when social sciences investigate relationships between physically perceivable phenomena, their studies could fall under the exact sciences category. For instance, we could examine the correlation between years of education (i.e., factual data found in records) and hours spent on sports (i.e., factual data to be collected through observations). We can consider this an exact science, as long as we compare similar contexts (e.g., low variability of education programmes' quality; equal opportunities for spare time and access to sports).

However, a study gathering opinions from individuals to offer explanations would not qualify as an exact science study. Not that each participant cannot express themselves honestly, but each opinion will heavily rely on various factors. These include, for example, the meaning of words and phrases participants use (e.g., insufficient motivation, family pressures), easiness to recall events with accuracy (e.g., how frequently they do sports) and effects of the interactions with the researcher (e.g., participants offering socially desirable answers). Besides, the researchers' interpretations may differ from participants' intentions.

Hybrid sciences typically use a mixture of observational data with information from questionnaires and interviews, or solely information from participants. When collecting information about immaterial energy from participants, the clearer the connections with material energy are, the more valid the results become.

For example, a study wants to investigate the relationship between curiosity and risky behaviours. Researchers collect data on these variables using participant information and observations. Certainly, the definitions of curiosity and risk will play a huge role when collecting data and information. As such, clear communication of definitions is crucial between researchers, participants, and observers. Different understandings of curiosity and risk will weaken the validity of the results.

For instance, regarding curiosity, a researcher could ask, 'How curious are you?', and present answer options like low, medium, and high. If also having provided no or a weak definition of curiosity, this case would generate highly subjective answers of limited validity. Would the study include a similar question for the 'risky behaviours' part of the study (e.g., 'How risky are you?'), the results would have an overall poor validity because of the lack of specificity in the questions for both constructs.

Another option would be to infer curiosity through events, asking participants something like, 'On average, how frequently in the same day do you want to find more about the world around you beyond the first information you receive?'. The researchers could offer answer options such as rarely, often, almost always. Here, the chances of obtaining better validity increase compared to the question formulation and the answer scale above. If this second option includes more specific scales (e.g., 1–2 times/day, 3–5 times/day and 6 or more times/day), validity could increase further. Of course, this still assumes the ability of the participants to recall information and that they answer truthfully.

The validity of the research outputs and anticipated outcomes and the credibility of any professional or scientific analysis increases with:

- more specificity in the definitions of the constructs of interest,

- answers focussing on stronger connections between inferential and abstract constructs with physically perceivable events, and
- more specific measurement scales.

Of note, regardless of the pursuit of reliability and validity, researchers must also be extremely mindful of how they conduct and communicate their studies, especially those involving data and findings about humans, and who sponsors their research. In our era, many countries, states, and research institutions have established codes of research and ethical practices suggesting how to avoid dependencies that could lower the level of objectivity in studies. Professional practice when performing projects with data collection and analyses would highly benefit from adopting such practices.

9.2 Scholarly Synergies

The previous section argues that clear definitions and measurements matter more in inexact than hybrid sciences. A study investigating the relationship between intelligence and empathy by employing no event-type construct will be excessively vulnerable to relatively higher invalidity. Research lacking robust and commonly understood definitions might not generate science in its narrow meaning. If researchers cannot meet this principal condition to the extent possible, then they can just hold arguments and join dialogues about the meanings and impacts of the results with no solid verdict. Collecting and analysing data by using scientific methods does not always produce science.

Inexact and hybrid sciences can increase their 'exactness' over time. The challenge is that collaboration in immaterial energy sciences may appear as less strong than in the exact sciences. In the latter, analysts regularly share findings and gather to explore common grounds and apply their knowledge towards commonly agreed definitions, answers and solutions (e.g., the definition of time, the development of a vaccine). Also, there are other constructs that science develops to group a previously observed, measured and clearly defined set of behaviours and properties of material energy (e.g., the flu disease).

Contrary, in inexact/hybrid sciences, researchers rarely use identical definitions, methodologies, techniques and tools to verify findings over time and across different populations. In the name of innovation, growth of knowledge, personal interest and reputation and other reasons, each scholar examining immaterial energy might add, remove, or change something from the work of previous research to perform their unique study. This prevents inexact/hybrid scientists from speaking with one voice to each other and the public.

Undoubtedly, we should never discourage diverse and new ideas. Nevertheless, researchers can study the link between immaterial and material energy using longitudinal studies, building on past research. For example, you might disagree with a definition of philanthropy if it does not align with your understanding or experiences. This does not mean that you must change or reject the specific definition if there is no newer study contradicting the results of previous research when conducted under the same conditions. There must be a healthy balance between testing the old and changing or rejecting it by default without verifying, complementing, or improving previously published work.

For instance, in the safety management discipline, there are many definitions, approaches, and measurement instruments regarding 'safety culture'. Those are regularly shared through scientific and professional publications, online posts and blogs, seminars, workshops, consultancies, conferences, and other channels. Safety culture is a term first introduced in the investigation report of the Chernobyl nuclear disaster in 1986.

However, back then, there was an inadequate understanding of what the report's authors meant and how they conceived this abstract construct. Since then, there have been many debates about meanings, characteristics, safety subcultures, and assessments in hundreds of papers, tens of books and chapters, roundtable discussions, and any other form of interaction. The absence of a bottom-up definition of 'safety culture', based on real-world observations, has led to this problem. A shared understanding of 'safety culture' is lacking because it was not defined from the ground up through observation and analysis.

Instead, many have largely followed the inverted path of decomposing safety culture into whatever elements they believe it includes. This is not a wise direction to take for immaterial energy constructs like this one. At least, we would expect that after decades of discussions and studies, scholars would have agreed on a shared definition and basic constituents of this construct and any similar one, preferably with links to observable events. Yet, 'safety culture' presents a different situation.

Undoubtedly, abstract constructs, though imprecise, guide professional decisions and organisational strategies. Terms like 'safety culture' and 'employee engagement' help people in the field communicate and work together, even if they are hard to measure precisely. Their utility lies in their ability to encapsulate multifaceted ideas that are otherwise difficult to articulate or operationalise. However, reliance on such constructs must be balanced with efforts to develop rigorous methodologies for their validation. By employing mixed methods, longitudinal studies, and clear operational definitions, researchers and practitioners can strengthen the reliability and validity of these constructs, ensuring they are not only useful in practice but also robust enough to inform evidence-based decisions and scalable interventions. This dual approach—valuing the utility of abstract constructs while striving for greater scientific precision—enables professionals to bridge the gap between theoretical insights and practical applications effectively.

To facilitate the above, it would be immensely beneficial for the professional world if scholars would converge their works every 5–10 years, agree on definitions, conceptual components, and representative unity behaviours and report back to the industry and the society. In the meantime, academics could organise scientific conferences as forums to debate, exchange ideas, and spark new studies without extensively disseminating to the industry each piece of idea and research that has not been sufficiently discussed, tested and connected with other concepts.

The approach above would reduce confusion and unproductive conflicts between professionals favouring different approaches, often based on subjective and not solid criteria. After sharing their common voice every few years, researchers would continue their discovery voyage, disputes, and debates and reconvene regularly to refine their approaches and definitions. Certainly, the specific proposition in this era can sound utopian given the commercial and conflicting interests, personal agendas and pressures in academia to leave their mark on industry and community practice and persuade public and private sources of providing funding.

9.3 Interplay of Sciences

Undeniably, all scientific families have contributed incredibly to our civilisation, sometimes negatively because of their misuse, but this can happen to any construct. Science led to producing nuclear power which we can use to generate electricity or destroy and annihilate. Some can use the results from social sciences to understand and help different groups (e.g., workers and employers) or discriminate and isolate. Such phenomena are sometimes outside the control of scientists.

Nonetheless, possibly, a strong opponent of subjectivity could be fast to declare superiority of exact sciences. However, it is paramount to acknowledge that immaterial energy sciences are typically the driving force of material energy sciences under a continuous interplay between them. For instance, curiosity generates ideas, both curiosity and ideas belonging to the area of immaterial energy. Such ideas primarily represent abstract and imaginary pictures of the unobservable or incomprehensive world or reasons behind physical observations. Ideas become theories, leading to hypotheses tested through experiments and discoveries.

Engineers do not only measure, design, test, and review by using mathematics and instruments. They converse with colleagues about methods to realise ideas. They discuss with clients to understand their needs and expectations. They collaborate with other technical experts to address challenges. They pitch solutions to management to secure funding. None of those activities belongs to exact science.

Interestingly too, sometimes exact sciences build immaterial constructs about unobservable or unexplained phenomena and develop theories. This often occurs when science cannot derive visible and measurable explanations of observable behaviours (e.g., theories about Bing Bang, dark matter) or when it groups the properties and behaviours of material energy. As the following paragraphs highlight, regardless of whether someone accepts it, immaterial energy is the starting and ending point of the scientific spectrum.

The medical field is a representative example. For example, at a first glance, stomach pain is an inferential construct for the general health practitioner and the patient; we cannot see and touch pain. A patient feels something physically unpleasant somewhere in their body, which can also affect their cognitive and emotional state. The doctor tries to explain the pain despite the initial ignorance of what is really happening inside the body of the patient.

During this first diagnostic phase, inexactness prevails. The patient might not have expressed their symptoms accurately, the first clinical picture might resemble tens or more of possible health problems and causes, and so on. Hence, at the first stage of pain investigation, someone has only information and no factual data; there are potential explanations and no established causes.

Specialists can determine the cause of pain with additional exams. Also, neuroscientists have thoroughly explained the mechanisms of pain as interactions of specific body elements, and empirical research has well-explored the emergence and intensity of those interactions. If the construct of pain had never been there (e.g., no complaints by humans who would passively accept any unpleasant feeling), and the construct of sympathy was not existent, we would never be driven to explain pain and relieve its bearer through exact sciences.

Patients may distrust medical advice due to superstitions, misinformation, bad experiences, or other factors. Also, they might not endorse the proposed therapy because of fear and nervousness or high tolerance to pain. All of those are not related to exactness. This example started with an immaterial construct and ended with another immaterial construct, while it also referred to material constructs and exact science.

The concepts of physical pain, its diagnosis and treatment above apply to all constructs used in professions. The interplay between sciences and the role of immaterial energy as a starting and finishing point becomes even more obvious in mental health and diseases. The sphere of immaterial is the initiator and the last point of our endeavours to explain, discover, change, support, and of any other activity.

9.4 Roles and Contributions

One concept underlining the arguments I presented in the sections above is that the study of physically observable causes-effects is the domain of exact sciences. Hybrid and inexact sciences are interested in explanations and interpretations, respectively, as they deal with the sphere of the physically unperceivable. They study the interactions within immaterial energy and its interplay with material energy. Thus, understanding physical causes through exact sciences does not mean ignoring the possible effects of immaterial energy. Similarly, the difficulty or reluctance to study and comprehend immaterial energy is not a good reason for doubting the existence of physically perceivable causes-effects.

The primary role of immaterial energy sciences in professions and the civilisation is to raise awareness of the society. Their influence extends to all involved in exact sciences and the entire life cycle of activities and products. Inexact and hybrid sciences help us reflect on reasons and factors and contemplate any material and immaterial aspects that drive the development and use of material energy within and outside unities. Inexact/hybrid scientists observe activities, outputs, and outcomes to generate new ideas and adjust existing theories about the relationship between material and immaterial energy. They study the 'nature' of immaterial energy through interdisciplinary scientific collaboration.

Scientifically unexplained from the perspective of exact sciences does not mean impossible from the perspective of inexact and hybrid sciences. The latter, however, can provide indications and advice but cannot offer definite solutions and boundaries. Equally crucial, immaterial energy sciences are the guardians of humanity. This is especially significant when exact sciences drift from their mission to serve us under the ethical principles applicable to each era, professional group, and geographical region. None of the ethics schools and principles I presented in Chapter 1 is a result of any exact science.

Most importantly, inexact sciences are the ones who lead the development and change of ethics. Of course, scientists and professionals focussed on precision might struggle with the ambiguity of inexact sciences. Nevertheless, together with their hybrid counterparts, inexact sciences play a critical role in the derivation of invisible but plausible relationships to counterbalance extreme deduction with insightful induction, obsession to detail with necessity for an overview, rejection of misbehaving parts with improvement of the system. Immaterial energy sciences are essential to counter extreme mechanistic views that reduce living beings, including humans, to mere raw material.

For instance, decades ago, the medical profession approached pain management primarily through physiological metrics (e.g., blood pressure readings, heart rate monitoring, and facial muscle contractions). Doctors would often make treatment decisions based solely on these mechanical measurements, treating pain as a purely biological response that could be quantified through physical markers. This mechanistic approach led to several critical issues. For example, chronic pain patients were often undertreated because their physiological markers did not match expected patterns. Also, patient anxiety and fear were overlooked as pain amplifiers, and the nocebo effect (i.e., negative expectations leading to negative outcomes) was not considered.

In the meantime, research by anthropologists, psychologists, sociologists and other scientists professionals in humanities disciplines revealed that pain expression varies significantly across cultures, social support affects pain perception, personal history influences pain tolerance, and other findings. This yielded a holistic pain assessment integrating physiology, culture, psychology, social support, personal narratives, family input, non-verbal cues, and spirituality.

The case above shows how humanities and social sciences helped transform a purely mechanistic approach to pain (i.e., treating humans as biological machines that merely 'react and interact') into a comprehensive understanding that honours the full human experience of pain, including thoughts, feelings, and social context[5]. However, it is imperative to appreciate that exact sciences are more exposed to scrutiny and criticism. That is because they deal with physically perceivable entities

---

[5] Cooney, M. F., & Quinlan-Colwell, A. (2021). *Assessment and multimodal management of pain an integrative approach*. Elsevier.

and phenomena that we can verify through implementing the constructed verification and validation criteria we have commonly accepted.

Indeed, some scholars blame system designers and engineers, who overwhelmingly rely on exact science, for their imperfect decisions. Surprisingly though, many of these scholars cannot or do not provide support as tangible, tested, and sustainable solutions beyond cliché statements and terms. Phrases like 'context matters', 'embrace variability', 'complexity of sociotechnical systems', and 'respect diversity' are typical. Undoubtedly, such statements have incredible value in nudging us and others think and reflect further. However, if remained in the conceptual domain and cannot be actioned, they lose credibility before the eyes of professionals.

Therefore, it is not about which scientific domain is better or more necessary to inform good professional practice. It is about how the scientific areas dealing with immaterial and material energy can understand and assist each other and work in unison while maintaining their distinct characteristics. For instance, engineering (i.e., mostly informed by exact sciences) changes the environment that influences behaviours. Humanities (i.e., mostly informed by inexact sciences) influence humans who change their environment. In parallel, management (i.e., mostly informed by hybrid sciences) regulates the material resources available, defines priorities, decides on beneficiaries and exerts an influence on the immaterial energy of others.

As a reminder of concepts which I discussed earlier, inexact sciences and many hybrid scientific fields deal mainly with unobservable information or perceptions. Exact sciences are based on observable evidence and data. Evidently, different persons can agree more easily on what they physically sense rather than what they conceptually perceive, understand, and believe. Thus, in professional practice and studies, it is paramount to discern between expressed thoughts, which comprise information, and observable acts, which constitute data and evidence. Interpreting acts of self and others is perception, whereas the visible effects of acts on other unities could be data.

For instance, imagine two professionals, ProA and ProB, collaborating on a project. Observable data and evidence would be that ProA submitted their part of the project two days after the agreed deadline, ProB's subsequent work was delivered three days later than planned, and the final project was completed five days behind schedule. Other evidence could be that three scheduled team meetings were cancelled, ProA attended 4 of the 5 project meetings, ProB attended 3 of the 5 meetings and neither sent advance notices for missed meetings.

Perceptions/interpretations that comprise information would be that ProA believes that ProB is unreliable because the latter missed meetings, ProB thinks ProA is disorganised because the latter was late with their project part, and ProA feels ProB is passive-aggressive in the emails exchanged. Other information could be that each believes the other is controlling, responsible for delays, and that their own communication and work ethic are superior.

The example above shows how we can readily agree on countable, observable events (i.e., data) but form different perceptions about the meaning behind those events (i.e., information). The same observable actions often lead to different interpretations by each of us based on our understanding, beliefs and conceptual frameworks.

Also, experiments in exact and some hybrid sciences are physically perceivable in their design, execution, and outputs and move us from theories, faiths and hypotheses to trustworthy/credible stories of cause-effect relationships (Chapter 7). Regardless of the scale we use, opinions and perspectives are not experimental outputs, even if they are called ‘evidence’ at times. However, experiments depend on them for their conception, execution, and analysis. As such, the interpretation of any exact science is a perfectly inexact process.

We cannot be judged for our immaterial energy stored, as it is externally unobservable. You, I, and any individual can think and imagine whatever we want without implications. However, when decisions, emotions, thinking, and anything that characterises immaterial energy manifest into observable phenomena, there are exposure and judgements against professionally and socially built constructs. Whether or not any judgement is fair changes over time, as exactly do all human-made constructs. The most important thing to acknowledge is that immaterial and material energy interact and influence each other constantly within and outside each of us and any unity.

Gratefully, despite the observations and arguments above, lately the large families of science have come closer and deal with modern challenges in tandem. This has had positive effects and beneficial ramifications to the professional field. It is encouraging that several professionals have acknowledged that their extreme specialisation has deprived them of the bigger picture. They admit their intense focus on their fields blinded them to other viewpoints and backgrounds. This acknowledgment has given rise to several studies and applications using inter-disciplinarity (i.e., adding components from different disciplines), multi-disciplinarity (i.e., co-creation with overlaps between disciplines) and trans-disciplinarity (i.e., integration of disciplines).[6,7]

In Fig. 9.2, I show the connections between sciences and summarise the perspectives mentioned earlier. The key message is that exact sciences show causes and effects. Hybrid sciences explain these, and inexact sciences interpret them. This distinction can help us move forward and not stick with unproductive arguments about what cause is or is not. As professionals, we need to acknowledge the roles, contributions, and boundaries of science. You should be cautious of ‘exact’ individuals who claim they can describe, predict, and fix everything. You should be alert of ‘inexact’ persons who believe they can interpret everyone. You better remain wary of ‘hybrid’ professionals who allege they have an answer and explanation for everything.

---

[6] Alvargonzalez, D. (2011). Multidisciplinarity, interdisciplinarity, transdisciplinarity, and the sciences. *International Studies in the Philosophy of Science, 25*(4), 387–403. https://doi.org/10.1080/02698595.2011.623366.

[7] Schroeder, M. J. (2022). Multidisciplinarity, interdisciplinarity, and transdisciplinarity: The tower of babel in the age of two cultures. *Philosophies (Basel), 7*(2), 26-. https://doi.org/10.3390/philosophies7020026.

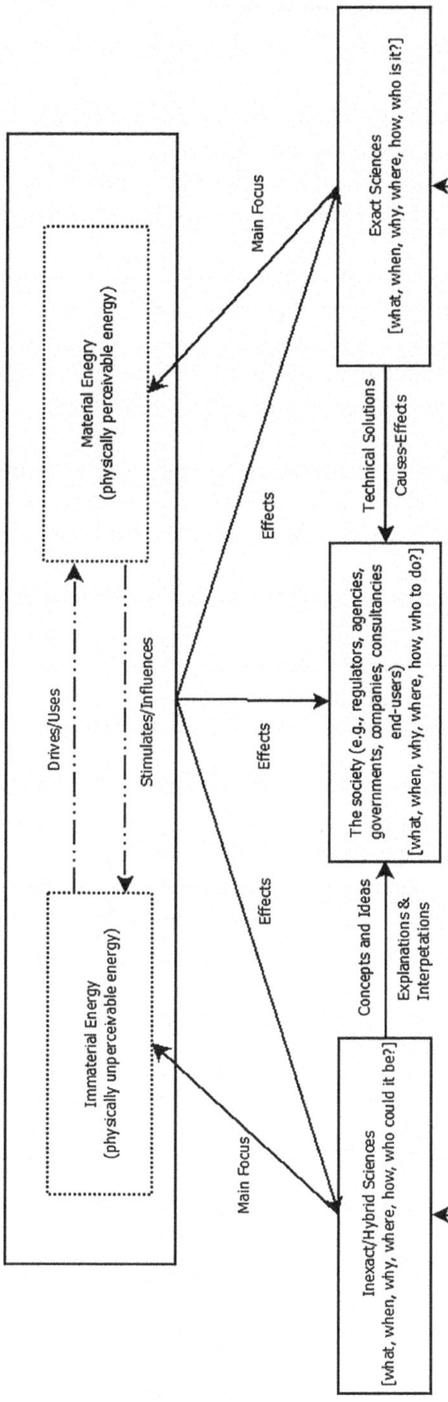

Fig. 9.2 Exact, inexact and hybrid sciences

Science Dialogues: Key Reflections and Actions

Reflections

- Professional dialogues about science are often shaped by the interplay of scholarly synergies, scientific methods, and disciplinary perspectives.
- The reliability of scientific narratives depends on the rigour of the methodologies used and the credibility of the sources. These must be critically evaluated in any professional setting.
- Collaboration between sciences—formal, exact, hybrid, and inexact—can reveal synergies that enhance understanding and problem-solving but require openness to diverse approaches.
- Misconceptions about the relative superiority of certain scientific disciplines can hinder productive dialogue. Recognising the complementary nature of these disciplines is essential.
- The roles of science extend beyond problem-solving to include fostering innovation, challenging norms, and enhancing ethical decision-making.

Actions

1. Evaluate Scientific Narratives: Critically assess the methodologies, assumptions, and sources behind scientific claims in your field. Seek evidence that supports the reliability and validity of these narratives.
2. Embrace Scholarly Synergies: Explore opportunities to collaborate across scientific disciplines. Identify areas where diverse methodologies and perspectives can address complex challenges.
3. Challenge Superiority Myths: Reflect on any biases you may hold about the value of certain sciences. Promote a culture that respects the contributions of all scientific types to professional practice.
4. Promote Interdisciplinary Learning: Encourage discussions and learning opportunities that bridge disciplines. Share insights from your field and actively seek knowledge from others.
5. Advance Ethical Science Dialogues: Use scientific dialogues to inform ethical decision-making. Incorporate diverse perspectives to address questions about equity, impact, and sustainability.

By fostering critical evaluation and interdisciplinary collaboration, you can enhance the effectiveness of scientific dialogues and contribute to more innovative and inclusive professional practices.

Part III
Energy Flow Concepts

Chapter 10
Collections

10.1 General

As I presented in Chapter 5, exposures exist when a unity transmits material energy, and another unity receives it. If the receiver responds to the transmitting unity, interaction occurs. If a unity transmits energy and no unity is exposed to the whole or part of the transmitted energy, there is no interaction. For instance, if worker A emailed colleague B through their computer (i.e., a collection of interacting unities under a single constructed name), and colleague B never noticed it, there was no interaction between these two individuals. However, there was some interaction between worker A and their computer because the worker had to spend some energy and use hardware and software to type and email the message.

Also, that a unity does not action back (i.e., exposed unity) does not mean the absolute absence of interactions. When energy is received, there is always some form of activity on the side of an exposed unity, even if this activity is not immediately visible, acknowledged or triggering a reaction towards the energy emitter. To continue the example above, if worker B notices the email message from worker A but decides to not respond, there is some interaction. Worker B was exposed to material energy which worker A transmitted and reflected some of the worker A's immaterial energy. Worker B reacted differently than Worker A anticipated, however, interaction occurred.

Another example, when someone gets exposed to radiation as part of their job activities, their body reacts invisibly to radiation energy regardless of any actions the individual could take regarding the radiation source. This person might be aware or not of how the internal unities of their body react to the reception of radiation. Radiation affects the body's sub-unities regardless of awareness.

Also, when I get criticised, something small or big reacts inside me despite deciding to remain silent. If I decide not to act upon it, it does not mean my immaterial and material energy and its elements remained untouched. The material energy

N. Karanikas, *Professional Generalism in a Hyper-specialised World*,
https://doi.org/10.1007/978-981-96-4039-3_10

received, which was used to transmit immaterial energy from the critiquing persons, has influenced me in some way.

10.2 Unity Systems

Most, if not all, scientific and industry fields use the construct of systems.[1,2,3,4,5,6] After reconciling various definitions from diverse sources and disciplines, I define a *typical system* as:

- the collection of two or more periodically interacting unities, including the means of their interactions, which,
- exchange (part of) their energies to achieve at least one *Explicitly Agreed and Defined Objective (EADO),*
- within a specific timeframe or continuously regardless of the distance of these unities in space and time.

For instance, two professionals collaborate to produce a management report in two weeks using technology. Agreed objectives can refer to the conceptualisation, creation, implementation, communication, modification and decommissioning of any construct. This can involve completing tasks, achieving results, conducting research, agreeing on ideas, developing concepts, or changing energy states of unities.

Agreed objectives can encompass aspects of:

- Quantity (e.g., how many products, services, outputs),
- Quality (e.g., the characteristics of the outputs), and,
- Time (e.g., deadlines, intermediate milestones).

Of note, cost is not listed as an aspect above as it corresponds to the energy required or available to achieve agreed objectives EADOs. As such, energy can be an enabling or limiting factor to deliver with specific quantity and quality within a specific timeframe, but it is not an aspect of the core objective. Also, the more an EADO covers the three aspects above, the higher its inclusiveness. For instance, this month's objective (i.e., time aspect) is to produce three tons of printing paper (i.e., quantity aspect) suitable for laser printers (i.e., quality aspect).

---

[1] Surya, S., McGranaghan, M. F., Dugan, R. C., & Beaty, H. W. (2012). *Electrical power systems quality* (3rd ed.). McGraw-Hill Education.

[2] Fairley, R. E. (2019). *Systems engineering of software-enabled systems.* John Wiley & Sons, Inc.

[3] Buijs, R. M., & Swaab, D. F. (2013). *Autonomic nervous system.* Elsevier.

[4] Costa, J. (2023). *Health as a social system: Luhmann's theory applied to health systems.* An Introduction, Transcript Verlag, Belefeld.

[5] Nugent, W. (2009). *Analyzing single system design data.* Oxford University Press, Inc.

[6] Friedman, L. M. (1975). *Legal system, the: A social science perspective.* Russell Sage Foundation. http://www.jstor.org/stable/10.7758/9781610442282.

Literature refers to additional characteristics of objectives, but all these connect with the definition of agreed objectives EADOs and the quantity, quality, and temporal aspects of each objective presented above. For example, with the well-known SMART criteria,[7,8] Specific (S) and Agreed (A) are contained in the EADO definition, Measurable (M) and Realistic (R) relate to quantity and quality under specific conditions and agreements, and Time (T) corresponds to the temporal factor.

Theoretically, the smallest typical system comprises three unities, two of them having established an agreed objective and interacting through media constructs. The third unity enables interactions between the remaining two. However, the number of distinct unities included in a system depends on the level of abstraction or detail. This depends on where the focus is.

For example, at the most basic level of abstraction, a car factory itself could be considered a single unity. This unity produces cars under agreed objectives EAODs, and its interactions with other external entities (e.g., suppliers, customers and the government) are its relationships. At a more detailed level, we could break down the factory into its various departments, like production, engineering and quality control. Here, each department then becomes a distinct unity with its own specific functions and interactions to deliver its own EADOs. At an even more granular level, you could focus on individual workers, machines or even components within the factory. Each employee, machine or component would then be considered a separate unity, interacting with other unities to achieve their individual EADOs.

The number of distinct unities within a system depends on how we choose to define and categorise them. The level of abstraction determines the granularity of our analysis. All unities belonging to a system exchange and transform their energies. Any unity with no assigned and direct role in achieving the objectives agreed can be part of a system's *proximal environment* if it:

- directly interacts with a system physically (i.e., *active interaction*), or
- unidirectionally transmits energy to the system (i.e., *active exposure*), or
- has the potential to directly interact with a system physically (i.e. *dormant interaction*), or
- could unidirectionally transmit energy to the system (i.e., *dormant exposure*).

All other external unities belong to a system's *distant environment*. For instance, there can be three colleagues work collaboratively to complete a fruit sorting task by using a sophisticated machine. A supervisor that provides some basic safety reminders to the three workers is an active interaction in the proximal environment, as this person does not directly contribute to the task's output. The lighting also belongs to the proximal environment and represents an active exposure as it transmits material energy to the workers. Coworkers who might interact with those workers

---

[7] Conzemius, A., & O'Neill, J. (2011). *The power of SMART goals: Using goals to improve student learning*. Solution Tree.

[8] Dobson, M., & Wilson, S. B. (2008). *Goal setting: How to create an action plan and achieve your goals*. AMACOM.

represent dormant interactions. The air conditioner represents an active (if switched on) or dormant (if switched off) exposure.

A system can welcome exposures and interactions from the environment that contribute to agreed objectives EADOs. Conversely, interactions and exposures from the proximal environment would not be welcome if perceived as disturbances and threats to the achievement of any EADO. In the example above, the workers could believe that some discussions with their supervisor can help them complete their EADOs, whereas on other discussion occasions, they could feel unnecessarily distracted by the supervisor.

Also, irrespective of its perceived utility, incoming energy from interactions and exposures with the proximal environment always takes part in the energy exchange and transformation within a system. The incoming energy becomes part of the system when it is received by at least one unity of the originally defined system, a case denoting the change of the system's energy state. As such, continuing the previous example, the light energy beamed from the bulbs becomes part of the system's energy.

An agreed objective EADO can regard a new or modified unity or changes in the energy states of unities belonging to the system. For example, during a university session, learning outcomes are EADOs aiming at generating changes in the energy states of students (e.g., students become aware and can recall information about the causal relationship between two unities). Those changes can remain undefined or invisible if not discussed or assessed at the end of the class. The lecturer could employ a formative or summative assessment to gauge the understanding of students, but this does not mean that all students would take part in this activity. Hence, the EADO-learning outcomes can be partially or completely visible or invisible.

The observable unity outputs and outcomes (e.g., deliverables, services, products and their effects) which a system generates as per its agreed objective EADOs might partially or wholly be part of the system or transferred to the environment. They can also interact with the material and immaterial energy of unities within or outside the system. In the teaching example above, the degree of achieving the learning outcomes could also affect the energy of the teacher (e.g., thoughts about the complexity of the content, emotions about the impact of their teaching) or be used beyond the class in the improvement of next course offerings and pedagogical approaches.

I illustrate the definitions above in Fig. 10.1. For the sake of brevity, the figure includes only limited examples of the concepts above. As such, it does not depict all interactions within a system and it, proximal and distant environments.

10.3 Other Unity Collections

Directly interacting unities can also form collections that do not fall under the typical system definition above. More specifically, *network* is a collection of unities where:

- there are irregular or random interactions occurring amongst unities, and
- these interactions do not associate with any agreed objective EADO.

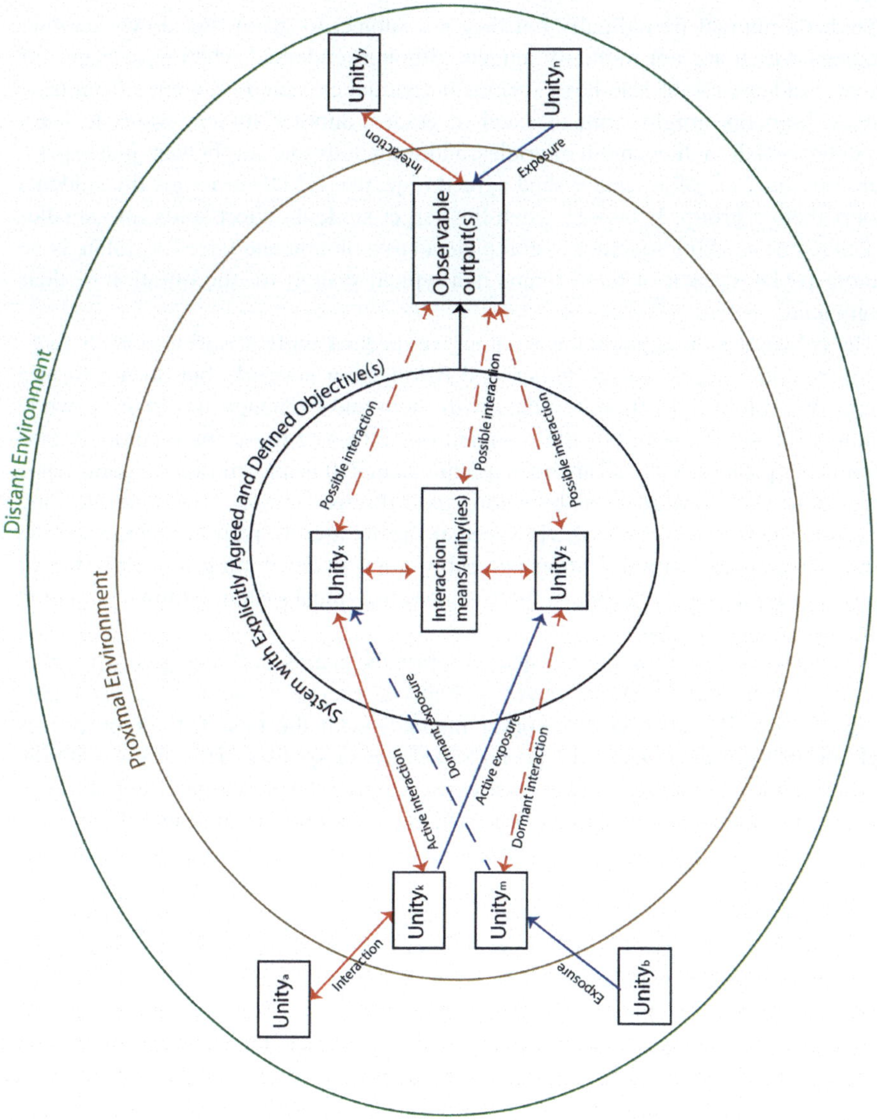

Fig. 10.1 System, proximal and distant unities and interactions

If only the first condition above is violated (i.e., there are periodic interactions but still not an EADO), then the unities form a *group*. If only the second condition is violated (i.e. there are irregular/random interactions with an EADO), the unities shape an *atypical system*. Below are some examples to illustrate further the definitions above.

Students interact periodically but they are subject to given, top-down learning outcomes which are not mutually agreed, although endorsed when registering for classes. Students might also have various individual expected outcomes from their courses. Someone might want to excel in grades, another student wants to learn deeper beyond the achievement of grades, and somebody else might want just to pass. Therefore, the lack of an established agreed objective EADO amongst the students renders them a group. However, when this larger student cohort splits into smaller student teams working together to complete an assignment and have formulated one or more EADOs, each of these teams is a typical system for the duration of their assignment.

The colleagues or acquaintances whom we meet casually at various events (e.g., meetings, conferences, social gatherings) belong to a network, but do not form a system. We might hold friendly chats with them and exchange information while attending the same event, but the intended objectives of those interactions can be different per professional and are not explicitly stated. It is uncommon for conference delegates to start conversations by stating their discussion objectives and checking if the other person is on board. However, if during a conversation or presentation at the conference, communication agreeably aims at developing a partnership or clarifying a topic correspondingly, there can be an atypical system within the specific interaction's timeframe.

When a worker randomly looks at a poster on the aisle's wall, they get exposed to energy (i.e. reflected light) that carries immaterial energy elements (e.g., an important message). Thus, while the worker interacts with the poster, their objectives might differ from the ones of the poster's designer or sponsor. This aligns with the network definition. Networks also exist when we irregularly/randomly interact with artefacts of technical nature, or when such artefacts interact amongst them (e.g., computer processors exchanging information but executing functions with different local objectives).

In most human–machine interactions, technology does not converse with humans to form agreed objectives EADOs. If such interactions are periodic, there is a group (e.g., when somebody watches the news on the TV every evening or when my tablet's chips continuously exchange data bits). The above, of course, exclude sophisticated technology like generative artificial intelligence where theoretically human and machines can collaboratively create EADOs and form typical or atypical systems. In Table 10.1 I present a summary of the definitions and parameters discussed above.

Table 10.1 Types of collections

Active Interactions	Explicitly Agreed and Defined Objective (EADO)	
	Yes	No
Periodic	Typical system	Group
Random	Atypical system	Network

10.4 Zooming In and Out

Larger collections might engulf various unities. Those can include various interaction means (e.g., communication and feedback channels) and supportive unities (e.g., equipment and tools, defences against internal and external disturbances). Depending on the focus, a collection can be approached as part of a larger collection where the former becomes a unity, usually referred as a subsystem (or subgroup or subnetwork). If we focus exclusively on the previously defined subsystem, then this becomes the collection of interest, and the previously larger system now becomes the proximal environment.

Therefore, what is a unity in one discussion or study could be a system in another case, depending on the focus. As such, in this book, most of the concepts I present apply equally to unities and collections when referring to any of those terms, unless otherwise stated. Likewise, when referring to sub-unities of unities, it includes the cases of unities of collections.

For example, a human can be a unity of a collection (e.g., business, community, sports team) when we are interested in the latter. However, in another instance, a human can be a collection when an analyst wants to study its health, state, behaviour, and so on. Likewise, in the case a particular human is of interest, anything outside belongs to the proximal or distant environments. Hence, the term environment, as defined above, can refer to anything outside we arbitrarily define as a collection, even if in another case the particular collection is seen as a unity. The key point is to clearly define the level of granularity/abstraction preferred.

A car moving on the road is another example. One could first arbitrarily define a collection comprising the car with all its components, the driver, and, possibly, other passengers. Assuming there is an agreed objective EADO amongst the driver and the passengers (e.g., arrive at work safely not later than a specific time), you could name this collection as a system, with the car facilitating the interactions towards achieving the EADO. Here, the physical environment (e.g., nature, weather elements), the technical infrastructure (e.g., road, signs, traffic lights), and other unities and systems (i.e. other cars moving or not) can take part in active or dormant interactions with the defined collection and constitute the proximal environment as they lie outside the boundaries of the defined collection.

The fuel in the car's tank is part of the system, while the oxygen needed for burning the fuel belongs to the proximal environment and is incoming energy. The fuel production and transport unities and collections (e.g., process power plants and fuel transport companies) belong to a distant environment as nobody from our defined system directly interacts with those entities currently. However, if the focus shifts to the fuel combustion chamber as the collection of interest, then the rest of the car unities, including the passengers, fuel tank, and all other technical collections and unities, become the proximal or distant environment.

Therefore, each unity can belong to more than one system, network, or group where it can play the role of the sender, receiver, or medium. Defining the boundaries of a collection and understanding the roles of its unities is key. Also, networks or groups operating within a system can include interactions whose outputs are used throughout the system and other collections. For instance, the chips in my computer's monitor might be a network or group, depending on the regularity of their interaction. Their interactions result in displaying information before my eyes. Likewise, the monitor and me constitute a group (e.g., when using it regularly to perform my work activities) or network (e.g., when using it randomly). In this example, the user-monitor group/network uses the outputs of the chips' group/network.

10.5 Explicitly Expected

When purchasing a product with given specifications, functions and capabilities to deliver the output desired, you would argue there is an agreed objective EADO, and, by extension, a system. For example, you bought a monitor to view digital information, and the monitor was made for this purpose. You can rightfully claim an EADO because the monitor has a clear purpose that is understood by everyone involved (e.g., designer, manufacturer, reseller). However, as explained above, EADO regards the unities interacting directly, whereas in this example, the other unities belong to the distant environment.

In such cases, instead of an agreed objective EADO, which characterises only systems, there is an *Explicitly Expected and Trusted Objective (EETO)* between any unity and its distant environment unities or amongst unities within networks and groups. EETOs are typically bidirectional like EADOs and reflect something that is normatively expected by the unities involved, although those unities have not explicitly formulated any objective. EETOs are typically formed by normative references like statutory legislation and regulations, organisational policies and rules, community practices and customs, organisational norms, etc. Systems do not have EETOs, as their definition above requires EEDOs. As such, EETOs apply to groups, networks and distant environments.

Continuing the example above, many assume buyers will use the product correctly. The buyer assumes the product will meet its specifications and be free of any flaws for a reasonable period. This is because there are national and international frameworks that facilitate building such expected objectives EETOs between consumers and vendors. EETOs can also be formed through social interactions, media, and other channels, even without set frameworks (e.g., what a guest will enjoy when visiting a museum).

Expected objectives EETOs originating from distant environments or formed amongst network groups, conveyed through active interactions, correspond to *moderated interactions* involving *moderated unity collections* (i.e., moderated system, group or network). This applies when agreed objectives EADOs at the collection level cannot be directly operationalised by its sub-collections, and they become EETOs for the latter. In this case, those typical sub-systems within a larger collection can establish EADOs with specific outputs and outcomes. This way, generic EETOs originating from collection-level EADOs can be translated into more locally focussed, scoped, and concrete EADOs.

For instance, a company with various organisational levels and departments is usually a moderated collection where expected objectives EETOs can be created and transmitted multi-directionally amongst several sections and staff. Although normatively expected, it could be an illusion to contemplate that any agreed objective EADO formulated at the organisational level can apply in its original form directly to lower organisational levels. This is because the exchange and inevitable transformation of energy through any moderated/distant interaction will inflict changes to any transmitted EADOs regarding organisational-level objectives.

Senior management can consult with staff and define policies (i.e., a form of an expected objective EETO) that are operationalised through tailored and contextual agreed objectives EADOs across levels and departments, aiming for an alignment between EADOs and EETOs. There can be an EETO between senior management at the top organisational level and supervisors at the worksite level about worker productivity. Another EETO can regard the work conditions staff expect to enjoy because of managers investing in staff's welfare, health, and safety beyond legislative compliance.

However, as energy flows and transforms amongst various sub-collections and unities, there will be always gaps between transmitted and perceived versions of the same expected objectives EETOs and between EETOs and agreed objectives EADOs focussing on the same objective (Chapter 16). In Fig. 10.2, I illustrate the above, noting that EETOs and EADOs can refer to multiple proximal and distant environments within the same moderated collection, but EADOs only apply to unities within systems or between directly interacting sub-systems.

10.6 Implicitly Assumed

Besides any explicit objectives, either agreed and defined EADOs or expected and trusted EETOs, unities within collections might also have various *Implicitly Assumed and Trusted Objectives (IATOs)*. Those regard objectives that remain internalised, such as ambitions and expectations, which unities assume and trust they will be achieved within collections additionally to EADOs/EETOs. It is atopic to believe that the formulation of EADOs, which is an integral characteristic of a system, covers all expectations of the unities belonging to the system and collections and unities of the proximal and distant environment.

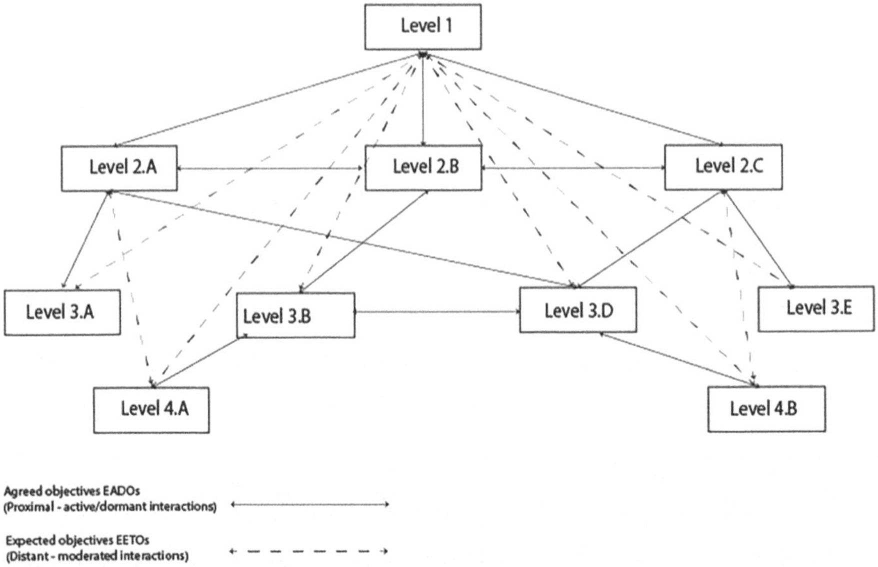

Fig. 10.2 Examples of Explicitly Agreed and Defined Objectives (EADOs) and Explicitly Expected and Trusted Objectives (EETOs) in a moderated collection

When an assumed objective IATO is externalised and not temporarily or entirely rejected by a collection, it becomes an expected objective EETO. Especially for proximal unities and systems, the EETO emerging from the communication of an as IATO should be ideally transformed into one or more agreed objectives EADOs. If no transformation of an emerging EETO into an EADO occurs, or if the externalised IATO is rejected or shelved, the respective collections are characterised by *Unsettled Side Objectives (USOs)*. Those supplement any EETOs/EADOs and remain valid as long as at least one unity of the collection supports or needs them.

The different objective types are interconnected in several ways. Different objective types influence each other due to energy exchange at varying abstraction levels (Fig. 10.3). For instance, EADOs at one level (e.g., company directorate) might spur IATO development at the same and lower levels (e.g., company departments) or higher organisational levels (e.g., company board of managers). All combinations of interactions are possible.

The example below shows how different objectives are created multi-directionally. There was a senior professional in the Human Resources field. This person worked in recruitment, advertising jobs and finding candidates. He reviewed applications, ranked them, and advised organisations on the best candidates. In the contracts between the organisations and the recruiter, there were several agreed objectives EADOs (e.g., broad advertisement, correct implementation of the criteria, recommendations for suitable applicants).

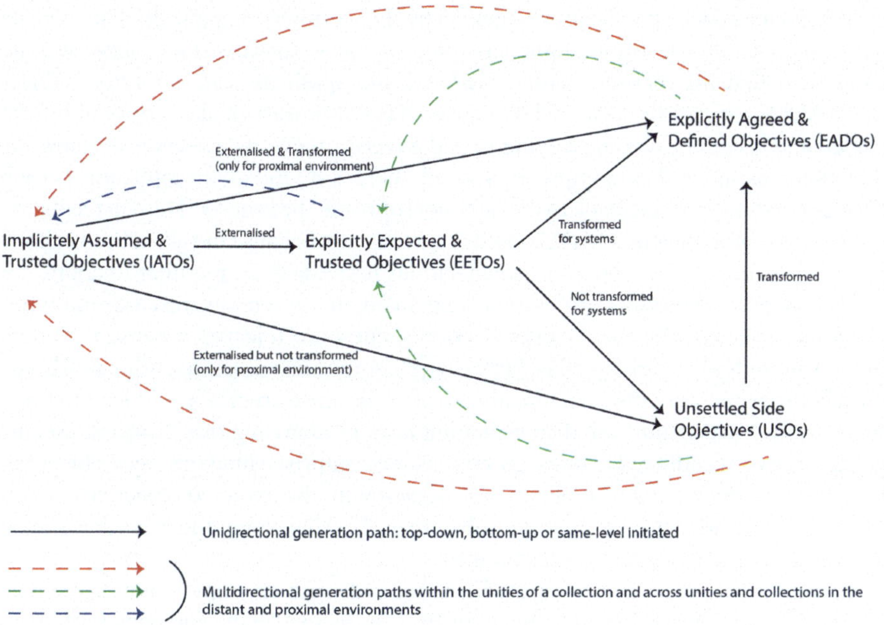

Fig. 10.3 Explicitly Agreed and Defined Objectives (EADOs), Explicitly Expected and Trusted Objectives (EETOs), Implicitly Assumed and Trusted Objectives (IATOs) and Unsettled Side Objectives (USOs)

There were also different expected objectives EETOs (e.g., skills and experience of the recruiter's staff, compliance with applicable legislation) and assumed objectives IATOs (e.g., renewal/extension of the contract between recruiter and organisations if the latter would remain satisfied). As discussed above, those agreed EADOs, expected EETOs and assumed IATOs were born by and giving birth to each other in a continuum. For instance, to secure an extension of the contract (i.e., IATO), the recruiter should have staff with relevant qualifications and skills (i.e., EETO) who would offer to the organisations the best possible solution with competitive rates (i.e., EADO).

The more satisfied the customers were and the more the contracts earned with different organisations (i.e., internally agreed objectives EADOs), the more someone would expect the recruiter employing highly experienced workforce (i.e., expected objective EETO), which generates the assumption of even more satisfaction and future contracts (i.e., assumed objectives IATOs). Correspondingly, when considering the interactions between the recruiter and job applicants, there was no typical system to formulate EADOs, but there could be EETOs. For instance, it was expected that job applicants address all advertised criteria with veracity. There could also be IATOs. For example, applicants might assume success if qualified or receive feedback if unsuccessful.

When I asked the specific professional why the recruiter company does not consistently send feedback to job applicants, he gave three answers. First, there was no agreement that the recruiter would feedback the applicant (i.e., no agreed objective EADO), despite the assumed objective IATO of professional courtesy to inform someone who put efforts in replying to and advertisement and deserves to know the rejection reasons so that to improve. Second, there were too many applicants per job to offer personalised feedback to the ones not fulfilling the criteria. Third, a feedback-related expected objective EETO could not even exist because the advertised criteria were just a subset of the ones the organisations had asked the recruiter to apply.

Indeed, as the particular professional explained, there were several cases the applicants met successfully the advertised criteria but were rejected because the client organisations had hidden agendas. For example, some businesses discriminated based on school, gender, or ethnicity. Openly advertising those criteria would lead to sanctions, as they are against antidiscrimination laws in many regions. Nonetheless, the recruiter covertly adhered to those criteria, which comprised hidden agreed objectives EADOs with the clients, completely misaligned with the assumed objectives IATOs of applicants and with the expected objectives EETOs stemming from legislation and representing community expectations.

Employment is another example. Someone will sign an employment agreement or contract, including expected objectives EETOs decided at the company level (e.g., broadly defined annual performance expectations). Shortly after the person begins work, they would agree with their direct manager/supervisor on specific agreed objectives EADOs for a defined period (e.g., specific deliverables within 12 months). Those EADOs must expectedly align with the company-level EETOs, or at least, not being controversial. The achievement of these EADOs is what the new staff member discusses with their manager in any annual performance review meetings.

Also, the manager and the recruit can state additional agreed objectives EADOs not derived from company-level expected objectives EETOs (e.g., contribution to the local activities of the department). Moreover, they might have assumed objectives IATOs not verbally expressed (e.g., the new worker expects a timely alert from the supervisor if the latter notices that something does not look right with this person's work).

Any assumed objectives IATOs cannot be part of review meetings, although they are existent within the minds of each of the interlocutors, unless they are externalised as expected objectives EETOs or unsettled objectives USOs. However, IATOs, EETOs and USOs stored in the immaterial energy of both parties (or noted somewhere through material energy) will still play a role in worker-manager interactions. Over time, those types of objectives might be transformed to agreed objectives EADOs following respective initiatives of the manager or the employee.

Another more generic example can be when someone gets the bus to commute to work. The passenger trusts the driver will operate the bus safely (i.e., expected objective EETO), and they will reach the desired destination within a reasonable time (i.e., assumed objective IATO). The driver expects the passenger will observe the safety rules posted on several positions in the bus, will give seating priority to persons with special needs and conditions and will not consume food and drinks (i.e., EETOs). These objectives usually source from the agreed objectives EADOs set by the authority responsible for public transport and regard drivers and passengers. These and other EADOs must have been translated by the transport organisation into EETOs and transformed into EADOs between the driver and their direct manager.

The various posters and messages around the bus are also expected objectives EETOs the company communicates to the passengers. However, although these can be also verbalised through announcements and assuming the passengers understand them, they can remain unsettled objectives USOs. Under regular conditions, there are dormant interactions between the driver and the passenger and active exposures of the passenger to the posters/messages/announcements on the bus.

In the case a passenger does not observe a rule, the driver might raise concerns and, if the situation is escalated, they might get into a conflict. For instance, a passenger might not respect the corresponding expected objective EETO and start consuming food on the bus. Any driver action will create an active interaction, where several assumed objectives IATOs of the driver and the passenger might manifest (e.g., setting the tone of the conversation, expectations to exchange personal details).

Of note, the non-delivery or partial achievement of an agreed objective EADO does not mean there is no system. Notably too, system-focussed and business literature differentiates between networks/groups and systems by adding to the latter traits, such as common goals and shared understanding. However, such collection traits, while useful in sparking and mobilising discussions and the exchange of opinions and ideas, cannot be used to define a system clearly. This is because definitions of unity collections based on invisible properties can take various meanings and be perceived in dramatically different ways. Such intangible collection features mostly correspond to assumed objectives IATOs, expected objectives EETOs and unsettled objectives USOs and remain abstract and often inferential constructs.

Agreed objectives can be the test to examine whether a collection is a system, network, or group. For instance, two moving cars in a state of active interaction (e.g., the drivers can see each other) constitute a network. The drivers might have common overall goals (e.g., they want to arrive uninjured to any destination each time they drive) but their desired outputs at each time-point can differ (e.g., they want to arrive at different locations). Therefore, they are not a system.

Each of the drivers holds expected objectives EETOs for the other drivers around, stemming from the agreed objectives EADOs and EETOs stated in road traffic rules and regulations. They most probably expect that other drivers will maintain safe distance and indicate when changing direction. Also, drivers might have several assumed objectives IATOs, such as the courtesy of giving priority to a car changing lanes. All those objectives do not render all cars and their drivers at a specific time-point and location a system.

Collections: Key Reflections and Actions

Reflections

- Collections, whether systems, networks, or groups, are foundational to understanding professional and organisational dynamics. Each type has unique structures, interactions, and objectives.
- Systems are defined by explicitly agreed goals and interconnected components working towards those goals, emphasising coordination and integration.
- Networks rely on irregular relationships and interactions amongst entities, often with implicitly assumed objectives and more flexible structures.
- Groups, while sharing some characteristics with systems and networks, are typically defined by explicitly expected objectives, often shaped by cultural or contextual norms.
- The ability to 'zoom in and out' of collections—examining both their micro and macro aspects—enables a deeper understanding of their dynamics and interdependencies.

Actions

1. Identify Collection Types: Reflect on the collections you engage with in your professional life. Determine whether they function as systems, networks, or groups and assess their defining characteristics.
2. Clarify Objectives: For each collection, distinguish between explicitly agreed, explicitly expected, and implicitly assumed objectives. This clarity helps align actions and expectations.
3. Examine Interdependencies: Analyse how elements within a collection interact and depend on one another. Recognise how these interdependencies influence overall performance and outcomes.
4. Adapt to Contexts: Tailor your approach based on the type of collection you are dealing with. Systems may require structured planning, while networks and groups may benefit from more flexible, relationship-driven strategies.
5. Encourage Multi-Level Analysis: Practice shifting perspectives to understand collections at different levels of detail. This 'zooming in and out' enables you to address both immediate issues and broader systemic challenges.

By understanding and adapting to the unique characteristics of systems, networks, and groups, you can foster greater cohesion, efficiency, and adaptability in your professional and organisational contexts.

Chapter 11
Activities

11.1 General

When exposed and interacting, all unities involved are subject to influences and changes because of the exchange of energy. Depending on the level of abstraction/detail preferred, the activity of any unity or collection, regardless of the activities of its sub-unities or collection unities respectively, can be classified as:

- *Reaction (RE)* to incoming energy, or
- *Self-Change (SC)* triggered mainly by incoming energy, or
- *Transformation of Others (TO)* through mainly energy transmission.

Reaction RE happens always to any unity when energy is received and occurs inevitably, deliberately, or not. Self-change SC regards living unities and includes the cases of inevitable *Adaptation (AD)* to incoming energy and wilful *Self-Transformation (ST)*; I especially discuss adaptation in Sect. 11.3 and Chapter 17). Last, transformation of others TO also regards living unities and is always deliberate; the TO activity is not to be confused with the inescapable effects of RE on other unities, as explained below. It is important to note that:

- The types listed above regard activities and not actions, as activities typically include several actions. The term activity in this book also covers the case of a single incidental action.
- Reaction RE, self-change SC and others' transformation TO can occur simultaneously as a unity can receive, process, and emit or transmit energy from and to different unities concurrently.
- As we cannot always directly observe rigid and clear boundaries between these activities, their distinction is conceptual and concerns how unities respond to incoming energy and direct available energy.

N. Karanikas, *Professional Generalism in a Hyper-specialised World*,
https://doi.org/10.1007/978-981-96-4039-3_11

Importantly, whereas reaction RE can happen with no other activity:

- Self-Change presumes Reaction [i.e., *Reaction PLUS Self-Change (RESC)*], and
- Transformation of Others presumes Reaction and Self-Transformation [i.e., *Reaction PLUS Self-Change PLUS Transformation of Others (RESCTO)*].

More specifically, reaction RE happens when any unity from the environment transmits material energy, and the unity of interest is exposed to it and reacts to this exposure:

- internally: the energy received is directed towards the exposed unity's internal sub-unities and generates internal effects, and possibly,
- externally: the exposed unity transmits energy of the same or different type and magnitude to other unities in its environment, leading to external effects.

In humans and other living unities, reaction RE is driven by developed associations in cognitive energy and/or referents in their affective energy when material energy is received from a source. The more familiar a unity is with the context of its exposure to energy, the more predictable the reactions to incoming energy can be. Also, energy exchange through RE, apart from changes in material energy, might or not lead to new or changed associations and referents within the exposed unity. Such internal changes and modifications, which alter the overall energy state of an exposed unity, may or not be acutely realised by the unity or even welcome, but they can still occur.

For example, a person can experience a traumatic event like a severe car accident, which involves significant exposure to energy. Such an event typically triggers intense fear and the release of stress hormones. In response to those changes in affective energy, the brain may form new neural pathways associated with fear and hypervigilance. Also, the individual may develop post-traumatic stress disorder, characterised by intrusive memories, flashbacks and avoidance behaviours.

All immaterial energy effects above could also be accompanied by physical changes, such as increased heart rate, difficulty sleeping, hyperarousal, and potential for chronic pain. Many of these changes occur unconsciously. The changes may be subtle and gradual, making them difficult to pinpoint as direct consequences of the trauma. Also, the person may not fully understand the underlying mechanisms driving their symptoms. The effects of trauma can be long-lasting and significantly impact the person's life, even if they are not consciously aware of the underlying causes. Moreover, the individual may actively resist acknowledging or addressing the trauma.

The case of Reaction PLUS Self-Change (RESC), besides the material energy exchanged, denotes energy investment to enable internal reconfigurations and rearrangements. When a unity changes itself, it is because it has reacted first to incoming energy, and then proceeds with further energy exchanges amongst its sub-unities and with other external unities in the environment. Hence, RESC denotes the usage of energy by a unity to modify its material energy state and generate new cognitive associations and affective referents or change existing ones.

Especially Self-Transformation (ST), which is the expression of deliberate self-change, assumes self-knowledge.[1,2] This means awareness of a unity about its current/previous physical, cognitive, and affective energy states, so that to self-transform by channelling energy where most needed. For instance, a researcher receiving peer review comments on a scientific article could not just react to this news (e.g., feel disappointed, inform other co-authors) but decide to self-change. This could be achieved through understanding of the weak and strong points of the manuscript, search for opportunities to improve this and future articles, and so on. Those ST actions assume some level of self-awareness.

Reaction PLUS Self-Change PLUS Transformation of Others (RESCTO), besides material energy exchange with others and energy investment in self-change, involves energy investment in willingly affecting or changing other unities. RESCTO, additionally to self-knowledge necessary for self-transformation, assumes awareness of material and immaterial energy states within the target unities. Several disciplines acknowledge this as extremely necessary to increase the chances of successful transformation.[3,4,5,6,7]

Transformation could create new associations and referents or alter existing ones in other living organisms. However, it will definitely influence their material energy, as with any exposure and interaction. Because of those effects on material and immaterial energy, when especially humans become the target of transformation, ideally, they must be acceptive to changes which much occur as per the ethical principles of the respective context (Chapter 1). However, there can be cases where legal frameworks and social norms do not require seeking consent when aiming at transforming other. This happens, for example, during mandatory education in several countries (i.e., we do not ask children whether they consent to attend school) or when intervening medically to treat a patient in comma, under sedation, etc.

In several human collections (communities, groups, teams, organisations, etc.) achieving self-change SC before transforming others TO can be a normative expectation, forming the special case of RESTTO. Such norms suggest that before trying

---

[1] Gonzalez, M. (2012). *Mindful Leadership the 9 ways to self-awareness, transforming yourself, and inspiring others*. Jossey-Bass.

[2] Bunting, M. (2022). *Vertical growth: How self-awareness transforms leaders and organisations*. John Wiley & Sons, Incorporated.

[3] Bosher, S. D., & Pharris, M. D. (2009). *Transforming nursing education: the culturally inclusive environment*. Springer.

[4] Aluchna, M., & Aras, G. (2015). *Transforming governance: New values, new systems in the new business environment*. Taylor & Francis Group.

[5] Uitto, J. I., & Batra, G. (2022). *Transformational change for people and the planet: Evaluating environment and development*. Springer Nature.

[6] Vanka, S., Rao, M. B., Singh, S., & Pulaparthi, M. R. (Eds.). (2020). *Sustainable human resource management transforming organizations, societies and environment*. Springer Singapore. https://doi.org/10.1007/978-981-15-5656-2.

[7] Ahmed, R., Al-Maruf, A., & Jenkins, J. C. (2023). *Transforming Bangladesh geography, people, economy and environment* (1st ed. 2023.). Springer International Publishing. https://doi.org/10.1007/978-3-031-45093-8.

to change others in a certain area (e.g., influence through persuasion, change through education, enforcing through rewards and penalties), we should first change ourselves in that area, especially through self-transformation ST, not just adaptation AD. Indeed, if we preach others to treat humans with dignity, we must first become an example. We could rightfully advocate waste management changes for the benefit of the planet, provided we have adopted already some recycling and energy efficiency habits.

Each transformation activity cannot be generalised beyond the context it targets, and it can become invalid in many other instances. For example, a surgeon can perform surgery on a patient without operating on themselves first. As such, there are cases when the self-transformation ST is not required of someone before or during transforming others TO. However, the person aiming for TO might have invested energy to acquire information about how to implement the change. Hence, this activity type can be merely reaction-adaptation-transformation of others driven (READTO), without this being negative by default, depending on the context and reasons.

READTO could occur when an individual perceives their energy state as satisfactory or believes they need nothing beyond inevitable adaptations before transforming others TO. Also, maybe somebody cannot secure additional energy to facilitate deliberate internal changes. Furthermore, there could be time constraints concurrently with rapid environmental changes that do not afford time and energy investment in self-transformation. Besides, TO could begin while self-change SC has also started but not completed.

11.2 Energy Investment and Changes

In Fig. 11.1 I show how each activity is nested, with the transformation of others TO requiring the most energy, followed by self-change SC, and then reaction RE. When looking over time and across various contexts and cases, someone might have spent more energy in one activity category than others. For example, some individuals might just react to energy exposures more often than changing themselves or attempting to transform others. Besides, in relative terms and assuming comparable contexts and energy resources, in mid- and long-term:

- RE lasts shorter than reaction and self-change RESC,
- RESC lasts shorter than reaction, adaptation, and transformation of others READTO, and
- READTO lasts shorter than reaction, self-change, and transformation of others RESCTO.

All three activity levels lead to some form of change to a unity, collection, and possibly the environment because they involve the exchange of energy regardless of whether a unity realises instantly that a change occurs. The unity of interest might

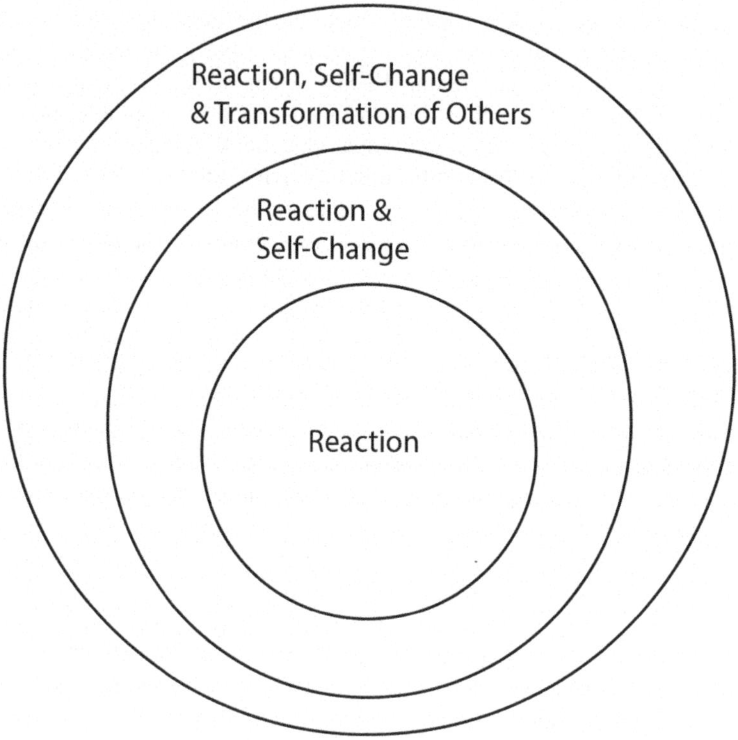

Fig. 11.1 Energy investment in reaction, self-change and transformation of others

be conscious or not about the ongoing changes in its energy state during reaction RE. However, a unity is always conscious, at least for part of these changes, during self-transformation RESC and transformation of others (RESCTO or READTO), which are deliberate and typically preceded by reaction RE to energy.

Of note, all the above apply to the unity of interest. This means that if an external unity tries to transform the unity of interest and the latter does not realise this, it just reacts and, possibly, adapts to the energy received. If the unity of interest realises and accepts the transformation, it can react or also initiate self-change, assuming it is aware of the consequent changes in their physical, cognitive and affective energy states.

For example, when a virus enters the body-unity of an individual, dedicated body parts (i.e., sub-unities) defend and try to kill the virus. The individual may never notice this exchange of energy unless this battle is uneven and they develop symptoms like fever and a runny nose. The virus and body sub-unities reacted, self-changed, and enforced changes to each other with no conscious decision from the individual. However, somehow, the unities of this scenario ‘knew’ and carried out various processes and interacted.

The energy exchanges above were something the individual did not directly control. Still, the individual could proactively support body sub-unities to run their reaction RE, reaction and self-change RESC or reaction, self-change and transforming others RESCTO activities. For instance, based on available medical and health promotion information, the individual can follow a balanced diet, exercise regularly, and avoid exposing body sub-unities to toxic unities (e.g., dangerous chemicals and highly processed food). The overall aim of the actions above is to maintain the individual's capability to perform their activities, condition their body sub-unities through safe micro-exposures (e.g., vaccinations) and so on.

Yet, the specific person does not instruct their sub-unities. They do not know exactly how all those actions will result in tangible benefits. The individual just supports their sub-unities in their functions because it seems the sub-unities somehow know. Of course, it can happen that these preventative strategies do not work always and for the particular individual to the extent expected. Here, body sub-unities might not be able to deal with the external unity/virus, and the person could notice further pain, fever, and other symptoms. Next, the individual could see a doctor, take medicine, rest more, and do other things to conserve and boost their energy. This corresponds to additional self-transformation by using internal and external energy.

In Table 11.1 I present examples of the activity types for three different unities. Reaction always precedes and accompanies Self-Change (i.e., Adaptation and/ or Self-Transformation) and Transformation of Others. Although for the sake of simplicity, in the particular Table I mention examples from unities, the concepts apply to collections as well, depending on the level of abstraction.

11.3 Typology of Laws

To deepen our understanding of how energy dynamics influence activities, it is essential to consider the principles or 'laws' that govern these interactions. These laws provide a structured lens through which we can examine the predictable and variable aspects of energy investment, exchange and transformation. Categorising these laws helps us interpret behaviours of unities and create a foundation for analysing the interplay between reactions, self-changes, and transformations. The typology of laws introduced in this section serves as a crucial bridge between abstract energy concepts and their application to the diverse activities that underpin professional and organisational practices.

Reaction-type activities RE can be subject to *Natural or Innate Laws*, as for example, the exchange of electrons between atoms and the self-healing of physical bodies when injured. Such laws represent universally accepted truths for similar unities in similar states irrespective of temporal factors. Although the activities, outputs, and outcomes related to those laws can be observed, their origins remain largely unknown. For example, if a living unity does not replenish the calories spent, it will gradually become slimmer and weaker; this is a natural law that we do not really know how it was formed.

Table 11.1 Examples of activity categories

Activity category	Example A—Human	Example B—Plant	Example C—Animal
Reaction (RE)	A1. Someone receives comments on their technical report (energy received), they feel frustrated (inwards effect of energy) but they finally decide (internal use of energy) to repair the report (outwards direction of energy) and reply to the reviewers (outwards direction of energy)	B1. A flower is exposed to sunbeams (energy received). The energy from the sun is directed inwards to the flower for its growth (inwards effect of energy), and, at the same time, triggers the expenditure of energy from the flower to move its leaves towards the sun (outwards energy direction)	C1. A bee sensed a predator bird (reception of light and/or sound energy), causing the bee to revise its original plan (inwards energy effect) and change its route (outwards energy direction) to avoid the bird predator
Reaction PLUS Self-Change (RESC)	A2. *In addition to the activity A.1 (reaction) above*, the person spends time to reflect on their performance and how they could improve their weak points for future work	B2. *In addition to the activity B.1 (reaction) above*, the flower changes its length to reach the sunbeams easier	C2. *In addition to the activity C.1 (reaction) above*, the bee avoids in the future any flying routes adjacent to locations where predatory birds build their nests
Reaction PLUS Adaptation PLUS Transformation of Others (READTO)	A3. *In addition to activity A.1 (reaction) above*, the person chooses not to self-transform, although some adaptive changes might unconsciously take place internally (internal use of energy). However, the person shares the comments of the reviewers with colleagues to render the latter aware so that they can possibly avoid the same mistakes. The person assumes their colleagues are interested in the information shared (outwards energy transmission) and their self-improvement	B3. *In addition to the activity B.1 (reaction) above*, the flower chooses not to self-transform, although some adaptive changes might unconsciously take place internally (internal use of energy). However, it produces toxic substances to discourage other plants from getting closer to it and block the sunbeams. The flower might somehow 'know' that other living organisms would die if they got in contact with the toxic environment it has created (outwards energy transmission)	C3. *In addition to the activity C.1 (reaction) above*, the bee chooses not to self-transform, although some adaptive changes might unconsciously take place internally (internal use of energy). However, it informs other bees about the areas that bird flocks have been detected. The bee might somehow 'know' that other bees would consider this information (outwards energy transmission) to prolong their biological living time

(continued)

Table 11.1 (continued)

Activity category	Example A—Human	Example B—Plant	Example C—Animal
Reaction PLUS Self-Change PLUS Transformation of Others (RESCTO)	A4. *In addition to A.1 (reaction) & A.2 (self-change) above*, the person shares the comments of the reviewers and their improvements with colleagues to render them aware so that they can possibly avoid the same mistakes. The person assumes their colleagues are interested in the information shared (outwards energy transmission) and their self-improvement	B4. *In addition to B.1 (reaction) & B.2 (self-change) above*, the flower produces toxic substances to discourage other plants from getting closer to it and block the sunbeams. The flower might somehow 'know' that other living organisms would die if they got in contact with the toxic environment it has created (outwards energy transmission)	C4. *In addition to C.1 (reaction) & C.2 (self-change) above*, the bee informs other bees about the areas that bird flocks have been detected. The bee might somehow 'know' that other bees would consider this information (outwards energy transmission) to prolong their living time

Also, reaction can be based on the knowledge each unity acquires from the cause-effects associations (i.e., cognitive energy elements from past and ongoing interactions and exposures), in combination with a unity's perceived position relative to other unities (i.e., affective energy elements). When cause-effects associations become integral parts of a unity over time and affective referents are established, unities develop automatic stimuli-reaction pairs (if …, then …), which represent its *Fundamental Laws.*

An example of a fundamental law is when I apply brakes after realising a very short distance between my vehicle and the preceding one. This is a fundamental law and not a natural one; it does not apply to all drivers and me across all contexts and time-points. Although it is expected that when drivers see their vehicle getting too close to other movable or immovable objects, they must immediately apply brakes, other parameters (e.g., distractions, fatigue) might lead to a delayed application or misapplication of the law (e.g., using another pedal). Fundamental laws can be altered over time and exhibit varying degrees of difference across similar unities, even under similar conditions.

Literature refers to fundamental laws as 'System 1'[8] and automated/skilled behaviours.[9] It views these laws as naturalistic decision-making and acute responses to familiar stored in long-term memory (i.e., the area and process of ultra-fast retrieval of stored associations). Other cases are subject to stimuli-decision-action processing before reacting. Literature refers to these as 'System 2'[8] rule-based or knowledge-based behaviours[9] that combine working-memory processes (i.e., slower processing of data/information) and retrieval of information from long-term memory. System 2

[8] Kahneman, D. (2011). *Thinking, fast and slow*. New York: Farrar, Straus and Giroux.

[9] Reason, J. (1990). *Human error*. Cambridge University Press.

cases denote a mixture of naturalistic (i.e., rapid recognition of patterns) and rational decision-making (e.g., searching for environmental cues, and weighing options to anticipate outputs and outcomes).

Rule-based behaviours represent the application of *Basic Laws* and involve more cognition energy and time than fundamental laws when confronting relatively (un)familiar situations. In the cases of basic laws, the 'if-then' pairs of fundamental laws are extended to combinations of 'if-then-else-or-…' combinations. Basic laws are the ones known but not applied with a frequency that would convert them to fundamental laws. For example, calculating derivatives takes time without regular practice, even if you understand the concept.

Knowledge-based behaviours necessitate even more energy investment before reacting. They correspond to situations where unities combine several basic and fundamental laws to make sense of the situation and cope with what they sense. Such conditions lead to the development of *Emerging Laws*, which over time can become basic or fundamental laws.

For instance, to diagnose a rare disease, the doctor cannot rely on simple pattern recognition or established procedures. They must analyse a complex set of symptoms, considering various potential diagnoses, and synthesise information from multiple sources, including medical literature, patient history, and the latest research findings. This requires a deep understanding of fundamental medical principles and the ability to apply them creatively to a unique situation.

Admittedly, science cannot define measurable and clear boundaries of the cognitive and behaviour types mentioned above to differentiate indisputably between System 1 and 2 or between automated, rule-based, and knowledge-based reactions. The reason is that all those refer to invisible processes and entities in the immaterial energy space. To differentiate unities of the same characteristics and in the same state regarding their reaction type, we can only to compare their response times to similar stimuli. The shorter this time, the more the application of fundamental laws, and the longer the relative time, the more the development of emergent laws, we could presume.

Neuroscience has significantly advanced our understanding of these mechanisms through research. However, Chapter 5 explains that this field focusses on analysing physical interactions and stimulus-response within the body. Analysts are unable to observe and analyse the exact nature of emotions, memories, mental models, decisions and other cognitive and affective energy aspects themselves. To-date, all these remain immaterial energy constructs.

11.4 Consciousness

As stated in Sect. 11.1, self-change involves self-knowledge of a self-unity/collection *capabilities*, meaning its material and immaterial energies stored (i.e., capacity) and ability to mobilise them. Self-change can also be classified as deliberate/conscious (i.e., Self-transformation) or inevitable/unconscious (i.e., Adaptation) depending on our definition of unity/collection and focus area. Unconscious adaptation falls under what Carls Darwin named as natural selection and evolution.[10]

However, unconscious adaptation applies when we view the living being of interest as a single and distinct unity. Here, adaptation corresponds to the concept of Natural/ Innate Laws I discussed in Sect. 11.3. When examining a living being as a collection and diving deeper into its constituent unities, we would discover that these unities somehow hold 'knowledge' of themselves to react and self-change. This occurs regardless of whether the bigger unity/collection realises it.

For example, famous social experiments and case studies such as the ones related to conformity[11] and groupthink[12] have approached participants as interacting unities and concluded that adaptations were occurring unconsciously. Indeed, these findings stand true when examining humans as unities. Had we examined deeper the participants' sub-unities, we could have discovered that these internal sub-unities were 'knowing' what they were doing, and that they were behaving 'consciously'.

Therefore, whether we call something (un)conscious depends on the abstraction/ analysis level and our knowledge of the unity/collection of interest. Also, if we accept that subconsciousness merely controls us as humans, there is no reason to talk about influencing and improving human performance and behaviour, as everything would be predetermined. However, this exact awareness of the possibly subconscious, along with the opportunity to influence it, constitutes one of our unique traits as humans compared to other living beings, at least according to today's knowledge.

Also, as noted in Sect. 11.1, transformation of others goes beyond reaction and self-change by involving energy investment in external units. Because energy is directed intentionally, transformation ideally requires knowledge of 'others' regarding their material and immaterial energy states. Ethically, changes must not negatively impact the unities involved. Although this suggests that transformations always happen consciously, perhaps there might be unintentional transformation cases (e.g., side effects of energy exchange on other unities).

It is possible to unintentionally affect others with your reactions and self-change efforts. However, in such cases, the energy receiving unities would just react or self-change to the energy they were exposed from the emitting source. Still, this would not be classified as transformation. The latter always entails purposefully directing energy to affect other unities. Certainly, the targeted unities can be informed and acceptive about the transformation attempted or remain ignorant of the intentions of the energy transmitter. This does not change the fact that they are subjected to a consciously initiated transformation activity another unity started.

---

[10] Darwin, C. (1859). *On the origin of species by means of natural selection, or the preservation of favoured races in the struggle for life*. John Murray.

[11] Asch, S. E. (1952). *Social psychology*. Prentice Hall.

[12] Paul't Hart. (1991). Irving L. Janis' victims of Groupthink. *Political Psychology, 12*(2), 247–278. https://doi.org/10.2307/3791464.

11.5 Humans Versus Other Unities

If we zoom out and view teams, communities, organisations and all other social collections as large unities, we could wonder whether the reaction RE, reaction and self-change RESC and reaction, self-change and transforming others RESCTO activities described in this chapter can take place without each of those large unities being centrally conscious. Hence, you could contemplate whether these activities can occur within and across the various groups, levels, departments, functions, and members of a collection without these resulting from the collection's central consciousness.

Indeed, all the above happens and are inescapable. The unities of a collection and the sub-unities of any unity are unities themselves and subject to a continuous exchange of energy. Regardless of their type and size, all unities carry some autonomy and 'know-how' to react to lesser or larger degrees, even how to self-change when it is about living organisms.

Especially humans hold an additional activity type which, to date, has not been found in other living beings. Not only do we react, self-change, and transform others, but we also *theorise*. This activity includes the use of available/retrievable information, personal discovery/experimenting, development of experiential knowledge, and generation/modification of information available to others. We theorise about the present, past, and future, test hypotheses, and try to validate the present and the past.

If we would only copy and paste from each other via physiological channels (e.g., genetic codes), adapt to the environment alone, and merely influence and transform others through immaterial and material energy, we would not differ from animals and other living creatures. If we were simply subject only to natural evolution, there would be no reason, sense, or meaning to converse, reflect, debate, and doubt. We should let things happen 'naturally' and strive to survive and proliferate as all other living beings.

Theorising stimulates sensing, composing and decomposing, re-sensing, re-composing, and re-decomposing unities, and so on. We will keep going until we have enough information to understand how similar units react, adapt, and transform. For example, biologists learn by dissecting unities into small parts and applying their findings to similar parts. They also share this information with other fields to help support life. This is how analysts have constructed biomarkers to sense potential health problems and intervene, which is a form of transforming others, to improve well-being.

Doctors do not perform surgery on every patient to check for diseases. They infer what is happening based on what is known from similar cases in the past. Theorising triggers repeatedly gathering and processing such information from humans and other living things. Analysts continue this iterative process until they construct an adequate model of the material and immaterial energy interactions and exposures that drive reaction, self-change, or transformation and how unities experience the impacts of those activities.

Theorising is when we wonder about ourselves, and everything around and sometimes feel reluctant to adhere to prescribed processes and rules religiously. Often, we even attempt to alter what we view as natural and intervene in the mechanisms of natural evolution. Whatever rules and procedures we comply with are mainly reaction-type activities, typically sourcing from the 'why' of others and not answers to our own 'whys'.

Another point of contemplation is when humans can be subjects of a transformation of others TO strategy, and who is legitimately authorised to implement this. As I articulated earlier in this chapter, current professional ethics dictate we are not authorised to transform other humans unless those have agreed to the process. Before starting any human-focussed TO activity agreed and expected objectives (Chapter 10) must be agreed upon. Simply put, TO activities can involve changing other humans only when these receivers are aware of these activities, including the risks and expected outputs and outcomes, and have endorsed them. Similarly, although we cannot secure consent from animals, there are codes when aiming to study and intervene in such living unities.

Under this lens, social engineering, can be considered an unacceptable type of manipulation, regardless of the intention behind it. This is because its underlying philosophy is to transform others without their consent. Although lately social engineering has focussed on cybersecurity threats,[13,14] it is also well hidden in practices towards enforcing behaviours, promoting services, and marketing products. Such practices are unfortunate examples of how findings from exact and hybrid scientific fields (e.g., neuroscience and experiments about human sensing and processing) are misused.

Moreover, it seems many neglect that the third law of Newton 'For every action there is an equal and opposite reaction' applies only to raw material. Newton never meant to derive laws for humans and other living beings. For living organisms, the direction, form and amount of the energy exchanged during reaction varies. Besides what I argued in Chapter 9 when discussing sciences, many still apply the third Newtonian law to humans.

For instance, courts base their arguments about fair or not self-defence depending on the amount of the energy the victim transmitted to the attacker. Judges and juries expect the victim should not transmit much more energy to protect itself than the potential of the energy received. However, someone would doubt whether this criterion can be widely applicable and sensible, especially when considering the interplay of material and immaterial energy under non-deterministic ways and often unpredictable outcomes. Matters such as material energy features (e.g., mass and size of the attacker) and cognitive and affective energy interactions (bullying, coercion, etc.) can impact on a victim's decision on whether and how to respond to an attack.

Thankfully, contemporary inexact and hybrid sciences declare their objections and stress that physical laws cannot apply to humans. This, of course, acknowledges the effects of the unobservable, immaterial energy. Otherwise, if we were purely

---

[13] Ozkaya, E. (2018). *Learn social engineering*. Packt Publishing.

[14] Hadnagy, C. (2018). *Social engineering* (2nd ed.). Wiley.

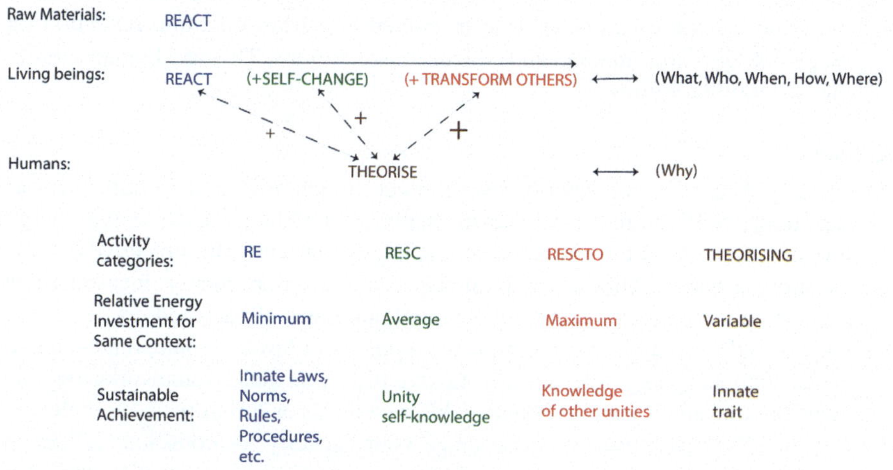

Fig. 11.2 Overview of activity types per unity type

material unities, we should obey the Newtonian or other universally tested laws of material energy. In simple words, such newer positions rightly underscore our stochastic nature and reject determinism.

Several inexact/hybrid scientists accept the presence and effects of the unobservable immaterial energy within humans, which renders human activities and behaviours stochastic. However, it is paradoxical that several of these scientists deny the existence of unobservable, immaterial energy outside human unities. They prefer to label such external immaterial energy as paranormal, metaphysical, supernatural, and so on. To me, this signals selectivity and double standards. In Fig. 11.2 I summarise the principal concepts I covered in this chapter.

Activities: Key Reflections and Actions

Reflections

- Professional and organisational activities can be categorised into three fundamental types: Reaction, Self-Change, and Transformation of Others. These categories reflect distinct ways unities engage with their environment and allocate energy.
- Energy investment is a critical aspect of these activities. Whether reacting, adapting internally, or influencing others, effective energy management ensures optimal performance and sustainable outcomes.
- Activities are interconnected, with energy flows between them, influencing how individuals and organisations adapt, respond, and innovate.
- The typology of laws provides a framework for understanding the principles that govern activities.

- Consciousness plays a pivotal role in human activities, enabling reflection on energy use, decision-making, and ethical considerations. This sets human activity apart from other unities.

Actions

1. Classify Activities and Energy Use: Reflect on activities and classify them as Reactions, Self-Changes, or Transformations of Others. Analyse the energy investment required for each type and its alignment with your objectives.
2. Optimise Energy Allocation: Evaluate whether your energy investment is proportionate to the demands and potential outcomes of each activity.
3. Understand Activity Laws: Examine the typology of laws—innate, fundamental, basic, and emerging—relevant to your activities. Use these frameworks to guide decisions and adapt your approach to different levels of certainty and complexity.
4. Enhance Reflective Practices: Leverage your capacity for conscious reflection to assess the effectiveness of your actions and energy use. Identify areas for improvement and adjust strategies accordingly.
5. Foster Interconnected Activities: Recognise how reactions, self-changes, and transformations of others influence one another. Seek to balance these activities for cohesive and integrated professional practices.

By integrating energy investment principles, activity classifications, and the typology of laws into your professional approach, you can enhance efficiency, adaptability, and ethical decision-making within your organisational context.

Chapter 12
Energy Exchange

12.1 General

When attending to the visible world, it becomes apparent that everything is about regular or irregular exchange of material energy, often carrying immaterial energy information. This happens everywhere, from within tiny particles to between entire countries. For example, when I host a dinner party, everyone exchanges material energy which uses, influences, and stimulates immaterial energy. I use my body (material energy) and mind (immaterial energy) to cook (using material ingredients) for my guests. Cooking involves the exchange of material energy between me, the food, and the equipment.

During dinner, I use my body parts (mouth, tongue, teeth, hands, etc., the movement of which necessitates material energy) to share news, exchange ideas, express opinions, imply (dis)satisfaction, and transmit several other cognitive and affective information (immaterial energy). In return, guests visit me (material and immaterial energy to travel) and engage in conversations, using their material and immaterial energy to share thoughts and ideas. They might also bring some gifts (material energy) that I might like or not (immaterial energy).

When you work, you invest material energy (body movements) and cognitive energy (knowledge, mental skills, etc.) in return for some income, which represents mainly material energy, and some recognition. The latter reflects immaterial energy transmitted by colleagues through physical channels (e.g., encouraging conversations) and affecting your material and immaterial energy. Also, our negative mood (affective energy) can generate physical stress and changes to our body (material energy), like high blood pressure and increased heart rate. These bodily changes might generate additional thoughts, worries, and decisions (immaterial energy).

At broader levels, commercial trading regards predominantly the exchange and conversion of material energy (e.g., raw and processed material, goods) via immaterial energy (e.g., reasoning, persuasion, trust). Contrary, interactive art (i.e., concerts and performances) is primarily about the exchange of immaterial energy through

N. Karanikas, *Professional Generalism in a Hyper-specialised World*,
https://doi.org/10.1007/978-981-96-4039-3_12

material means (e.g., sound and light). Even more widely, consider the underlying reasons for cooperation and disagreement between nations.

Most of the time, it is all about how countries will share and exchange material energy (e.g., physical materials, electricity, technology) by using their immaterial energy to convince others. They could even use material energy (e.g., weapons, hard borders) and immaterial energy (e.g., diplomatic skills) to enforce their wills. Besides, the material energy purchased from claimed from other countries is expectedly used to increase the material and immaterial energies of its citizens (e.g., better living standards).

There is nothing free from energy exchange. Everything is about material and immaterial energy, which interact continuously and affect each other within and amongst us and other unities. International conventions and national, regional, and local legislations aim to impose how we are expected to use our material and immaterial energy. They also dictate how the total energy under each jurisdiction must be exchanged and distributed to the subjects of the law and anything outside them.

We may not steal because we must not deprive others of their legitimate energy, material most of the times but also immaterial if it comes to intellectual property and cognitive and emotional aspects. We may not kill other humans because several ethics and laws suggest we have no rights of exerting force and control over the existence of other persons, meaning terminating others as distinct unities with their own individual material and immaterial energy. Also, bullying is banned in many countries, meaning it is prohibited to use material and immaterial energy to degrade the material and immaterial energy of others.

Every law and regulation is about the possession, distribution, and expected use of energy, and shapes our normative references of the what, where, who, how, and when to do with our energy. The development of such formal normative artefacts is what we trust in the ones we elect or endorse (e.g., governments, councils, boards, communities). We authorise them to come up with enforceable measures and guidance on how available energy is supposed to be sourced, stored, used, and so on. Legislation does not dictate what and how to think and feel, but it regulates the way we use material energy, which also carries cognitive and emotional information (e.g., meanings).

We have legislation about proprietary rights and taxation obligations, meaning how material energy is shared and distributed. There are also rules about healthcare that direct the use of material and immaterial energy of some society members for the well-being of the rest of the society and the access to services which, once more, comprise material and immaterial energy. Laws about education dictate how immaterial energy, especially cognitive energy, will be shared through physical energy within boundaries of expressing affective energy.

Every legislation, regulation, code, and standard relates to energy exchange. The same goes for unwritten laws in communities and societies, which also shape unities' normative references. Those express expectations of how we are allowed or not to use the material and immaterial energy available for the benefit of others or, at least, for avoiding harming fellow citizens. Regardless of any laws and rules, expressed or implied expectations, which notably change over time, the question is. 'What drives you to use your energy and for the benefit of whom or what?'. The concepts I unfold in the following sections suggest that normative references alone, such as laws and procedures, do not suffice.

12.2 Needs and Desires

Unsurprisingly, you would first legitimately ask, 'How much material and immaterial energy does someone need?'. Answering this question is crucial to understanding what drives energy exchange from the specific person's perspective. Theoretically, the answer would be 'the minimum useable energy MUES (i.e., material MES and cognitive CES energies) necessary for an individual to survive within a specific environment' (Sects. 5.3 and 5.4).

However, our needs are moderated by our acceptable useable energy state (AUES) and desired useable energy state (DUES) reflecting our preferred living standards. Those standards are part of our cognitive energy as types and quantity of material energy possessed, overall energy levels and created thresholds and read lines (e.g., minimum levels). Such living standards can be pursued both willingly (e.g., someone's plan is to achieve 50% more material energy in 10 years) or through our conformity to a specific environment (e.g., somebody's pursuit to buy a luxurious car because everyone else has one).

To clarify further and minimise confusion, it is important to note that acceptable and desired energy states indeed play a dual role in influencing how we feel (i.e., affective energy) and what we pursue (i.e., cognitive energy). Somebody might feel sad about their energy situation, but this does not always mean they are prepared to seek energy from others. The specific person can even donate part of its low energy to other suffering people or other living being. This is an example of the non-exclusive and non-linear interplay between cognitive and affective energies that render their outputs and outcomes largely non-deterministic. Indeed, literature suggests the interconnections of constructs like motivation with both cognition and emotion,[1,2,3] acknowledging the continuous and inevitable interactions between cognitive and affective energies (Sect. 5.4).

Nowadays, rarely do we accept and desire the minimum energy that is necessary to maintain physical existence. This could be driven by several parameters, such as people having experienced energy loss down to the minimum energy levels to survive. This could generate anxiety, frustration and other unpleasant feelings about their

---

[1] Ferguson, E. D., & Wee, B. E. F. (2000). *Motivation: A biosocial and cognitive integration of motivation and emotion.* Oxford University Press.

[2] Dai, D. Y., & Sternberg, R. J. (Eds.). (2004). *Motivation, emotion, and cognition: Integrative perspectives on intellectual functioning and development.* Taylor & Francis Group.

[3] Masmoudi, S., Yun, D. D., & Naceur, A. (Eds.). (2011). *Attention, representation, and human performance: Integration of cognition, emotion, and motivation.* Taylor & Francis Group.

ability to survive. Also, external information could have suggested that someone's future energy state will dramatically drop (i.e., anticipated energy < current energy).

There might be also several 'positive examples' of individuals around with higher current and anticipated energies, which become models for us. Furthermore, others could have expectations of us regarding the use of our energy, even when it is inadequate to meet those expectations. Therefore, what energy we accept and desire does not always equal the minimum energy we need.

For instance, the minimum material needs of an individual (e.g., 2,500 calories intake to maintain weight) might be lower than what they accept (e.g., nothing less than 3,500 calories available during a single day). They might even desire to reach 5,000 calories availability. It can be that excessive material energy boosts their affective energy as it makes them feel better.

It could also be the case that more material energy protects their affective energy (e.g., they want to shape a very muscled body which can appeal to others). Maybe they are afraid that if they only had 2,500 calories available, something could (un)expectedly deprive them of the minimum energy level needed to maintain their current energy and sustain their lives. I could also desire more energy just because others have more energy. There can be numerous reasons for that.

As another example, someone might need specific knowledge and cognitive skills to perform a task. However, they could decide to undertake the particular task even with a lower cognitive energy level than the minimum necessary because they feel it is imperative to perform the task under any means. Perhaps they could also worry about the implications of not executing the task.

Someone might meet minimum job requirements (i.e., usable energy) but wants to learn more (i.e., cognitive energy increase) because of social pressure or personal goals. Somebody might have all the material and cognitive energy they accept and need, but they want to store more because they are aware of or have experienced adverse circumstances which might harm their future energy levels.

Regardless of its current energy state, when considering the gaps between minimum useable energy MUES, acceptable usable energy AUES and desired useable energy DUES for a particular individual, we can symbolise per time-point the following three internalised constructs of Energy State Tolerance Region, Energy State Upgrade Region and Energy State Motivational Envelope.

Energy State Tolerance Region (ESTR)

$$\begin{aligned}&\textit{Energy State Tolerance Region ESTR} \propto \textit{Acceptable usable energy AUES}\\&\quad -\textit{Minimum usable energy MUES}\end{aligned} \tag{12.1}$$

When acceptable ACUES > minimum MUES, then tolerance ESTR > 0 and represents how much energy someone could acceptably lose without this threatening their physical existence. ESTR reflects the distance from the minimum energy level that a person perceives as safe. If AUES = MUES, then ESTR = 0, and the person perceives their minimum energy state as an acceptable condition. When AUES < MUES, then ESTR < 0, and the individual does not mind if they become physically inexistent.

Energy State Upgrade Region (ESUR)

$$\begin{aligned}\textit{Energy State Upgrade Region ESUR} &\propto \textit{Desired useable energy DUES}\\ &\quad - \textit{Acceptable usable energy AUES}\end{aligned} \tag{12.2}$$

If desired DUES > acceptable AUES energy, then energy upgrade ESUR > 0. This corresponds to how much more energy someone wishes to gain to move from the acceptable to their ideal state. When DUES = AUES, then ESUR = 0. Here, the person accepts nothing less than their desired energy state or they do not seek more energy than the state they have accepted. The case of DUES < AUES, meaning ESUR < 0, is possible but has no actual meaning. If an individual desires less than what they accept, then it automatically leads to DUES = AUES.

Energy State Motivational Envelope (ESME)
The combination of the above could symbolically offer per time-point the *Energy State Motivational Envelope (ESME)* of an individual (12.3).

$$\begin{aligned}\textit{Energy State Motivational Envelope ESME} &\propto \textit{Tolerance ESTR} + \textit{Upgrade ESUR}\\ &= (\textit{acceptable AUES} - \textit{minimum MUES})\\ &\quad + (\textit{desired DUES} - \textit{acceptable AUES})\\ &= \textit{desired DUES} - \textit{minimum MUES}\end{aligned} \tag{12.3}$$

When desired DUES > minimum MUES energy, including the case desired energy DUES = acceptable energy AUESU, then motivation ESME > 0. This reflects how far from their minimum physical existence energy point someone wishes to grow their energy state. If DUES < MUES, then ESME < 0, and the person, for some reason, prefers to become physically inexistent, similarly to the case AUES < MUES above. When DUES = MUES, then inevitably AUES = DUES = MUES. Here, the individual does not want and wish for anything more than the energy necessary to exist within a given environment.

Interestingly, the acceptable energy AUES construct does not appear in the motivation envelope ESME symbolic formula above. Although purely conceptual, this generates important observations. First, AUES could be just a transitional stage somebody welcomes when moving towards achieving their desired energy levels DUES. As I discuss in more detail in Sect. 17.3, this can be attributed to the fluidity of AUES originating from the constant conditioning and adaptation of someone to their changing physical, social and technical environments.[4,5,6,7] This suggests that DUES is relatively more constant than AUES.

For instance, although one believes they should earn $100,000 from their work, they can accept a salary of $80,000 considering their minimum energy needs and the situation in the job market currently. Indeed, a $5,000 raise would be welcome and could constitute this person's new acceptable level, especially when deciding to look for a job elsewhere. Nevertheless, their desired income can remain the same. Also, because of financial problems in a business, employees could accept fewer team-building activities, without this meaning they would not still desire more team-building opportunities. Also, they could think of team activities requiring less energy.

As a second observation, the difference between what is absolutely necessary for somebody and what they wish to achieve will dramatically motivate the when, where, how, and what of exchanging energy with others. This does not mean that the minimum energy MUES is immovable. However, unlike the desired energy DUES, which expresses wishes and could change more frequently, MUES represents the energy state required for survival and expectedly changes less often.

Indeed, someone's minimum energy state can lower or increase with time as well. If we find ways to use our energy more efficiently, we can do the same activities with less energy, meaning we have a lower minimum energy necessary than before. If we must execute a task that requires more cognitive energy than what we have, our necessary minimum energy gets higher.

Therefore, while both energy tolerance and upgrade affect daily decisions, desired energy DUES will have the most significant effect. The higher the DUESU is, the more the motivation of an individual to increase their energy state. Motivation will be shaped not only by the gap between DUES and minimum energy MUES of someone, but also by similar gaps of others around.

Comparisons of tolerances ESTRs, upgrades ESURs and motivations ESMEs amongst individuals can reveal full or partial overlaps or a complete divergence. Hence, the results of such comparisons could also stimulate cognition to discover reasons and possibly redefine someone's desired energy DUES. Why, for example, has somebody set a desired energy state lower or higher than other people around? Why is someone's ESUR lower or higher than the one of others? In Fig. 12.1 I present some of such comparison cases.

For the sake of brevity, in Fig. 12.1 I only picture cases where minimum energy MUES is lower than desired energy DUES and the fluid acceptable energy state AUES lies between them. However, as mentioned above, there can be instances where DUES is lower than MUES. This, for example, covers cases of suicides or sacrificing energy for any reason they deem worth it (e.g., betterment of others).

---

[4] John, M.T., & Roberts, D.G. (1996). Cultural Adaptation in the Workplace. Routledge

[5] Chandler, T. J., & Brown, L. E. (2008). *Conditioning for strength and human performance*. Wolters Kluwer Health/Lippincott Williams and Wilkins.

[6] Little, M.A., Dyson-Hudson, R., & Smith, E.A. (1983). *Rethinking human adaptation: Biological and cultural models*. Routledge

[7] Kahn, P. (2011). *Technological nature: Adaptation and the future of human life*. The MIT Press.

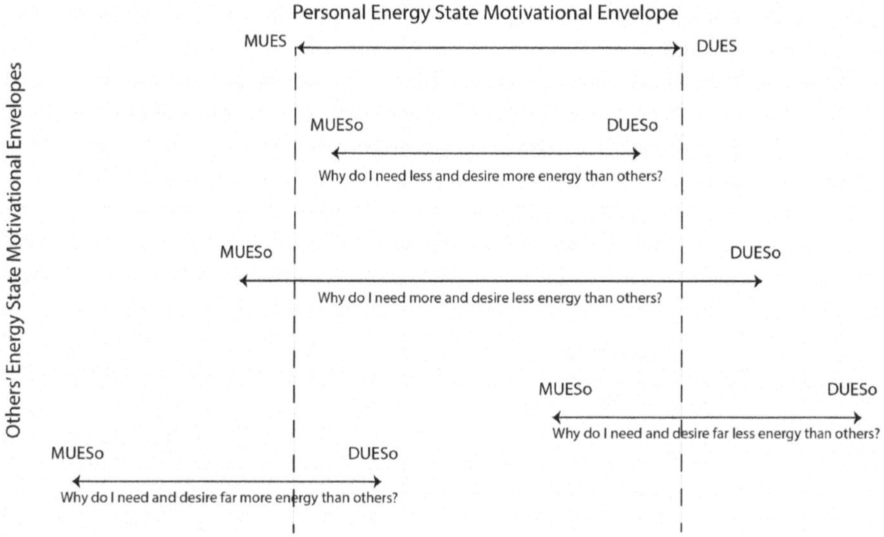

Fig. 12.1 Comparisons of energy state motivational envelopes

12.3 Energy Investment and Outcomes

As I discussed in Sect. 12.2, motivation ESME varies per individual depending on a multitude of factors. These change over time through the individual's interactions with other unities, including other humans. Similarly important, although conceptually reasonable, it is unfeasible to compare the minimum energy states amongst individuals. The reason is there is no solid reference point for what constitutes the lowest necessary level of material and cognitive energy for a person to sustain life within a specific environment.

The main challenge in establishing solid comparison references is the diversity of characteristics of different individuals, the constantly changing environment, our inability to measure cognitive energy (e.g., knowledge and memories) and several challenges with material energy measurement (e.g., stored in several forms, converted continually from one form to another). Although there have been energy limits for material energy, below which physical existence could be threatened (e.g., daily calories intake for humans with different ages and weights), those still constitute indications and do not uniformly apply to all humans.

Indeed, many people have survived solely on bread and water for extended periods. It may seem unnatural, but that claim is only valid from a narrow perspective of what natural is. Such individuals might have developed highly efficient uses of their energy, minimising interactions that absorb their energy, controlling their material energy through cognitive and affective energy mechanisms unknown to most and other mechanisms and practices. The possibility we cannot explain the above adequately through current scientific knowledge does not mean that these cases and the humans involved are unnatural.

Finding explanations and making comparisons regarding the minimum and desired energy levels of unities and collections can be a never-ending endeavour. Instead, we could focus on how each unity or collection uses their energy, corresponding to how a unity or collection exchanges energy. As I argued in Sect. 12.1, put plainly, energy use means energy exchange. Theoretically, there could be an ideal unity that does not exchange energy and still secures its existence: a *self-sustained unity*. However, it seems such unities do not exist. Even raw materials undergo energy exchanges with their environment, which can slowly result in their degradation.

Indeed, non-living unities like raw material do not need to exchange energy to physically exist, regardless of whatever energy they are exposed to and transforms them. However, such material energy changes do not mean that energy is lost. It simply denotes that a specific unity or collection (e.g., office building, precious stone, stainless steel) does not maintain over time the characteristics paired with its constructed definition (i.e., the number and types of its sub-unities). Because of exposures, energy is transformed, absorbed, converted, etc. as per the law of energy conservation in physics. Therefore, for the sake of setting a reference point, we can conventionally accept that non-living unities are *self-contained unities*.

All living unities rely on others, they are *dependent unities*. We and other living beings rely on interactions with other unities to sustain our existence and perpetuation of species. For example, plants use ingredients from the ground (e.g., water, metallic elements, and organic compounds) and light energy to grow and survive. They interact with other living organisms to ensure pollination (e.g., insects finding nutritious substances in a flower). Similarly, we and animals depend on other unities, biological and not, to live the longest possible and secure the continuation of species.

Hence, given those dependencies and earlier arguments in this chapter, *Wilful Energising Investment (WENI)* would be a useful comparison construct. WENI is shaped by the person's energy motivation envelope and represents the wilful contribution of a person to the overall energy of other unities or collections. The terms I introduce and the examples I provide in the rest of this section equally apply to humans and their collections, depending on the preferred level of abstraction (Sect. 10.4).

A person using their energy for the benefit of other unities (i.e., increase in overall energy OES_O) would be assigned a positive WENI, the value of which will increase with the amount of energy invested and the positive change achieved. Likewise, a person using their energy for harming other unities (i.e., decrease in OES_O) would be assigned a negative WENI, the value of which will decrease with the amount of energy invested and the negative impact inflicted.

Hence, in its simplest form in Eq. 12.4, for the period between the employment of useable energy by a person UES_P at time-point t and the later time-point of interest T, wilful energising investment WENI is symbolically defined by the *Wilful Energy Investment Rate (WEIR)* multiplied with the *Intended Energy Exchange Outcome (IEEO)*.

$$WENI_T \propto WEIR_t * IEEO_T \propto \left(\frac{UES_{P,t} \text{ invested in direct interactions}}{\text{Available } UES_{P,t} + \text{Anticipated Energy Exchange}_T} \right) * \left[\frac{(OES_{O,T} - OES_{O,t})}{OES_{O,t}} \right] \quad (12.4)$$

More specifically:

- Wilful Energy Investment Rate (WEIR) is the rate of:
  - the usable energy UES_P (i.e., material and cognitive energy) a person consciously employed when interacting with other unities in their proximal environment at time-point t, by
  - the person's available useable energy UES_P at time-point t and anticipated energy exchange at time-point T (Sect. 5.5),
- Intended Energy Exchange Outcome (IEEO) is the targeted change to the overall energy OES_O of the external unities directly involved in and indirectly affected by these interactions between the time-points t and T.

One advantage of the construct of wilful energising investment WENI is that it avoids direct comparisons between energy states (e.g., comparing the wealth status of individuals) that can often be unfair (e.g., it is not someone's 'fault' they inherited lots of material energy). Also, WENI does not cover the inevitable reactions and adaptations during energy exposure and exchange that occur beyond the control of any living unity (Sects. 11.3 and 17.3). Instead, WENI reflects how much of their energy individuals purposefully use and with what intended outcomes, as explained below, while also meeting their needs and satisfying their desires. Therefore, WENI can be a more useful proxy for inferring the invisible, internal energy motivation envelope.

12.4 Sponsors and Antagonists

The construct of wilful energising investment can be useful for classifying individuals regarding their energy use. When interactions deliberately aim to benefit the overall energy of other unities OES_O in the proximal and distant environments, without foreseeable or expected energy gains reciprocally, the person of interest is a *selfless energy sponsor*.

Higher energy investment rate and intended positive outcomes result in higher wilful energising investment WENI. For example, donating money to a philanthropic organisation aiding the disadvantaged benefits both the local and distant environments. In the specific context, the higher the donation offered, the higher the WENI is, and if you expect nothing in return, you can be classified as a selfless energy sponsor.

If there is an expected reciprocity when investing usable energy UES_P for the benefit of other unities (e.g., money donation is deductible from taxed income), then the person is a *reciprocal energy sponsor*. When the reciprocity in energy exceeds the usable energy invested, the individual is a *selfish energy sponsor*. Energy sponsors sacrificing most of their energy UES_P for supporting others with no expected reciprocity are *sacrificial energy sponsors*; those are persons we usually name as absolute heroes. For example, sacrificial sponsor is someone who does not spare their physical life to save others from a dangerous situation. The more the overall energy OES_O increases, the more sacrificial the energy sponsorship is.

When useable energy investment harms others without expected energy gains, the individual is a *selfless energy antagonist*. For example, selfless energy antagonist is someone who harms the environment by contaminating the ground (e.g., spills most of the toxic materials they possess) and expecting no energy gains in return. If there is an expected reciprocity when investing useable energy in degrading other unities, then the person is a *reciprocal energy antagonist*. For instance, this involves someone taking credit for another person's work to their own advantage. If the energy self-gain is higher than the energy invested, the individual becomes a *selfish energy antagonist*.

An antagonist investing most or all their usable energy in harming others with no energy reciprocity becomes a *sacrificial energy antagonist*; those are individuals we typically name as absolute villains. For instance, sacrificial antagonist is somebody who gets themselves fatally injured to ensure solely that others get harmed (e.g., suicidal attack to the public as a manifest of opposition to a government decision). The more the OES_O decreases, the more sacrificial the energy antagonism becomes.

A person might have no intentions to use their useable energy UES_P for the benefit or harm of others. If the person employs their UES_P only to ensure they meet their needs and not intentionally increasing their energy levels, they are a *selfless energy exchanger* (e.g., babies and little children). Of course, when a balanced individual interacts with others because those unities threaten the individual's usable energy, the person will temporarily exchange energy and probably become a *defensive energy exchanger*. For example, children can become defensive when others take their food away or claim their toys. If an energy exchanger aims to increase their useable energy UES_P, they become a *selfish energy exchanger*.

In Fig. 12.2, I illustrate graphically the classifications presented above. I want to re-emphasise strongly that these categories are fluid. Individuals can shift between them depending on context, intention, and perspective. The horizontal axis in Fig. 12.2 presents the denominator of energy investment rate WEIR (i.e., $AvailableUES_{P,t} + AnticipatedEnergyExchange_T$), and the vertical axis represents the product of the WEIR's nominator by the intended outcome IEEO (i.e., $UES_{P,t}investedindirectinteractions * \left[\frac{(OES_{O,T} - OES_{O,t})}{OES_{O,t}}\right]$).

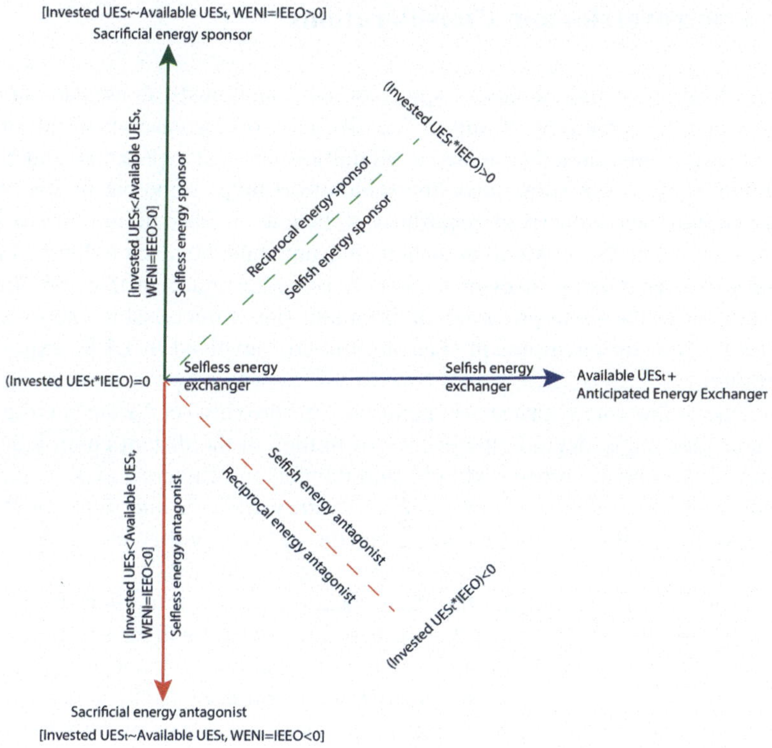

Fig. 12.2 Sponsors and antagonists

In literature, energy antagonists are typically labelled as toxic,[8,9] while sponsors are described as benefactors, supportive, and nurturing. However, those classifications can be divisive as they often focus deterministically more on the actual outcomes than on the intentions. They often oversimplify and generalise without considering the timeframe, context and motivation of energy sponsorship or antagonism, as I discuss in Sect. 12.5. A snapshot at a time-point to label a person or collection as a sponsor or antagonist can be misleading (Chapter 14).

[8] Arabi, S. (2020). *The highly sensitive person's guide to dealing with toxic people: how to reclaim your power from narcissists and other manipulators*. New Harbinger Publications, Inc.

[9] Kusy, M., & Holloway, E. (2009). *Toxic workplace!: Managing toxic personalities and their systems of power*. Jossey-Bass.

12.5 Controversies and Considerations

The classification of individuals as sponsors and antagonists above can serve its purpose when the same type of impact (i.e., increase or decrease of overall other's energy OES_O) is intentionally directed to all unities involved in proximal and distant environments. However, sometimes, the same effort helps some but harms others. Energy beneficiaries or deprived, regardless of the intended benefit or harm to them, can belong to either the proximal or distant environments. For each individual time-point of wilful energising investment, it is reasonable to accept that the affected unities belong to the same proximal environment (i.e., direct usable energy UES_P recipients) or distant environment (i.e., not directly involved in UES_P exposures/ interactions).

When the usable energy invested benefits only the proximal or distant environment and would knowingly degrade the energy of unities in the distant environment or proximal environment, correspondingly, and the person of interest expects nothing in return, they are a *controversially selfless energy sponsor and antagonist*. The controversy lies in the fact that the same person and energy they use leads to both positive and negative effects on different unities and collections.

For instance, a professional who offers valuable advice to a client-friend (i.e., proximal environment) also knows that the beneficiary client will misuse their energy to degrade others who are distant environment for the professional (e.g., the client unfairly competing with others to win a bidHere, the professional becomes a controversial energy sponsor (for the proximal environment) and antagonist (for the distant environment). If there is also some gain expected (e.g., a gift from the client-friend) lower than or equal to then energy invested, the professional would be a *reciprocal and controversial energy sponsor and antagonist*. If the gain is higher than the invested energy, the individual becomes a *controversially selfish energy sponsor and antagonist*.

Likewise, a person could invest most or all their usable energy to promote other's energy OES_O in proximal or distant interactions but degrade OES_O in the distant or proximal environment, respectively. Here, the individual who sacrificed (almost) everything is a *controversially sacrificial sponsor and antagonist***.** For instance, someone gets severely injured when fighting and killing a carnivorous animal (i.e., proximal environment) to protect others who would encounter it (i.e., distant environment). Environmentalists may find the action unacceptable (i.e., sacrificial antagonist), while others may view the same person as a saviour (i.e., sacrificial sponsor).

Hence, if wilful energising investment WENI only considers the overall energy OES_O of the unities closer or accessible, any evaluation can be highly biased and deceptive. The lower the radius of the circle that we draw to determine WENI through intended outcomes, the more biased and unfair the result could be. Hence, WENI evaluations depend on access to unities in the distant environment and any OES_O information about them.

Also, the time-points which wilful energising investment considers play an important role. The shorter the *T-t* period, the higher the confidence that the changes to overall energy OES_O of other unities can be attributed to the investment of usable energy by the person of interest. When the timeframe is longer, it is more difficult to develop confidence in attributing OES_O changes to a particular person because there could be other individuals and variables that can influence OES_O.

Wilful energising investment WENI in Eq. (12.4) can have longitudinal power to capture the cases where useable energy is used to deprive unities of some of their energy temporarily, under the expectation this will lead to more benefits in the mid- or long term. For instance, a teacher can be strict when marking assignments, leading to a lower overall energy OES_O of students in the short term. However, the goal is to help students build resilience and achieve greater professional success, meaning facilitating higher OES_O in long term. As such, whereas students could label the teacher as an energy antagonist today, the teacher can function as an energy sponsor. It depends on the selection of T time-point.

The closer the time of evaluating wilful energising investment WENI to the marked assessment results, the more likely WENI will be negative, and the students will view the teacher as an energy antagonist. The more the teacher repeats the same practice, the more time it will take until the WENI reflects the intended positive outcomes, as the student will regularly experience a lower overall energy. In the long-term, it would be also less certain whether any professional success would be primarily or solely attributed to the strategy of the particular teacher or other factors.

Likewise, the wilful energising investment WENI equation can also be used where a person employs their useable energy to benefit the energy of other unities OES_O at the present, while knowing that this might lead to lower OES_O in the mid- and long-term. For example, providing teenagers with salty and processed food can increase their OES_O temporarily (e.g., great taste and many calories) but could harm their health in the long-term. Thus, whereas the food chain actors can initially be seen as energy sponsors, they can prove energy antagonists.

Here, the outcome again hinges on the chosen T time-point. The closer the evaluation time-point to the food consumption time-point, the more probable the wilful energising investment WENI will get a positive/high value. The consumers, who could be unaware of the latency of health issues, would view food chain unities as energy sponsors.

If the consumption of such unhealthy products is repeated often, then the positive wilful energising investment WENI value is reinforced and the actual harmful results suggesting a very negative WENI might be realised late or even ignored (e.g., public health campaigns). Nonetheless, by the time the adverse health effects manifest, it can be problematic to claim that the consumption of low-quality food was the principal or sole factor.

Although in Table 12.1 I present the classifications introduced above and in Sect. 12.4, the examples in this section illustrate the challenges in establishing causal relationships in complex social systems despite any conceptual energy investment classifications we can adopt.

Table 12.1 Energy user types

Energy user type	Usable energy invested: Some (S) or (almost) all (A)	Intended energy recipients and effects		Reciprocal energy gain anticipated: Yes > energy invested (Y>E), Yes ≤ energy invested (Y≤E), No (N)
		Proximal: Increase (I) or Decrease (D)	Distant: Increase (I) or Decrease (D)	
Outcome-indifferent individuals				
Selfless energy exchanger	S	—	—	Y≤E
Selfish energy exchanger	S	—	—	Y>E
Energy reciprocity individuals				
Selfless energy sponsor	S	I	I	N
Sacrificial energy sponsor	A	I	I	N
Selfless energy antagonist	S	D	D	N
Sacrificial energy antagonist	A	D	D	N
Energy non-reciprocity individuals				
Selfish energy sponsor	S	I	I	Y>E
Reciprocal energy sponsor	S	I	I	Y≤E
Selfish energy antagonist	S	D	D	Y>E
Reciprocal energy antagonist	S	D	D	Y≤E
Energy-controversial individuals				
Controversially selfless energy sponsor and antagonist	S	I	D	N
	S	D	I	N

(continued)

Table 12.1 (continued)

Energy user type	Usable energy invested: Some (S) or (almost) all (A)	Intended energy recipients and effects		Reciprocal energy gain anticipated: Yes > energy invested (Y>E), Yes ≤ energy invested (Y≤E), No (N)
		Proximal: Increase (I) or Decrease (D)	Distant: Increase (I) or Decrease (D)	
Controversially sacrificial sponsor and antagonist	A	I	D	N
	A	D	I	N
Controversially selfish energy sponsor and antagonist	S	I	D	Y>E
	S	D	I	Y>E
Reciprocal and controversial energy sponsor and antagonist	S	I	D	Y≤E
	S	D	I	Y≤E

Energy Exchange: Key Reflections and Actions

Reflections

- Energy exchange underpins all professional and organisational interactions, encompassing material, cognitive, and emotional energy. Understanding these exchanges is key to navigating complex systems and relationships.
- Needs and desires drive energy investment, shaping how individuals and organisations prioritise, allocate, and balance their resources.
- Patterns of energy exchange, such as the Energy State Tolerance Region and Energy State Motivational Envelope, highlight the boundaries and incentives that influence behaviour and performance.
- Energy sponsors and antagonists play crucial roles in energy dynamics, either supporting or obstructing efforts. Recognising these roles helps manage influences and align energy exchanges with goals.
- Controversies and considerations, such as ethical dilemmas and power imbalances, often arise in energy exchanges. Addressing these thoughtfully is essential for sustainable and equitable outcomes.

Actions

1. Map Energy Exchanges: Reflect on the flows of material, cognitive and emotional energy in your professional context. Identify where energy is being invested, lost, or underutilised.

2. Assess Needs and Desires: Evaluate how your needs and desires, as well as those of others, drive energy exchanges. Ensure these align with and balance fairly between organisational objectives and personal or team priorities.
3. Monitor Energy Tolerance, Upgrade and Motivation: Analyse the Energy State Tolerance and Upgrade Regions and Motivational Envelope in your interactions. Recognise when energy levels are strained or when motivational gaps may hinder performance.
4. Identify Key Influences: Distinguish between sponsors who facilitate energy gains and antagonists who obstruct it. Develop strategies to leverage supportive influences and mitigate challenges posed by opposition.
5. Address Controversial Dynamics: Reflect on ethical considerations and power imbalances in your energy exchanges. Engage in open dialogues and adopt equitable approaches to foster sustainable and inclusive practices.
6. Optimise Energy Outcomes: Design workflows, team dynamics, or organisational strategies to maximise the effectiveness of energy exchanges. Balance energy investments across short-term needs and long-term sustainability.

By understanding and managing the dynamics of energy exchange, you can enhance collaboration, drive performance, and create equitable and sustainable outcomes in your professional and organisational environments.

Part IV
Management Concepts

Chapter 13
Management Redefined

13.1 General

Like unities, collections can be characterised by physical aspects and event constructs (e.g., size, number of interactions, observable events of systems) and calculative and inferential constructs (e.g., system reliability, safety, productivity). Typically, depending on the nature, composition and other contextual parameters, such constructs can be useful in the entire lifecycle of a collection (e.g., design, planning, implementation, deployment, monitoring, analysis, review, modification, and decommissioning). Collection-focussed constructs focus on measuring quality, quantity, and temporal aspects of inputs (i.e., incoming material energy), outputs (i.e., outgoing material energy), and activities (i.e., use of material energy).

For example, a vehicle is a collection characterised by its volume, length, number of parts/unities and other material features, and calculative constructs such as efficiency, fuel consumption, breaking performance, and acceleration. Evaluations of car performance constructs typically involve recording input parameters (e.g., fuel volume, type, and temperature), activity parameters (e.g., duration of mixing air and fuel and igniting), and output parameters (e.g., pressure and temperature of fumes). For each of these parameters, specific characteristics considered include quantity (e.g., how much air of fuel), quality (e.g., the octanes of the fuel) and time (e.g., how long it takes to ignite).

Similarly, social groups are human collections characterised by the number of members and their demographics and some constructs pertinent to their activities (e.g., number and frequency of meetings) and outputs (e.g., number of letters to external stakeholders). For instance, when a lecturer assigns an essay to a group of students, there are several inputs available to each student, such as information sources (e.g., lecture notes, literature), computer and stationary objects and ideas expressed from other students.

The activity of each student involves using the inputs available and transforming them into material energy like communication with other students, written notes and

N. Karanikas, *Professional Generalism in a Hyper-specialised World*,
https://doi.org/10.1007/978-981-96-4039-3_13

draft parts of the essay. Students use their interacting material and immaterial energy, and the energy exchanged between the students of their group. The completed essay is a form of material energy resulting from the exchange of immaterial and material energies between the students. It is the output the lecturer receives, assesses, and grades based on constructed criteria and expectations.

Depending on the relative time-point of using constructs related to monitoring behaviours and performance, literature refers to lagging indicators (after: output-focussed), or leading indicators (before: input-focussed) or process indicators (during: activity-focussed). There are plenty of other labels for these indicators and respective measurements, such as reactive, historical and retrospective for lagging indicators, and proactive and predictive for leading indicators. Monitoring such indicators can be periodical and typically considers predetermined thresholds of observable or perceived events.

If we monitor and act before we experience the event threshold defined (e.g., a serious injury, failure in exams, drop of sales more than X%), our monitoring is labelled as leading, and any actions stemming from monitoring are named proactive. If we observe and react to an unwanted event, meaning the one that exceeded any upper or lower threshold, monitoring can be labelled as lagging, and any remedial interventions can be named reactive.

Classifying temporal aspects (e.g., lagging and leading) is arbitrary and only makes sense for a defined collection/unity within its environment at a particular time-point. For instance, the number of traffic incidents can represent a lagging indicator for the road system-collection (e.g., regulators, divers, enforcement agencies). However, traffic incidents can be a leading indicator for planning in particular businesses (e.g., car dealers and repairers).

Any output characterised by 'lagging' aspects can be used again as a 'leading' input into activities of the same collection or unity. For example, farmers produce goods (i.e., outputs) which consumers use (i.e., inputs). For these goods, important 'lagging' indicators for the farmers could be the tons produced, volume of unsuitable/rejected goods, nutritional value, taste, and colour. The same indicators could be 'leading' indicators for the consumers, the agricultural sector and others.

In Fig. 13.1, I present a generic case of the concepts I discussed above. The main point to note is that classifications like the ones I presented in this section are remarkably relative and might create confusion. They rely significantly on who, where, when observes what and how they classified it. Furthermore, such classifications do not include the monitoring of unities and collections external to the ones of interest. This is another notable weakness, as external entities can still influence the ones of interest. Therefore, in the next book sections, I introduce alternative terminology and perspectives to reduce vagueness and confusion.

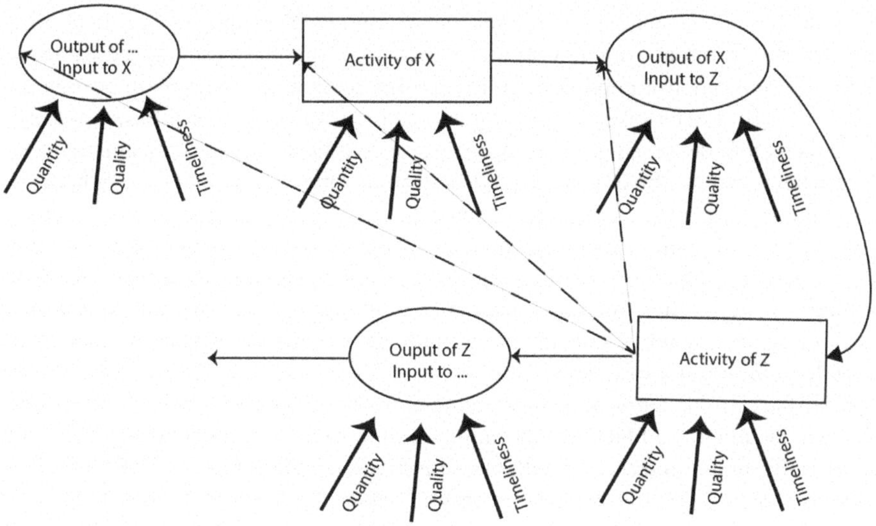

Fig. 13.1 Inputs, activities and outputs

13.2 Sensing

The more generic term 'sensing' can be used instead of monitoring as it has a broader scope applicable to humans, other living unities and any collection type. Sensing can be achieved through biological means (e.g., sensory receptor cells in our eyes and ears) or technology (e.g., motion sensors). Sensing is about detecting the status of and changes in the proximal environment through open and focussed sensing modes.

In *open sensing*, sensors are always exposed to any incoming energy from the proximal environment. Open sensing does not have a pre-planned focus and detects any changes. This mode of sensing typically associates with reactions or adaptations to incoming energy (Sect. 11.1) and can activate natural and fundamental laws (Sect. 11.3). For instance, receptors of human skin constantly sense any changes in environmental conditions (e.g., temperature and humidity). Those changes can mobilise material energy and lead body parts to alter their functioning (e.g., blood pressure changes) based on natural laws, whereas they could also drive someone to drink water with only little of thinking required (i.e., fundamental law).

Focussed sensing corresponds to the deliberate focus on specific areas, activities and other elements. It is employed when we want to examine the energy status and other aspects of other unities or collections so that to select deliberately the preferred activity type: reaction, self-change, or transformation of others (Sect. 11.1). Open sensing can stimulate focussed sensing (e.g., you ask others if they have observed or felt the same changes in the environment). Also, first-order focussed sensing results might drive us to second-order, deeper or broader, focussed sensing.

For instance, we can use focussed sensing to compare the aspects of a collection or unity against a reference point over time or once (e.g., whether a car is speeding above the limit). One can also employ focussed sensing to examine whether to change the aspects of self or external collections/unities (e.g., whether a car needs maintenance and replacement of some parts). Somebody else could use focussed sensing to investigate whether to establish new or modify current reference points (e.g., whether a car should be inspected at larger intervals).

Regardless of open or focussed mode, sensing can also be classified as native or external sensing, depending on the scope. *Native sensing* regards the entire collection of interest or its unities, their characteristics, interactions, and exposures. *External sensing* regards any unity and collection in the proximal and distal environments of the collection or unity of interest.

When performing native sensing of humans and living unities and their collections, there will be always a black box because sensing observes interactions of material energy only and not interaction with and of immaterial energy whose status can only be inferred when sensing material energy (Chapter 5). Therefore, *native assumptions* represent the black boxes for each collection/unity, meaning internal areas and aspects not directly sensed. Similarly, *external assumptions* refer to aspects, activities, and outputs of the proximal environment that cannot be directly sensed. Often, external sensing and assumptions are used to inform the design of native monitoring and interventions. Concurrent external and native monitoring represent the case of *anticipative sensing*.

For example, a business can conduct native sensing of its finances (i.e., energy status) at the overall company level (i.e., open native sensing) and in each of its sections with budgeting responsibilities (i.e., focussed native sensing). Depending on its financial targets, the business might act to adjust its activities, use of resources and other parameters. However, as businesses operate in the wider market and not in a vacuum, they also regularly sense the overall political, economic and competition environments (i.e., open external sensing) and possibly specific competitors or regions (i.e., focussed external sensing). Native sensing and this data will help shape business strategies, policies, and goals (i.e., anticipative sensing).

13.3 Management

Sensing triggers some processing that drives (in)actions (i.e., mobilisation or not of material energy). Typically, any (in)actions will retrofit the sensing stage under an iterative cycle of sense-process-(in)act-sense. From the viewpoint of energy exchange, any (in)action by humans and other living beings is:

- preceded by internal processing (i.e., immaterial energy) of the data sensed (i.e., incoming material energy), and

- shaped through the interplay between cognitive energy (i.e., cognitive associations) and affective energy (i.e., affective referents) related to the collections and unities involved (Sect. 5.4).

The sensing, processing and (in)acting stages embody the construct of *management* in its broader meaning, applying to all living unities and their participation in collections. Humans and every living unity are energy managers because they are exposed to energy, processes incoming or available energy and mobilise the energy accessible.

As such, in this book, by using the term management I do not refer to collections such as social and organisational systems, smaller or larger groups, and the environment, and I do not target physically unperceivable constructs such as quality, safety, security, and so on. In its wider meaning, management is neither about financial, production, health, safety, and other constructs, nor self-management, nor senior, department, and line managers. Such labels and classifications used in most management books can obscure the core notion of management's scope or purpose: energy sensing, processing, and (in)acting.

From a pragmatic perspective, for example, we cannot manage safety because it does not physically exist. However, we can manage energy with the goal of influencing whatever we have agreed the construct of safety represents. Similarly, we cannot manage quality but only the energy directed to areas related to what we have agreed that quality represents. The same applies to health, security, and other constructs.

Even further, we cannot manage social systems, teams, and individuals because the energy contained in humans does not belong to anyone. Organisational, department, team, and other managers do not directly 'manage people', as often implied. Instead, the role of a manager in any organisation and collection at any system level is to:

- gain a comprehensive understanding of the proximal and distant environments: sense what is happening inside and outside the collection and sense the capabilities of staff and other unities,
- process this information by considering Explicitly Agreed and Defined Objectives (Sect. 10.2), Explicitly Expected and Trusted Objectives (Sect. 10.5) and Implicitly Assumed and Trusted Objectives (Sect. 10.6), and
- distribute available energy (e.g., materials, information, instructions) across staff to achieve the objectives above.

Hence, for instance, a manager can allocate budget to departments and approve the purchase of new tools (i.e., increase energy), decide on success criteria (i.e., energy output quantity, quality, and timeliness), direct focus during different periods (i.e., when and where energy is to be used) and assign tasks to staff (i.e., who and how may use specific unities/energy sources). All the above do not correspond to managing directly people or systems but managing the energy available to self and those people and systems.

Understandably, as managing persons and organisations comprises standard terminology, the above can read controversial. Still, realising that someone manages the quantity, types, ways and other parameters of the energy that others use to deliver outcomes and does not directly manage others can help overcome the tensions between the constructs of management and control in organisational contexts.[1,2]

13.4 Processing

When managing, the rationalistic perspective claims that possible (in)actions must be the result of *analytic processing*: sense-analyse-(in)act.[3,4] Analytic processing engages mainly cognitive energy (i.e., cognitive associations) towards some form of decomposition of the units, collections, and constructs of interest in smaller parts. It is conducted typically through a top-down, deductive pathway, and can generate basic laws (Sect. 11.3).

For example, analytic processing is when a mechanic disassembles and tests different parts of complex equipment to identify the cause of a malfunction. A student might solve a complex equation by first breaking it down to smaller parts and then combining their results. A biologist studies a system through dissection and experiments to understand its parts and how they work together.

Synthetic processing is based predominantly on affective energy (i.e., affective referents): sense-synthesise-(in)act. Synthetic processing occurs principally with a convergent, bottom-up, inductive direction through the employment of schemas, stereotypes, beliefs, and other affective aspects to (in)act, without consistently engaging cognitive associations.[5,6] For instance, an experienced professional can classify some information as credible or not almost acutely without a thorough analysis.

Literature uses the term *naturalistic decision-making* to denote synthetic processing. However, this can lead to misperceptions that the opposite, that is analytic processing, is not 'natural' or 'realistic'. Besides, synthetic processing, also named in literature as System 2[7], can lead to emerging laws (Sect. 11.3). It is far faster and effortless compared to analytic processing, which is often called System 1.[7] Importantly, although focussed or open sensing mode will determine the area of interest, it

---

[1] Greenwald, H. P. (2007). *Organizations management without control*. SAGE.

[2] Sitkin, S. B., Sitkin, S. B., Cardinal, L. B., & Bijlsma-Frankema, K. (2010). *Organizational control*. Cambridge University Press.

[3] Tavana, M. (2012). *Decision making theories and practices from analysis to strategy*. Business Science Reference.

[4] De Felice, F., Saaty, T. L., & Petrillo, A. (2016). *Applications and theory of analytic hierarchy process—Decision making for strategic decisions*. InTech. https://doi.org/10.5772/61387

[5] Militello, L., Lipshitz, R., & Schraagen, J. M. (2008). *Naturalistic decision making and macrocognition*. Taylor & Francis Group.

[6] Salas, E., & Klein, G. A. (2001). *Linking expertise and naturalistic decision making*. L. Erlbaum Associates.

[7] Kahneman, D. (2011). *Thinking, fast and slow* (1st ed.). Farrar, Straus and Giroux.

does not directly define the processing mode. The processing mode can remain the same or alter between analytic and synthetic regardless of the sensing mode.

For example, when someone deals with a complex problem and is tired or exposed to adverse conditions (e.g., high temperature), they might not apply the same thorough analysis as under friendlier conditions. Instead of decomposing and systematically analysing (i.e., analytic processing) the situation of concern (i.e., focussed sensing), environmental stressors (i.e., open sensing) could lead this individual to synthesise quickly and converge whatever information they have perceived, or data collected (i.e., synthetic processing), and form a more abstract, possibly less accurate argument or less effective and sustainable solution.

Certainly, the processing mode could lead to the modification of the sensing mode and area before (in)acting. For instance, if a medical doctor believes the results of a generic blood examination (i.e., open sensing) cannot indicate categorically a specific health issue (i.e., analytical processing), they can refer the patient for additional tests with more specific biomarkers (i.e., focussed sensing). However, this actually corresponds to an action on the sensing activity. Switching between open and focussed sensing as well as changing the collection or unity of interest are forms of actions.

13.5 Urgency and Stability

In pragmatic terms, analytic and synthetic processing modes are not binary in the time continuum. They are usually blended, although they can take their extremes in smaller fractions of time. As such, *synthanaletic processing* is a reconciled point between analytical and synthetic processing. Two crucial parameters that can affect the processing mode are:

- the perception of urgency, which in professional settings normatively associates with the sense of responsibility, and
- whether the environment is relatively stable or dynamic, which partially implies controllability.

The higher the urgency and the more dynamic the environment, the more a unity moves towards synthetic processing. For example, acting as a first responder to a building under a fire will be most probably driven by synthetic processing. Conversely, preparing a presentation for a professional meeting under no time pressure might foster a more analytical approach.

The construct of urgency is typically linked to the perceived time availability to (in)act.[8,9] The less time we have before a deadline or negative outcome, the

[8] Magill, G., & Aramesh, K. (2016). *The urgency of climate change: Pivotal perspectives*. Cambridge Scholars Publishing.

[9] Spector, B. (2019). *Constructing crisis: Leaders, crises and claims of urgency*. Cambridge University Press.

more urgent it feels. However, although often the time available can be estimated, the sense of urgency can differ across individuals even under the same timeframes and conditions. Several books about time perception do not explicitly address the construct of urgency but agree that cognition and emotions play a determinative role in how we perceive time.[10,11,12]

Hence, from a more holistic approach that considers not only cognition and emotions but also material energy, *urgency* can be linked to the concept of overall energy state OES I introduced in Sect. 5.4 in conjunction with the time available. The greater the anticipated effects on OES of ourselves or other unities that we are concerned about or feels responsible for, the lower our perceived controllability in the specific context, and the less the time available, the higher our sense of urgency to (in)act.

Controllability represents collectively someone's:

- familiarity that allows them to employ cognitive associations for the specific context, and,
- confidence in considering different (in)action options and anticipating their effects on energy of themselves and others, and
- capability to mobilise their energy accordingly.

For instance, imagine an inexperienced professional receiving an unexpected request to report about a complex case (i.e., relatively low controllability), in a short time (i.e., short time available) and perceiving that a delayed or low-quality document would have negative consequences for the future of their employment (i.e., high effects on energy of self). This person would feel more urgency than an experienced professional who has dealt with several similar cases (i.e., relatively high controllability) who feels necessary or irreplaceable at work or confident of finding soon an excellent job elsewhere (i.e., acceptable or minor effects on energy).

Small deviations with a constant reappearance or low changing pace could create the impression there is still enough time to process and intervene. The impression is founded on the belief that future small deviations will be predictable and not lead to unfavourable consequences. Large deviations usually generate a pressure to process and act in a relatively short time, based on the presumption that such deviations would occur again, or their cascade effects could disturb several collections and unities directly or indirectly.

Effects on energy can include cases where material energy MES and affective energy AEB could be lowered (e.g., physical or psychological harm, loss of or damage to property) or where opportunities to increase or maintain MES or AEB are missed (e.g., someone is late at an important business meeting, one cannot join others in a

---

[10] Vatakis, A., Balcı, F., Di Luca, M., & Correa, Á. (2015). *Timing and time perception. Procedures, measures, and applications*. Brill.

[11] Grondin, S. (2019). *The perception of time: Your questions answered*. Taylor & Francis Group.

[12] Wearden, J. (2016). *The psychology of time perception*. Palgrave Macmillan UK. https://doi.org/10.1057/978-1-137-40883-9.

Table 13.1 Urgency levels

Urgency parameters			Urgency level
Anticipated effects on energy	Context-specific controllability	Perceived time available to (in)act before energy effects are realised	
HIGH	LOW	LIMITED	VERY HIGH
HIGH	LOW	ENOUGH	HIGH
HIGH	HIGH	LIMITED	
HIGH	HIGH	ENOUGH	MEDIUM
LOW	LOW	LIMITED	
LOW	LOW	ENOUGH	LOW
LOW	HIGH	LIMITED	
LOW	HIGH	ENOUGH	VERY LOW

conference trip). In Table 13.1 I present the different urgency levels based on energy, controllability and time availability.

In cases of very high urgency, irrespective of environmental conditions, we would expectedly get closer to synthetic processing. We would employ stored associations to cope with the situation swiftly and invest no-to-little time and cognitive energy in processing analytically the environment. For example, driving a familiar route, and suddenly hitting an unexpected obstacle, requires quick thinking.

Similarly, under a very low urgency level, we would again default to synthetic processing, as there would be no perceived need to invest cognitive energy in a more analytical processing. In the example above, if the driver is on a very familiar route, nothing irregular happens and there is no worry about arriving at the preferred destination at a specific time, they would not engage much in analysing the environment.

The difference is that in the former case of high urgency, the need to process more analytically might be acknowledged but remain almost impossible to meet, resembling the constructs of crisis and emergency.[13,14] In the second case, although the lack of urgency affords a more analytical approach, there is no perceived necessity for it, resembling the construct of complacency.[15,16]

In Table 13.2 I present the processing mode opportunities for various combinations of urgency levels and environmental conditions. I use 'opportunity' to avoid assuming a fixed level of maximum cognitive effort for each processing mode in Table 13.2.

---

[13] Farazmand, A. (2014). *Crisis and emergency management: Theory and practice* (2nd ed.). CRC Press.

[14] Blythe, B. (2016). *The manager's guide to quick crisis response: Effective action in an emergency.* Rothstein Publishing.

[15] Tushnet, M. (2005). *The constitution in wartime: Beyond alarmism and complacency.* Duke University Press.

[16] Gostin, L. O. (2003). *The AIDS pandemic: Complacency, injustice, and unfulfilled expectations.* University of North Carolina Press.

Table 13.2 Processing mode opportunities for urgency levels and environmental conditions

Urgency level	Environment	Processing mode opportunities
VERY HIGH	Any	SYNTHETIC
HIGH	Dynamic	SYNTHETIC
HIGH	Stable	MORE SYNTHETIC
MEDIUM	Dynamic	SYNTHANALETIC
MEDIUM	Stable	SYNTHANALETIC
LOW	Stable	MORE ANALYTIC
LOW	Dynamic	ANALYTIC
VERY LOW	Any	SYNTHETIC

This effort would range from minimum cognitive energy in synthetic processing to maximum cognitive energy investment during analytic processing.

Hence, a professional with opportunity for synthanaletic processing might process a developing situation more synthetically or more analytically than Table 13.2 suggests because of several reasons (e.g., feel more or less capable than they really are). Also, as all environments are dynamic to different degrees, the distinction between dynamic and stable environment in Table 13.2 is relative and associated with the construct of *predictability*. Whether people see an environment as stable or changing depends on how predictable they think it is.

The concepts I discussed above can be symbolically depicted as:

$$\textit{Processing mode} \propto f(\textit{urgency}, \textit{environmental stability}) \tag{13.1}$$

where,

$$\textit{Urgency} \propto f(\textit{anticipated energy effects}, \textit{controllability}, \textit{time available}) \tag{13.2}$$

13.6 Objectives and (In)actions

Instead of using the term threshold to label (in)actions as per current practice (Sect. 13.1), the broader construct of objectives, whether they are agreed EADO (Sect. 10.2), expected EETO (Sect. 10.5) or assumed IATO (Sect. 10.6), would be more inclusive to use. EADO, EETO and IATO capture more than agreed and established limits and boundaries regarding inputs, processes and outputs. EADOs, EETOs and IATOs can include those limits and boundaries, but encompass a wider range of activities, outputs and outcomes and their characteristics.

For example, the mandate for not over-speeding (i.e., EETO) is not exclusive to a specific speed limit-threshold. It regards both an activity (i.e., not to overspeed) and an output (i.e., the actual speed) with the intention to ensure safe outcomes for road users. The particular EETO regards limits in various contexts, such as 40 km/h in residential and school areas and 100 km/h in highways. Irrespective of location, someone should not drive over the applicable speed limit.

Objectives can be less deterministic and less focussed on the actual magnitude of constructs, rendering them even more inclusive. For instance, the objective of not harming others (i.e., expected objective EETO) captures all cases of physical and psychological harm without defining how much harm would be absolutely intolerable and by whom.

From an objectives' perspective, (in)actions are:

- *retrospective* when conducted after a collection or unity deviates from an objective.
- *prospective* when driven by indications of forthcoming deviations from an objective.
- *concerted* when they aim to change an objective.

Of note, concerted (in)actions are a special case and not triggered by foreseeable or actual deviations from the objectives, as such deviations would render any (in)action of objective prospective and retrospective, correspondingly. Concerted (in)actions source from external factors through external sensing (Sect. 13.2), such as when an organisation adopts best industry practices shared by a professional body.

In Table 13.3 I present the (in)action types based on the various combinations of time-points relative to meeting objectives and depending on the driving processing mode.

Management Redefined: Key Reflections and Actions

Reflections

- Management involves the orchestration of energy through sensing, processing, and (in)action, emphasising energy as the central resource in professional and organisational contexts.

Table 13.3 (In)action types for processing modes and objectives

Driving processing mode	(In)action types		
	After deviating from objective(s)	Before deviating from objective(s)	Changing the objective(s)
Preceded mainly by analysis and minimum synthesis	Retrospective Analytic	Prospective Analytic	Concerted Analytic
Preceded by some analysis and some synthesis	Retrospective Synthanaletic	Prospective Synthanaletic	Concerted Synthanaletic
Preceded mainly by synthesis and minimum analysis	Retrospective Synthetic	Prospective Synthetic	Concerted Synthetic

- Sensing requires gathering and interpreting signals from the environment, including material, cognitive, and emotional cues, to identify opportunities and challenges.
- Processing is the evaluation and prioritisation of sensed information, balancing immediate needs with long-term objectives to optimise energy allocation.
- (In)action reflects deliberate choices about when to act, when to pause, and how to direct energy, underscoring the importance of judgement in resource deployment.
- Urgency plays a pivotal role in management, requiring quick decision-making and energy-intensive actions. However, an overemphasis on urgency can destabilise systems if it undermines long-term stability.
- Effective management involves balancing urgency with stability, ensuring energy investments align with organisational goals and systemic sustainability.

Actions

1. Strengthen Sensing Capabilities: Evaluate the tools and methods you use for sensing environmental signals. Ensure they are robust enough to detect both urgent issues and slower-evolving trends.
2. Prioritise Urgency Thoughtfully: Distinguish between genuine urgency and perceived urgency. Avoid reactionary decision-making by assessing the actual impact and timing of each issue.
3. Optimise Energy Processing: Develop frameworks to process sensed information effectively. Use prioritisation strategies that account for both immediate needs and long-term stability.
4. Evaluate (In)action Choices: Reflect on situations where deliberate inaction might be more beneficial than hasty action. Consider how restraint can preserve energy and support stability.
5. Balance Immediate and Long-Term Goals: Integrate urgency management into your practices by aligning short-term responses with overarching organisational objectives and systemic resilience.
6. Promote Transparency in Urgency Scenarios: Communicate openly about urgency-related decisions. Ensure that team members understand priorities and the rationale behind energy allocations.

By balancing urgency with stability and integrating effective sensing, processing, and (in)action, you can foster sustainable, adaptive, and efficient practices that align with the dynamic demands of professional environments.

Chapter 14
Management Types

14.1 General

Considering the definitions and positions shared in Chapter 13, in Table 14.1 I suggest an alternative typology of management types aligned with the sensing, processing, and (in)acting constructs. The particular typology represents normative management types irrespective of temporal factors. In Table 14.1, the first classification variable regards the sensing scope and mode (i.e., where and what of sensing). The second classification variable corresponds to the focus of processing (i.e., what is under consideration). The third classification variable refers to the (in)action options (i.e., what can be possibly done, or not).

Of note, in Table 14.1, the term collection corresponds to the area of interest, with the term unity representing the collection participants. Both terms are subject to different levels of abstraction and decomposition (Sect. 10.4). Overall, the premise is that the type and mode of sensing drives various (in)action options which are supported by the processing focus.

The sensing concerned, for example, you can consider the entire collection (i.e., open sensing), and somebody else could sense unities or external collections (i.e., focussed sensing). Processing can focus on interactions (e.g., how and when staff interact), exposures (e.g., lighting levels to perform tasks), unities (e.g., specific clients), or characteristics of unities (e.g., health status of workers). (In)actions can relate to the organisation, design, alteration, improvement and maintenance of the area of focus, as those are defined in Table 14.1.

Regarding the (in)action options, perhaps removing unities or their interactions denotes alteration or improvement and not design and organisation, respectively. However, when you remove a unity or an interaction from a collection, you unavoidably change the proximal environment and its dynamics considerably. For instance, when a supervisor reduces the number of staff without changing the tasks and deliverables, the remaining staff might need to undertake the work of the removed

N. Karanikas, *Professional Generalism in a Hyper-specialised World*,
https://doi.org/10.1007/978-981-96-4039-3_14

Table 14.1 Normative management types

		Focus of processing				
		Relative: interactions with and exposures to proximal environment	*Exclusive: entire current unities**	*Restricted: characteristics** of current unities**		
		(In)actions options				
		Organisation: addition, replacement, removal or change of interactions with and exposures to proximal environment	*Design: addition, replacement or removal of current unities**	*Alteration: change of characteristics** of current unities**	*Improvement: adjustment of characteristics** of current unities**	*Maintenance: repair or recovery of characteristics** of current unities**
Sensing type (Sect. 13.2)	Sensing mode (Sect. 13.2)	Normative management types				
Native: collection of interest	*Open: entire collection of interest*	Prognostic Organisation	Prognostic Design	Prognostic Alteration	Prognostic Improvement	Prognostic Maintenance

(continued)

Table 14.1 (continued)

		Focus of processing				
		Relative: interactions with and exposures to proximal environment	*Exclusive: entire current unities**	*Restricted: characteristics** of current unities**		
		(In)actions options				
		Organisation: addition, replacement, removal or change of interactions with and exposures to proximal environment	*Design: addition, replacement or removal of current unities**	*Alteration: change of characteristics** of current unities**	*Improvement: adjustment of characteristics** of current unities**	*Maintenance: repair or recovery of characteristics** of current unities**
	Focussed: current unities, their characteristics and interactions or exposures	Diagnostic Organisation	Diagnostic Design	Diagnostic Alteration	Diagnostic Improvement	Diagnostic Maintenance
External: outside collections or unities	*Open or Focussed*	Extrinsic*** Organisation	Extrinsic Design	Extrinsic Alteration	Extrinsic Improvement	Extrinsic Maintenance

* Including medium unities facilitating interactions and exposures (Sect. 10.2)
** Physical aspects or inferential features (Sect. 2.3)
***Extrinsic types can complement prognostic and diagnostic types

ones, leading to some interactions vanishing and others emerging, weakening, or intensifying.

Effects like the ones above are not always apparent in the cases of alteration and improvement since these action options target principally the characteristics within unities to enhance their activities (i.e., react, self-change, and transform others—Sect. 11.1) and bring those and their outputs within the objectives' envelope. Like most interventions, these changes may affect the immediate environment. Still, all these effects are by-products of the main intended goal of these actions.

For example, a head of a department focusses on the interactions of its personnel with technology (i.e., relative processing focus) by monitoring them holistically without fixating on particular staff member or equipment (i.e., open sensing). The head could act through prognostic organisation to re-arrange these interactions (e.g., who and when to use what and where).

Another option would be prognostic design by replacing some equipment that can be detrimental or inconvenient to any staff. Also, prognostic alteration or improvement of some technical features of equipment could be considered for matching those with the job needs and the capabilities of staff. Prognostic maintenance would ensure the useful and necessary functions of the specific equipment are available to all workers when needed.

Of note, in the example above, the first management action was based on open sensing and relative processing focus, jointly representing the most abstract case of prognostic organisation. However, some of the subsequent (in)actions focussed on specific unities as we do not need to intervene in everything to ensure the desired objective.

Still, any (in)actions directed to particular parts of a collection should still aim to influence the 'whole' and be monitored for effectiveness through an 'open sensing' mode. Otherwise, the initially aimed holistic approach to managing a collection could drift to a localised and narrow scope of (in)actions. Ignoring this case might derail any management plans, and generate unintended side effects (e.g., specific staff members feeling targeted).

In Table 14.1 I do not suggest a hard line between the various management types. It does not mean to present them as exclusive cases with strict boundaries. At each time-point, management types for the same collection can differ depending on several parameters (e.g., resources, urgency, external pressures). The classification is introduced to inform management planning through the various options and, conversely, to identify more accurately the scope of processing focus and sensing mode of any management actions already applied.

As such, moving from the left to the right in Table 14.1 could correspond to contexts with diminishing available energy but also environments with finger-pointing, overly judgmental, and blameful approaches to failures. Therefore, the classification in Table 14.1 does not make a value judgement on management types, as there can be multiple factors influencing them.

14.2 Consistent Management

In principle, sensing and acting should align in their level of abstraction or detail, and (in)acting should be supported by the corresponding processing mode. This means that we should not judge the aspects of one unity when sensing the collection and having no monitoring mechanisms specifically tailored to its unities. Inversely, it is not sound to judge the aspects of a collection when sensing any of its unities specifically and having no monitoring mechanisms specifically tailored to the collection as a single entity.

Attributing collection success only to momentary activities and outputs of some of the unities relative to the entire time span the collection exists is illogical and unfair. Similarly, it is unreasonable to evaluate individuals based solely on overall collection performance. When you sense only a collection with a specific periodicity, you record information about the collection at specific time-points. Thus, from a logical and pragmatic perspective, you are not aware of its unities at those time-points and about the collection and the unities between those time-points.

The success or failure of a unity to achieve its objectives at some point, a case that can be revealed during a special investigation or inquiry, represents little to nothing about the overall performance of the specific unity throughout time. Correspondingly, if you sense some unities of a collection (e.g., because of resource limitations), you record information and can confidently conclude about the particular unities alone.

Any inference about the performance of the entire collection based on sensing some of its unities is illogical, if not dangerous, because of the arbitrary inferences and assumptions that can be made. To ensure consistency and fairness, you must sense and process a unity in its entirety before (in)acting on the unity in its entirety. You must sense and process a collection in its entirety before (in)acting on the collection in its entirety.

Thus, each of the normative management types derived from the correspondences between sensing, processing, and (in)acting presented in Table 14.1 reflects an alignment across them and represents *consistent management* (Fig. 14.1).

Hence, replacing whole unities after processing only some of their characteristics signals a misalignment: the processing regarded parts of the unity whereas the action affected the entire unity. For instance, if we monitor a company's performance at the level of departments, we are expected to process and intervene in the aspects representing the same level: the departments. This means we should consider the inputs, activities, and outputs of each department as a single unity.

Indeed, triggered by department-wide measurements, someone would process and action with a focus on a specific sub-section of a department because it was, for example, the one with the lowest achievement in any objective. Here, however, they would exclude unities or sub-collections of the department interacting with the particular sub-section (i.e., proximal environment). This could flag an incomplete and invalid approach.

In connection with the concepts introduced in Chapter 13, when somebody has fever, which is a body-wide sign of physical state (i.e., native, open sensing), they

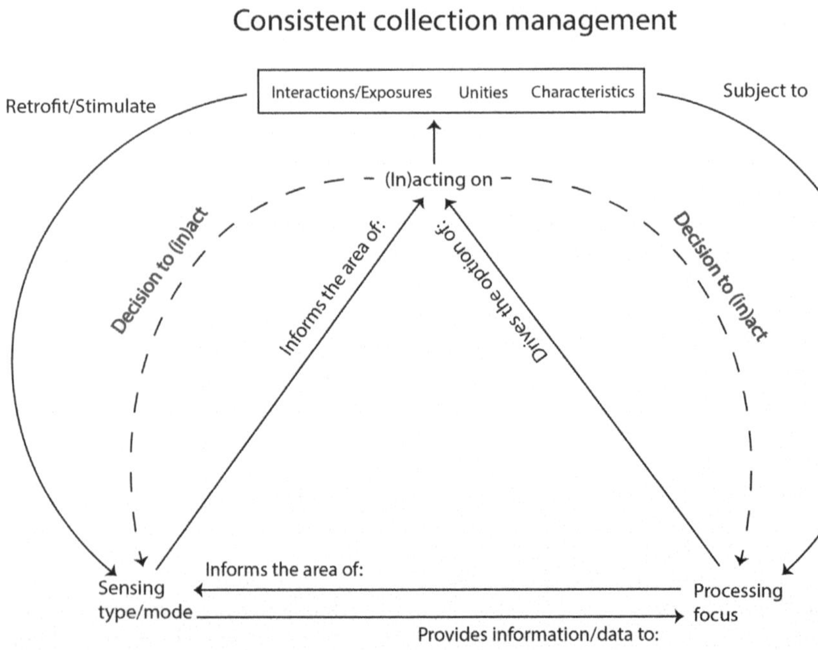

Fig. 14.1 Consistent collection management

usually want to action to protect themselves from any harm. Considering that fever represents a case where the body's temperature already exceeded a threshold (e.g., 37.8 °C for adults), the situation corresponds to retrospective action. If the person had acted because they sensed a rise in the temperature before reaching the level of fever, it could be proactive action.

Fever signals that something is happening with the individual's body sub-unities (e.g., antibody unities fighting bacteria unities). Using previous experience (i.e., own cognitive energy) or stored information from elsewhere (i.e., external sensing), the individual might just take paracetamol to fight fever (i.e., retrospective synthetic action). Here, they target the whole body-collection without knowing which of its sub-unities contribute to the problem at the time (i.e., prognostic improvement or maintenance).

If the body temperature drops, and the individual has no fever anymore, the only thing they know is that the drug somehow acted on the symptom. The person remains still unaware of the underlying problems that led to the unfavourable phenomenon of fever, which is a manifestation of material energy dysfunctions internally. Overall, management in the example above can be labelled as consistent. It represents cases where a collection-wide intervention (i.e., medicine) might have the desired results (i.e., lower the body temperature) without knowing how exactly this intervention worked and which unities and how were contributing to a deviation from an objective (i.e., not developing fever).

As I discussed in Sect. 8.2, cases like the example above sometimes occur with epidemiological studies, where reliable and repeated observations of associations between factors and diseases lead to decisions to implement preventive actions even before the exact mechanisms linking the factors with the diseases are known.[1] In an organisational setting, for instance, policies might have the desirable effect, although we cannot really know whether and how these policies worked for each collection and staff member and to what degree for each of them.

Additionally, it's hard to determine if the positive results were solely due to the specific policies or other factors within the organisation. The only information managers have is that after publishing the policies they observed a more desired output; nobody could establish any definite cause-effect relationship or explanation at this point.

In the fever example, had the individual inquired what might have caused the fever and had mitigated any factors, they would have demonstrated retrospective synthanaletic actions and consistent management. Somebody might not also actually know if the drop in the temperature occurred because of the paracetamol alone or in conjunction with other factors (e.g., their immune system had already started suppressing the bacteria).

There might be occasions that the fever returns often, or the medicine cannot offer any relief (i.e., native, open sensing). This is when someone could visit the medical doctor who would examine more specific unities (i.e., focussed sensing) that could provide clues about why the unwanted output-fever occurs. The doctor processes the data and information from focussed sensing, this indicating exclusive processing that can be analytic or synthanaletic depending on the degree to which the doctor has unambiguous data or uses judgement, respectively.

If, for instance, the left kidney is diagnosed with problematic functioning, the doctor can prescribe drugs or refer the individual to a specialist to restore the kidney's functions through an operation or other means (i.e., diagnostic maintenance) or, in the worst-case scenario, remove it or replace it (i.e., diagnostic design). Once more, the actions above correspond to consistent management. Another case could be that a few days after fighting the fever through medicine, the person visits their doctor to check if everything looks right. This case would represent a prospective analytic or synthanaletic action.

Now imagine a medical specialist removing a patient's kidney based only on the overall status of their health and without examining the kidney or other body sub-unities. This would be retrospective synthetic action and inconsistent management because it combined open sensing (i.e., generic health exam tests) with diagnostic design (i.e., removal of kidney). Should there be no timely access to focussed sensing (e.g., kidney-focussed tests) and the patient's biological life was at risk, inconsistent management would be the sole option. This is the reason Table 14.1 refers to 'normative' management types, as there can be several justifiable exceptions from the norm, as discussed further in Sect. 14.3.

---

[1] Gordis, L. (2014). *Epidemiology* (5th Ed.). Saunders.

Also, had the doctor sensed abnormal kidney's functions through special tests and proceeded with an operation without being very confident about the effects of other underlying or broader issues (e.g., blood quality, interactions with other organs), it would be retrospective synthanaletic action and still consistent management. On each occasion above, it would sound illogical if the person had cursed their problematic kidney and named it useless, although it was contributing to their physical well-being all the time before it was involved in a health problem.

The doctor and the patient might not be entirely sure that it was the kidney's contribution alone and nothing external to it such as poor blood quality (i.e., proximal environment of the kidney), which, in turn, can be affected by dietary habits and the physical environment (i.e., active interactions of the body with the proximal environment). Such probabilities can be investigated through further focussed sensing, based on information from external sensing and followed by respective analytical or synthanaletic processing before deciding to (in)act.

14.3 Misaligned Management

Misaligned management here does not mean phenomena like personal behaviours that conflict with formal objectives or priorities. When considering the definition of management in this book, misaligned management presents conditions where sensing, processing, and (in)acting do not accord with each other, as discussed in Sect. 14.2. Paradoxically, effective management does not always require perfectly aligned sensing, processing, and (in)acting. While consistent management is ideal, partial misalignment can still be effective. Some misalignments might be acceptable, or even advantageous in some cases.

For instance, in a large hospital's emergency department (ED), perfect alignment would look like detailed monitoring of each individual patient case, staff member, and piece of equipment (i.e., focussed sensing), in-depth analysis of each data point collected (i.e., analytic processing) and proactive interventions precisely matched to the level of data collection and analysis (i.e., prospective analytic actions). However, in real-world conditions, this theoretically perfect alignment would be paralysing in an ED setting. The time required to maintain such consistency could severely impact the department's ability to handle emergencies effectively.

Hence, from a pragmatic perspective, some misalignment would be beneficial and effective. Sensing could include a mix of broad department-level metrics (e.g., wait times and patient volumes) along with specific monitoring of critical cases. Processing could incorporate quick synthesis of department-level data for overall flow management, but detailed analysis only for serious incidents. Then, some actions would be taken at the macro-collection level (e.g., adjusting staffing or opening overflow areas) based on general trends, while other actions could be highly unity-specific (e.g., intervening in individual critical cases).

The key in the example above is that the misalignment is intentional and managed. The emergency department accepts some inconsistency between sensing, processing, and action levels because it serves the greater purpose of effective emergency care. However, extreme misalignment would still be problematic, like implementing major departmental changes based on a single case, or trying to manage individual patient care based only on department-level statistics.

We cannot discourage and deny interventions in unities when monitoring collection-level aspects only. If a particular unity does not meet an objective, there are options to replace, alter, improve, or maintain it, as per Table 14.1, subject to the respective processing mode. However, using only unity-focussed options will not automatically improve the collection's performance. This is because the unities of the proximal environment with which the 'underperforming' unity of interest was interacting have been excluded from focussed sensing and processing.

Focussing only on output-related objectives at specific time-points and not monitoring input- and activity-related objectives renders us ignorant of what was happening with particular unities before noticing a problem in the collection and discovering these unities underperformed. A focus on unities stemming from collection sensing and aiming at collection objectives represents *opportunistic management*.

Reversely, introducing collection-level changes when monitoring only specific unities corresponds to *presumptive management*. Although possible from a pragmatic perspective, none of the management types above can be named as perfectly consistent as they rely on pieces of general information to intervene in the specifics or exploit partial information to drive actions for the whole, correspondingly.

For instance, during a construction project, the site manager observes some delays in installing the hydraulic system. If for this reason the manager disciplines the team leader of the particular section or believes that the project planner was at fault and that 'fixing' those will improve project performance, it is opportunistic management. Similarly, poor plant performance should not justify replacing all similar plants on this or future projects. This would flag presumptive management.

14.4 Paradoxical Expectations

Despite having defined the construct of management more broadly in Chapter 13, as it has been typically linked to organisations, in this section, I cover some paradoxes in organisational settings. Those paradoxes equally apply to any human collection where people hold assigned roles, such as parents and children in families, authorities and companies in jurisdictions, and leaders and members in teams. Thus, the reference to the roles of manager and worker or similar terms in this section correspond to any human collection where there is a structure, typically an (atypical) system or group with agreed objectives and expected objectives (Chapter 10), and there are assigned responsibilities and accountabilities in managing available energy (Chapter 15).

First, not all companies review every small problem. (e.g., minor operational disturbance occurrences). The reason is that such deviations can be very frequent, requiring considerable resources to process, even with the support from modern technologies like artificial intelligence. Hence, some companies track objectives (e.g., degree of achieving a production target over time or in specific production lines) to inform focussed processing and possible (in)actions. A few other businesses handle deviations from objectives based on criteria like 'first time occurred'.

From a pragmatic perspective, any of the strategies above seem reasonable. Numerous deviations can occur daily at the workplace and can take different forms, such as small oscillations in the performance of equipment, the expiration of recalibration interval of a technical tool, and the inapplicability of procedures locally in specific circumstances. Typically, such deviations are not systematically captured and analysed unless they have significant effects. Analysing every deviation would rather look like half of a business managing [i.e., sensing, processing, and (in)acting] the other half.

However, interestingly, several organisations expect, and sometimes dictate, that workers must sense, process analytically and (in)act upon all deviations happening during their tasks. Whereas, as discussed above, it could be justifiable at the company level to not always and immediately act on deviations, many managers expect that when staff detect deviations, they should stop, think, collect data, ask for information, compare, assess, report and so on before proceeding or not with any (in)actions.

Thus, some managers may grant themselves the privilege of primarily synthetic processing when dealing with the frequent deviations they sense, and they may assume for themselves the authority to proceed or not with further (synth)analysis. However, the same managers might rarely recognise the same privilege to workers. Instead, personnel must always process deviations analytically and, at worst, synthanaletically. There are even managers who view workers' synthetic processing as unacceptable.

For instance, if a staff member responds intuitively to a situation (e.g., respond to a client's request) without synthetic thinking because of several reasons (e.g., inadequate time, fatigue), and the result is unfavourable (e.g., the client complains), some managers could see this a 'foolish' act. This judgement could be made although intuitive responses by the same worker in the past had resulted in happy clients, saved time, and increased productivity as the worker did not need to invest energy and time to process analytically each single situation. When those managers decide about the next important project or investment based mainly on intuition and some cursory information and not indisputable data, they would probably forgive themselves in case of a failure.

Another paradox regards change priorities and expectations. Large-scale interventions that necessitate a combination of action options, ranging from repairs to re-organisation, typically need increased energy investment. Sometimes, driven by the reality of limited resources, management can label such extensive changes as not urgent. Usually, the larger the intervention and the scarcer the resources, the lower its perceived urgency.

However, such changes expectedly source from intensive native and external sensing and synthanaletic or analytic processing, which logically underline the necessity of the changes. Someone would decide investing energy in implementing large-scale interventions only if these were deemed necessary. Hence, the paradox lies in the fact that despite the magnitude of the recognised need, management could postpone its satisfaction.

As an additional paradox, when managers finally decide to progress with any changes (e.g., introducing new equipment, revising standards and procedures, changing shifts and team compositions), they expect that employees will action those changes within presumably reasonable timeframes. Such expectations might neglect that these necessary changes, which from a desk-office perspective could seem simple or relatively easy to implement, may be resource-demanding from the perspective of individual workers.

Personnel might have to reorganise and redesign their proximal environment and their physical and cognitive states to action changes. This effort and the consequent emotional load and effects are rarely considered when planning. At best, these organisations will schedule some sessions to train the staff involved. In reality, workers might delay doing what managers want if it takes too much effort.

Under a condition of scarcity mentality,[2] where staff believe resources are limited and that they need to hoard or compete for them, they would prefer to complete other tasks and process smaller changes first to ensure productivity. This is how many individuals usually prioritise (in)actions despite literature suggesting that in various contexts it is advised to prioritise what matters most.[3,4,5] Instead, in the name of productivity,[6,7,8] several people often focus on the smaller tasks first because they require less time and energy.

Hence, staff might leave the more extensive and demanding tasks for later. Of course, in the meantime more of small, required actions could emerge, and the larger ones could be postponed further. As smaller tasks providing quick wins can emerge daily, the endorsement and effective realisation of bigger changes might be significantly delayed.

Ironically, managers sometimes criticise employee delays but excuse their own. For instance, the extensive project for the re-organisation and redesign of the work environment to comfort employees might seem beneficial, but it would not harm

---

[2] Mullainathan, S., & Shafir, E. (2014). *Scarcity: The true cost of not having enough*. Penguin.

[3] Shallenberger, R., & Shallenberger, S. (2021). *Do what matters most: lead with a vision, manage with a plan, prioritise your time*. Berrett-Koehler Publishers, Inc.

[4] Wilson, L. (2012). *Criminal major case management: Persons of interest priority assessment tool (POIPAT)*. Taylor & Francis Group.

[5] Harrin, E. (2022). *Managing multiple projects: how project managers can balance priorities, manage expectations and increase productivity*. Kogan Page, Limited.

[6] Allen, D. (2003). *Getting things done*. Penguin Putnam.

[7] Basco, M. R. (2010). *The procrastinator's guide to getting things done*. Guilford Press.

[8] Bate, N. (2015). *Boost your productivity: A shortcut to getting things done and getting your life sorted*. Capstone.

to delay its delivery for some time. However, any postponements in implementing changes management decided could be unimaginable.

Last, in theory, initial conditions of accurate sensing, low urgency, and a stable environment afford a more thorough decision-making process and space for securing resources and acting prospectively. However, nobody can guarantee that everything will be actioned as expected and will meet the intended objectives within the timeframes planned. This could mainly occur because of the low ability to mobilise material energy through interactions between material, cognitive, and affective energies (Sects. 5.3 and 5.4). Hence, inactions can result from such inabilities or difficulties and not any deficiency in the way energy was sensed and processed to decide the actions or endorse and implement them.

Someone might have processed information proactively and decided to act prospectively. Still, because of various energy-related factors (e.g., past negative experiences, difficulty to recall information), they could act with a delay and perhaps retrospectively instead of prospectively as originally planned. Numerous instances show individuals perceiving threats, prompting flight, but experiencing temporary or complete paralysis.

In organisational settings, it is not rare that managers assume employees understand what a change entails (e.g., workers attended training) but in reality, staff do not implement it to the expected standard because of several energy-related reasons (e.g., physically tired, mentally stressed, low job motivation). The potential of humans, other unities and collections to mobilise their material energy is a key factor, alongside processing, (in)action, and normative management types.

If there is insufficient energy, low-quality energy, or inaccessible energy, and if one's energies interact in ways that hinder timely and effective decision-making, then any well-planned management type could fail, even under conditions of ideal alignment between processing and actioning (Sect. 14.2). As such, maximum, partial, and minimum ability to mobilise the material energy available correspond to *strong management potential*, *average management potential*, and *weak management potential*, correspondingly.

The concepts discussed in the sections above can be symbolically depicted as:

$$\textit{Management potential} \propto f(\textit{normative management type},\ \textit{ability to mobilise available material energy}) \quad (14.1)$$

where,

$$\textit{Normative management type} \propto f(\textit{sensing mode}, \textit{processing focus}, (\textit{in})\textit{action option}) \quad (14.2)$$

Management Types: Key Reflections and Actions

Reflections

- Management can take various forms based on the alignment between sensing modes, processing approaches, and (in)action options. These types are broadly categorised as consistent, opportunistic, and presumptive management.
- Consistent Management aligns sensing, processing, and (in)actions coherently, ensuring decisions are evidence-based, deliberate, and effective across contexts. It emphasises stability and systematic planning.
- Opportunistic Management leverages emerging opportunities, often requiring quick adaptation and flexible decision-making. While it can yield innovative outcomes, it may carry risks if poorly timed or unsupported by thorough sensing.
- Presumptive Management relies on assumptions or incomplete sensing, potentially leading to decisions that lack grounding in current realities. While sometimes necessary in uncertain scenarios, it must be applied cautiously to avoid misalignment.
- Misaligned management—where sensing, processing, and (in)actions are disconnected—can result in inefficiencies, wasted energy, and negative outcomes. However, in specific contexts can be unavoidable and even useful.

Actions

1. Identify Your Management Type: Reflect on your dominant management approach. Consider whether it aligns with the needs of your role, team, and organisation.
2. Foster Consistency: Prioritise consistent management by ensuring that sensing, processing and actions are integrated. Develop frameworks that support alignment and long-term planning.
3. Balance Opportunism with Caution: When adopting opportunistic management, assess the risks and potential rewards thoroughly. Use sensing tools to validate opportunities before acting.
4. Recognise and Mitigate Presumptions: Identify instances where you rely on presumptive management. Seek additional information or perspectives to reduce assumptions and improve decision accuracy.
5. Address Misalignments: Analyse past decisions to identify misalignments between sensing, processing, and (in)actions. Use these insights to refine your approach and manage better similar situations in the future.
6. Adapt Management to Context: Acknowledge that different scenarios require different management styles. Be flexible in adjusting your approach to align with dynamic professional and organisational contexts.

By understanding the types of management and striving for alignment between sensing, processing, and (in)actions, you can optimise decision-making, adapt to changing circumstances, and achieve sustainable outcomes in your professional and organisational practices.

Chapter 15
Accountability, Responsibility, and Trust

15.1 General

This chapter explores accountability and responsibility in human systems using energy management as a framework. There are many publications about those constructs, although several works target more the corporate level and link accountability and responsibility with negative outcomes.[1,2,3] This is understandable, as there is a tendency to associate those concepts with legal proceedings and arguments.

Accountability and responsibility apply to every setting, and we should approach those terms from a broader viewpoint. As argued below, when managing energy, there is no option to avoid accountability and responsibility. Ignoring responsibilities and accountability does not make them disappear.

The energy we are authorised to manage is the material and immaterial energies within the boundaries of our physical bodies, the energy of the external material unities we possess, and the unities trusted in us as *energy custodians*. Possessions and unities trusted in anyone are defined by various *codes*, meaning the broad web of conventions, legislation, rules, agreements, contracts, and other similar constructs at international, national, regional, societal levels, and types of human collections.

As I discussed in Sect. 12.1, all those forms of written and unwritten codes deal with the possession, distribution, and exchange of energy. They express expectations of '*who, when, why, where, what and how' (5W&H)* of managing energy, and while changing with time, they remain relatively defined within particular time periods. Therefore, apart from ourselves, of which nowadays people have full ownership in most countries, those ever-evolving codes allow us to possess other material unities

---

[1] Crowther, D. (2016). *Accountability and social responsibility: International perspectives*. Emerald Group Publishing Limited.

[2] Dealy, M., & Thomas, A. (2007). *Managing by accountability what every leader needs to know about responsibility, integrity and results*. Praeger.

[3] Demirag, I. (2005). *Corporate social responsibility, accountability and governance: Global perspectives*. Greenleaf Pub.

N. Karanikas, *Professional Generalism in a Hyper-specialised World*,
https://doi.org/10.1007/978-981-96-4039-3_15

and collections such as dwellings, vehicles, books, tools, equipment, and so on either exclusively or partially (e.g., 50% share of a business).

We are also trusted in managing the energy of several unities temporarily. Material unities being shared or trusted are usually owned by other collections or individuals or by nobody. For instance, we all use material resources to perform our duties at work. Those resources do not belong to us, but they are trusted in us under the expectation we will utilise them to deliver according to agreed objectives (Sect. 10.2).

When you attend a meeting at the client's premises, there are shared facilities you can use (e.g., toilets and car parking). These facilities represent material energy you do not possess, but others trust in you for a short time under some expected objectives (Sect. 10.5). The same happens when I borrow money or anything physical from others, as the lenders trust in me the use of whatever I borrowed.

15.2 Accountability and Responsibility

Possession and trust sourcing from codes, which presumably accommodate the expectations of the majority or the ones most in need, assume *accountability* towards the individuals or human collections who allow us to manage possessed and trusted energy and inform them about the 5W&H of managing this energy. When a company rents a car to a person holding a driver's licence, and the company staff has explained and reiterated the codes applicable (e.g., when to return the car, mandate to maintain the vehicle in a good condition), the customer becomes accountable to the company. The company is accountable to the society and various agents through different codes to observe the 5W&H regarding the permitted use of the car possessed. For example, the insurance company might have set restrictions on who the company can let drive their rental cars.

Accountability is inevitable for every individual belonging to a human collection or interacting with individuals and human collections. Only if someone lives completely isolated from other humans and ensures their energy management does not knowingly influence the energy belonging to, possessed by, or trusted in others can be free of accountability. The ones who through societal evolution and social contracts have been delegated with the authority to introduce, change, withdraw, and communicate codes are accountable to the ones those codes target and represent. Governments, regulators, agencies, councils, boards, and any individual or human collection involved in decision-making and enforcement of codes are accountable to the ones they represent and serve.

In the example stated above, authorities are accountable to the society, including the company and the customer, about the quantity, quality, and timeliness of the 5W&H provided (e.g., about mandatory car inspections) and the infrastructure offered. The company personnel are similarly accountable to the authorities and the society about the codes communicated to their customers and the roadworthiness of the rental vehicles. Too much or too little, too complex or too vague, too late or too early can equally cause unwanted issues, as I explained in Sect. 10.2 about agreed objectives.

The ones who under current codes acceptably and consciously receive energy from somebody are expected to respect the defined 5W&H. They become automatically accountable for the use of the energy received and placed under their control. Therefore, the customer is directly accountable to the rental company (i.e., the possessor of the car) and the authorities and the society (i.e., the possessors of the infrastructure) when driving and parking the car. As the authorities and the society trust the customer-driver to use their car according to established codes (e.g., traffic and driving rules), there is the driver-authorities/society accountability line. Thus, within human collections, and especially social systems, accountability is cyclical and mutual even if we do not always realise this.

Flipping over the construct of accountability provides the construct of *responsibility*. Those constructs are not opposing or unrelated; they are the two sides of the same coin. Since we are all receivers and transmitters of energy during interactions, we are responsible towards the receivers of the energy we transmit and accountable towards the transmitters or trustees of the energy we agreeably receive, possess, or use. As with accountability, responsibility is also a cyclical and mutual construct within human collections.

Continuing the example above, the rental company is responsible for the energy transmitted to the customer: the car and the necessary rules. The driver is responsible towards the society for using the car and infrastructure as per the 5W&H decided by the authorities. We are all responsible for influencing authorities to shape, change, and cancel the respective codes when they do not further serve their purpose. Besides, authorities are responsible for defining and communicating those codes back to 'energy managers', such as infrastructure organisations, drivers, rental companies, and maintenance and inspection workshops.

Besides, if we exercise responsibility, meaning we are aware of the energy we manage and the degree to which we apply the expected 5W&H, then it is easier for us to express our accounts. If we are not aware of our responsibilities, then we cannot express any accounts; literally, we have no accounts to tell. Here, although accountable to the trustees, we render themselves 'accountless'. Accounts are stories which are subject to validity and reliability (Chapter 7); if responsibilities are not exercised, neither valid nor reliable accounts are feasible.

15.3 Retrospectively and Prospectively

We sometimes realise our accountability after negative events occur. In such cases, after comparing energy management practices and their respective outcomes against the defined codes, we realise late what exactly for we were responsible, hence expressing only *retrospective accounts*. When we are aware of our responsibilities, we might express *prospective accounts*. These include, for example, clarification requests, feedback on rules implementation, energy requests, and discussions about the quality and suitability of the energy we manage.

Also, although sharing energy resources renders all sharers accountable and responsible for collective outcomes, we all remain individually accountable and responsible for the energy we manage under any agreed objectives and 5W&H per unit of time. Personal responsibility is not replaced by, nor does it guarantee, collective responsibility and vice versa.

The most prominent example is the physical environment we all share. It belongs to nobody, but we are all trusted in managing it according to various formal and informal codes and objectives. Each of us does not manage the whole environment, but the part we interact with. However, the way each of us manages this energy part affects the overall environment and interacts with others' energy management. The outcomes of our management of energy proliferate to the entire environment.

By extension, adherence to objectives and codes when managing energy (i.e., own, possessed, and trusted energy) does not mean we are absolved from our accountabilities if the outputs of our energy management, which inescapably regards our proximal environment, threatens the energy owned by and available to others in the distant environment. We are all expected to minimise any foreseeable or reported side effects on others which might not be direct recipients of our energy management. Otherwise, we indirectly, but wittingly, interfere with the management of energy available to others, over which we have not been explicitly delegated the authority to influence.

The concept above can seem overwhelming when you contemplate how you would manage all the energy you get exposed to and evaluate how your actions might affect the energy of other unities close and far from you. Indeed, we cannot do this continually and reliably, although theoretically possible from a merely rational and mechanistic perspective.

Also, we always interact with incoming energy, the exposure to which we cannot always control. We cannot maintain continuous open sensing for too long as we must direct our resources to the management of energy for which we are responsible. Often, we cannot deal with everything at once and we inevitably filter, prioritise, evaluate, choose, etc. (Sect. 16.2).

This is the reason humanity relies on mutual trust and continuous energy exchange under agreed and expected objectives and respective codes to support each other. This is why we trust each other that we will not intentionally degrade the energy available to each one and will not wittingly neglect, reject, and disregard any inputs from others and the applicable codes without a good reason.

Admittedly, each code regards a particular area of energy management and exchange and is issued irrespective of the capabilities of unities and collections over time, the variances in those capabilities across unities and the necessity to manage more than one area concurrently. Thus, it can be that some individuals are not informed about all applicable codes or do not have the capability to memorise, comprehend, and realise several of them.

As such, the knowledge of yours can become useful information for everyone. Each one of us must function as a '*responsibility reminder*' for others who, for any reason, do not manage their internal, possessed and trusted energy as per the agreed and expected objectives and applicable codes. Each one of us must fearlessly function as an '*accountability guardian*' by holding others into account for intentionally mismanaging energy or neglecting their responsibilities.

Accountability, Responsibility, and Trust: Key Reflections and Actions

Reflections

- Accountability and responsibility are central to effective management and professional practice. They encompass acknowledging obligations, making informed decisions, and owning the outcomes of actions.
- Accountability is retrospective, focussing on being answerable for past actions and their results. It requires transparency, clear roles, and consistent evaluation mechanisms.
- Responsibility is prospective, emphasising proactive commitment to tasks, decisions, and their anticipated consequences. It involves foresight, planning, and readiness to adapt.
- Trust acts as the foundation for accountability and responsibility, fostering collaboration, mutual respect, and shared goals within teams and organisations.
- Balancing retrospective and prospective perspectives ensures that both lessons from the past and planning for the future are integrated into professional decision-making and actions.

Actions

1. Clarify Roles and Expectations: Clearly define roles, responsibilities, and expectations within your team or organisation. Ensure all members understand their obligations and accountability structures.
2. Promote Transparency: Establish open communication channels to share successes, challenges, and lessons learned. Transparency builds trust and enhances mutual understanding of accountability.
3. Foster a Trust-Based Culture: Actively cultivate trust within your team by demonstrating integrity, consistency, and empathy. Recognise that trust is both a prerequisite and an outcome of effective collaboration.
4. Balance Retrospective and Prospective Views: Regularly evaluate past decisions and their outcomes to inform future planning. Use this balance to refine your approaches to accountability and responsibility.
5. Develop Mechanisms for Accountability: Implement systems to monitor progress, evaluate performance, and ensure that responsibilities are fulfilled. These mechanisms should be fair, objective, and adaptable.
6. Encourage Shared Responsibility: Promote a sense of collective responsibility within your team. Encourage individuals to support each other in achieving shared goals while maintaining accountability for their contributions.

By integrating accountability, responsibility, and trust into your professional practices, you can create a cohesive, transparent, and collaborative environment that enhances both individual and collective performance.

Part V
Appraisal Concepts

Chapter 16
Differences and Gaps (DaGs)

16.1 General

As I discussed in Sect. 11.3, our decisions and deeds can be conscious or unconscious. The former case is attributed to engaging more our System 2 (i.e., serial, effortful, and rational processing of information) and the latter case relates to employing mainly System 1 (i.e., parallel, fast, and emotional responses to stimuli).[1] However, it does not mean by default that engaging System 1 would always lead to negative events and using System 2 would always yield fruitful results.

Both systems serve important purposes, and neither is inherently 'better'. System 1 often leads to positive outcomes (e.g., expert intuition, emergency responses) and System 2 can lead to suboptimal outcomes (e.g., paralysis by analysis, overthinking). Yet, there has been an unsubstantiated tendency to associate retrospectively unfavourable events with the prevalence of System 1 and positive outcomes with System 2.

This tendency is based on the mechanistic premise that the more information someone processes consciously, the more successful they will become. Indeed, this does not stand scientifically and pragmatically as many, if not most, daily activities and body movements of humans are 'automatic', meaning System 1 regulates them. Detailed plans based more on System 2 processes do not always guarantee success; projects can still be over budget and late.

The System 1–2 approach portrays effectively the opportunities for several gaps longitudinally for the same individual and cross-sectionally for different persons depending on which system is engaged, when, where, why, and by whom. I have excluded the 'how' from this list because if we knew how to (dis)engage any of the two systems, we would function under System 2 constantly; any contemplation of System 1 would be void. Only in hindsight can we realise we have predominantly used

[1] Kahneman, D. (2011). *Thinking, fast and slow*. Farrar, Straus and Giroux.

N. Karanikas, *Professional Generalism in a Hyper-specialised World*,
https://doi.org/10.1007/978-981-96-4039-3_16

System 1. Any 'conscious' transition from System 2 to System 1 would inevitably cancel the concept of System 1. One cannot be conscious that they are unconscious.

Longitudinal variabilities and disparities (VaDs) occur when people sometimes respond differently to the same situation at different times. We often perform the same job differently and sometimes make different decisions about the same topic over time. *Cross-sectional VaDs* happen when several people deal in different ways with the same situation simultaneously. For example, as professionals, we can have different viewpoints on a topic or perform an activity in our own unique way, even in the same conditions.

Longitudinal and cross-sectional variabilities and disparities VaDs can be unobservable for immaterial energy (e.g., different thoughts or emotions over time and across individuals) and observable for material energy (e.g., different activities over time and across individuals). These types of VaDs exist concurrently because the reality of the dynamic environment and the interactions of different individuals between them and with the environment mean that[2]:

- everyone carries different material and immaterial energies at different time-points,
- no individual carries the same material and immaterial energies as other individuals, and,
- everyone uses their energy across the Systems 1–2 spectrum differently over time, even under similar circumstances.

There can also be *objectives-outputs-outcomes variabilities and disparities VaDs.* Cognitive dissonance is a profound example of an objectives-outputs-outcomes VaD theory. It deals with the possible discordance between immaterial energy (e.g., what we believe, want, need, and desire), use of material energy (i.e., what we do), and how the results of the latter could feed back and influence our immaterial energy.[3]

Often, variabilities and disparities VaDs carry rather negative connotations. For example, literature discusses the impact of heuristics and biases, and cognitive dissonance often deals with distress. Still, VaDs are vital for activating energy. Our civilisation would not grow, at least with the pace historically observed, if VaDs did not exist as cognition does not grow without detecting and processing differences. Any living unity would hibernate in the eternity without VaDs, under a uniform reality which we would perceive, process, and (in) act identically.

Senses, the gates through which we receive material energy, trigger immaterial energy to detect variabilities and disparities VaDs, process them and (in)act. Cognitive associations together with affective referents shape our mental models for each context (e.g., meanings, functions, capabilities, interactions), and collectively form expectations, tolerances, and redlines. Those models change over time as we get exposed to more information and knowledge. When handling VaDs, anything that does not match current models and expectations is considered a post–pre *difference.* If it goes over any allowed limits, it becomes a post–pre *gap.*

---

[2] Smith, T. J. (2015). *Variability in human performance.* CRC Press. https://doi.org/10.1201/b17319.

[3] Festinger, L. (1957). *A theory of cognitive dissonance.* Stanford University Press.

Therefore, both *differences and gaps (DaGs)* exist only in hindsight. Differences regard primarily 'qualitative' aspects (e.g., different work group composition than planned; different style of leadership than envisaged; limited accessibility of resources). On the other hand, gaps correspond mainly to 'quantitative' aspects (e.g., more work pressure than expected, product delivery date past the agreed deadline, fewer resources than agreed).

Certainly, perhaps we often contemplate the possibility of such differences and gaps DaGs proactively based on experience and records, and we plan for buffers and alternatives accordingly. Although this is true, those plans are predominantly based on the anticipated energy exchange and generate or modify agreed, expected, and assumed objectives, which then will be compared with the actual objectives to determine the magnitude of (un)anticipated DaGs.

For instance, you can add 10% additional time to the timeline of a project to compensate for delays historically recorded, meaning retrospective DaGs. The revised timeline comprises a renewed objective, the pursuit of which will show any new emerging DaGs, which might be recorded to inform the next project.

Our immaterial energy handles identified differences and gaps DaGs between the perceived reality (i.e., how it looks now) and mental models (i.e., how it should look like), places on them values (e.g., good or bad, ethical or unethical) and drives (n)actions. The various DaGs (e.g., in meanings, wealth, knowledge, skills, health status) mobilise us and force interactions.

Differences and gaps DaGs cannot have the same sign for everyone within a specific context. The positive gap for someone means they are better off from others, which suggests that those others might experience a negative gap. For instance, I will feel positive about my promotion, while other unsuccessful candidates may feel negative (i.e., DaG: I got promoted and others did not).

In the two following sections, I illustrate various differences and gaps DaGs at the macro-level by considering humans within their environment (Sect. 16.2) and at the micro-level within humans (Sect. 16.3). While I focus on individuals, these concepts also apply to collections (e.g., between team members, amongst organisational departments).

16.2 Macro-Level DaGs

When considering a person within their environment and the reality of differences and gaps and variabilities and disparities I discussed in the previous section, in Fig. 16.1 I extend the energy concepts I presented in Sect. 5.4 and Fig. 5.2. More specifically, I elaborate on how the three types of energy (i.e., material, cognitive, and affective) interact and depend on each other over time.

I also illustrate how environmental variability generates demands which, under given energy states, can result in multiple differences and gaps. The terms coloured in red in the top frame of Fig. 16.1 collectively correspond to the *context* per unit of

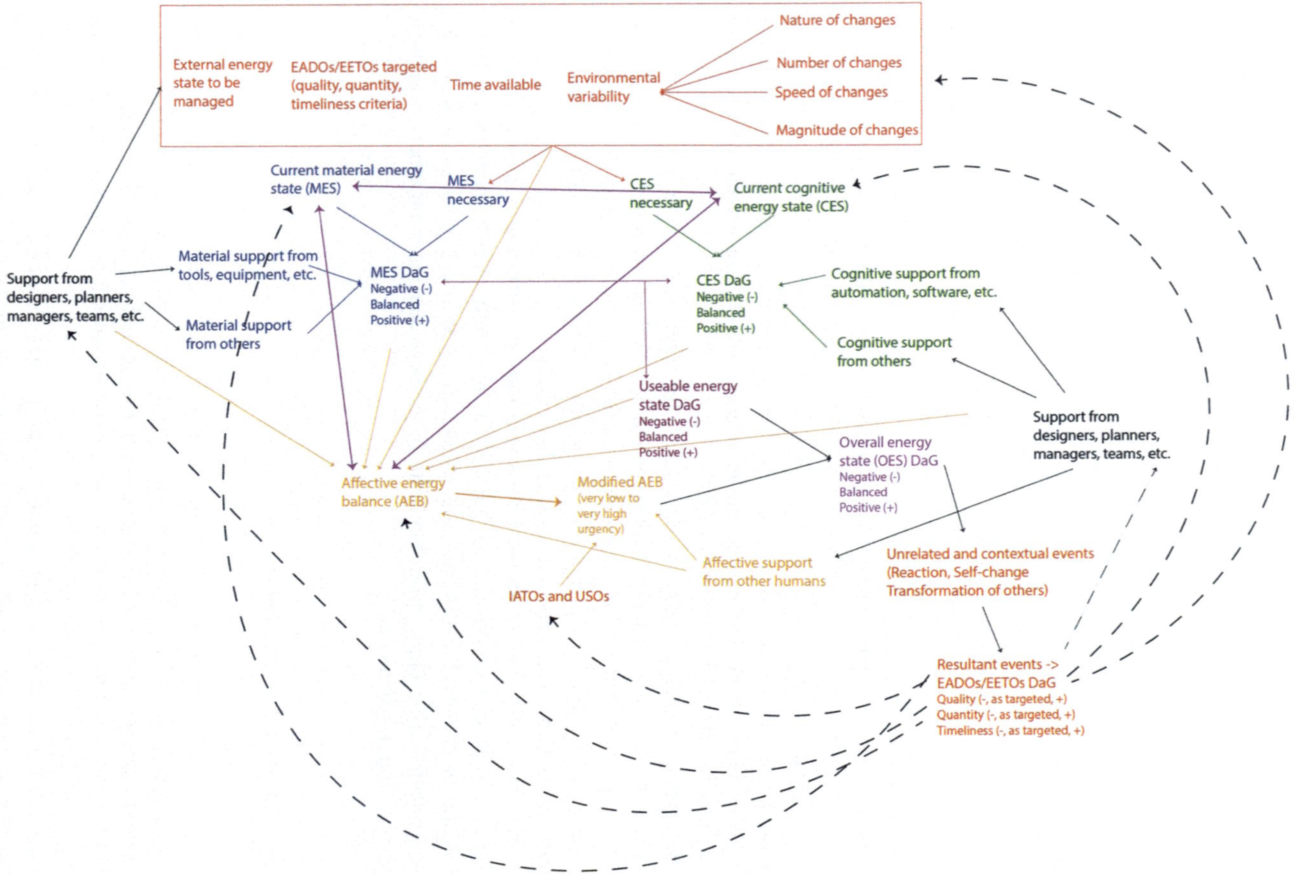

Fig. 16.1 Macro-level DaGs

time. They refer to factors that determine the physical and cognitive energy demands for an individual who per unit of time must:

- manage material energy with particular features (e.g., size, weight, toxicity, temperature),
- achieve Explicitly Agreed and Trusted Objectives (EATOs, Sect. 10.2) and Explicitly Expected the Trusted Objectives (EETOs, Sect. 10.5) within a specific timeframe,
- under the variability caused by changes in the environment, including the material energy to be managed.

Material energy MES and cognitive energy CES are defined by their quantity, quality, and accessibility parameters (Sect. 5.3). For instance, someone can have plenty of information stored but no idea how to use it. Also, they might hold the knowledge to process data but have limited access to the latter (e.g., problems with senses). Somebody else might have excellent physical elasticity and flexibility, but not enough energy to carry out jobs. Another might have stored much energy but have no physical skills to mobilise it.

The difference between the energy we have and the energy we need represents the energy state's differences and gaps DaG. When current material and cognitive energies and respective demands meet, there is a balance. When current energy exceeds demands, there is a positive DaG, meaning that an individual has more energy available to use. In the opposite case, a negative DaG signals a person lacks the energy necessary to manage the situation effectively within the given context (e.g., objectives, time, changes).

The interaction of material and cognitive energy can lead to a balanced usable energy state UES (i.e., material and cognitive energies) even when there is a surplus in one and a deficit in the other. Expectedly, cases with negative difference and gaps DaG in both material MES and cognitive CES energies will generate a combined negative UES. Similarly, when both MES and CES enjoy positive DaGs, UES will also be positive.

In cases of negative differences and gaps DaGs (e.g., someone lacks the physical strength or knowledge to manage a situation), external material and cognitive support from other humans and technology can contribute to decreasing DaGs and collaboratively improve usable energy UES. Such support can be directed to the context to ease the demands or can also be offered straight to the individual. Material support can be in a form that contributes to the physical force required to control material energy (e.g., tools or team members). Offering extra or clearer information, without adding to their mental load, is a form of cognitive support (e.g., using automation).

The overall energy state OES of the individual and the selected activity type (i.e., Reaction, Self-Change, Transformation of others—Sect. 11.1) will depend on the continuous interactions between the three energy types (i.e., material MES, cognitive CES, and affective AEB), a situation we cannot prescribe and predict as it varies over time and is affected by the environment. Especially, the initial and developing context, realising the differences and gaps DaGs in MES and CES, the sense of urgency (Sect. 13.5) and any Implicitly Assumed and Trusted Objectives (IATOs) or

Unsettled Side Objectives (USOs) (Sect. 10.6) will shape affective energy balance AEB.

The interplay of the parameters above with someone's own material and cognitive energy forms a complex web of interactions. As with useable energy UES, awareness of external material and cognitive support and direct affective support (e.g., encouragement, empathy) will influence affective balance AEB and, subsequently, overall energy OES.

When overall energy's OES difference or gap DaG is extremely negative, from a pragmatic perspective, the most probable activity would be just a reaction to incoming energy. As a negative OES DaG state corresponds to a high misbalance between external demands and useable energy UES, an individual might not have the energy and time for any other activity apart from a mere reaction. When we are overloaded with tasks and bombarded with information, demands, and expectations, we try to deal with the situation and survive. We only react based on what we already know, what others have done, what best practices suggest, and what innate and fundamental laws dictate (Sect. 11.3).

In such cases, we will also manifest a more synthetic processing (Sect. 13.4). We will start selecting, filtering, and omitting information (Sect. 16.2) or, when possible, seek external support. Indeed, we could still want to theorise during intense conditions. However, there is little time and energy left to formulate and fully and credibly answer the 'why' questions, transform those into hypotheses and test for their standing (Sect. 11.5). Under a negative difference or gap DaG, we might still attempt to find answers, but those would remain mostly in the sphere of the who, what, where, when and how already stored as cognitive associations and provided by others.

For example, consider a firefighter battling a large-scale house fire. The firefighter is facing immediate danger, physical exertion, and high levels of stress. As such, the priority is to contain the fire, rescue occupants, and ensure safety. There is little time to delve into theoretical questions. The firefighter is primarily concerned with 'who' needs rescuing, 'what' actions to take, 'where' the fire is spreading, 'when' to evacuate, and 'how' to use equipment effectively. A firefighter's main concern is immediate action and survival, not analysing the fire's cause or better firefighting techniques.

Any external support directed to an individual's energy (e.g., water and food, training) or relieving the burden would decrease negative differences and gaps DaGs. For example, when one provides a worker with a lever, the latter does not gain more physical strength but needs to apply less force to lift an object. This can contribute to lower DaGs and allow to invest energy somewhere else or for a longer period. However, sometimes, mistimed or unsuitable external support could have the opposite effect. For example, new tools may add complexity and require extra mental resources to learn.

Under neutral and positive differences and gaps, we have more capacity to wonder, question, and doubt. For instance, imagine a professional who does not undertake projects that are overwhelmingly demanding, and which do not require a significant investment of material and immaterial energy continually. This professional would have the opportunity to theorise about their choices, plans, professional connections, and other aspects.

In cases of capacity buffers, we might decide to explore the whys and, subsequently, reposition ourselves in the specific context, reconsider our reactions to incoming energy, and reflect on our interactions. Several publications on self-development, self-knowledge, and personal growth,[4,5,6] suggest how to achieve self-transformation beyond merely reacting to the unfolding reality (Sect. 11.1). Nonetheless, it is crucial to reiterate that if someone does not want to change, they would not feel the need for self-knowledge. Self-knowledge,[7,8] and self-transformation tightly couple together.

Considering the above and your own experiences, I am confident you can understand the non-deterministic nature of activities (i.e., unrelated and contextual events) that will drive outputs (i.e., resultant events—Sect. 2.3) and result in differences and gaps between those outputs and their outcomes and the originally agreed or expected objectives. Therefore, why we cannot claim we perform and deliver the same every day or hour, and rather every minute and second, even under relatively stable conditions.

There have been several heroic moments in our human history where people dealt with situations and triumphed against all odds and expectations, even when the differences and gaps in their material and cognitive energies had a highly negative sign. Similarly, sometimes humans do not meet expectations, even with the right material and cognitive energy states.

Last, everything that occurs through the exchange of energy in different forms and within an environment inevitably interacts with its environment (Sect. 12.1). Hence, resultant events and differences and gaps DaGs between actual outputs/outcomes and agreed/expected objectives will feedback and influence several areas. Each event and DaG might shape or change cognitive associations (e.g., the results of an experiment). It can modify or create affective referents, such as attitudes towards situations, humans, and other unities.

Additionally, those events and differences and gaps DaGs can affect material energy state, like resilience to exposure to toxins and bodily adaptation to increase its muscle strength and joint flexibility. Each event and DaG can influence other energy recipients or observers, shape the context, and potentially modify assumed and unsettled objectives. In Table 16.1 I combine the principles and concepts I discussed in this and the previous section, highlighting consequent implications and subsequent expectations.

---

[4] Francis, D., & Woodcock, M. (2002). *50 Activities for self-development*. HRD Press.

[5] Pedler, M., Burgoyne, J., & Boydell, T. (2013). *A manager's guide to self-development* (6th ed.). McGraw-Hill Education.

[6] Carr, A. (2020). *Positive psychology and you: A self-development guide*. Routledge.

[7] Strandberg, H. (2015). *Self-knowledge and self-deception* (pp. 1–237). Palgrave Macmillan. https://doi.org/10.1057/9781137538222.

[8] Gertler, B. (2011). *Self-knowledge*. Routledge.

Table 16.1 Macro-level DaG implications and expectations

Principle	Associated variabilities and disparities VaDs	Implications	Expectations
Individuals carry diverse physical, cognitive, and affective energies	Cross-sectional VaDs	The positive, balanced, and negative DaG[1] thresholds for MES[2], CES[3], UES[4], and OES[5] vary across different individuals in identical contexts	Different individuals might not perform/deliver the same event* in identical contexts
		The same external support can have various effects across different individuals in identical contexts	Different individuals might use in variable ways any uniform support provided within each context
The physical, cognitive, and affective energy states of each individual change over time	Longitudinal VaDs	The positive, balanced, and negative DaG thresholds for MES, CES, UES, and OES vary for the same individual over time in identical contexts	Any individual might not perform/deliver the same event* in identical contexts at different time-points
		The same type and level of external support can have various effects on the same individual over time in identical contexts	Individuals might use in variable ways the same type and level of support provided for identical contexts at different time-points
Cognitive and affective energies and their mutual and multidirectional effects with material energy cannot be empirically measured	Objectives-outputs-outcomes VaDs	The DaGs in MES, CES, UES, and OES can be experienced by each individual, but not externally validated	Individuals expect trust from others when sharing DaG-related experiences
		The total external physical, cognitive, and affective energy support necessary per context and over time cannot be accurately estimated	Individuals expect a readily-available pool of supportive material, cognitive, and affective resources to use as per their experienced needs (i.e., access to reserved energy—Sect. 5.4)

(continued)

Table 16.1 (continued)

Principle	Associated variabilities and disparities VaDs	Implications	Expectations
Nobody can completely control all factors influencing physical, cognitive, and affective energies	Cross-sectional and longitudinal variabilities and objectives-outputs-outcomes VaDs	The DaG signs of MES, CES, UES, and OES can change per unit of time and individual during the execution of the same activity	Individuals might perform and deliver variant events* during the same activity
		The total external physical, cognitive, and affective energy support estimated as necessary per activity might be insufficient	In perceivably highly dynamic environments, individuals expect an extra/back-up pool of protective and supportive material, cognitive and affective resources (i.e., passive and reserved energy—Sect. 5.4)

*Unrelated or Contextual event/activity or Resultant event/output characterised by Quality, Quantity, and Timeliness criteria

[1]DaGs: Differences and Gaps; [2]MES: Material energy state; [3]CES: Cognitive energy state; [4]UES: Useable energy state; [5]OES: Overall energy state

16.3 Micro-Level DaGs

The human brain is a complex network of nerves, synapses, and other sub-unities that interact rapidly and are difficult to monitor. Neuroscience concentrates on areas of the brain (e.g., amygdala and hippocampus) activated when we are exposed to stimuli. However, since such observations are descriptive and do not explain immaterial energy (Sect. 5.2), scientists still rely on theoretical models. By delving deeper conceptually, we could contemplate specific internal differences and gaps that result from the interactions between material and immaterial energies.

In Fig. 16.2 I map more detailed differences and gaps DaGs within humans per unit of time. I propose a conceptual model that illustrates the complex system of cognition and emotions, with material energy acting as both incoming energy and part of one's useable energy. This concept brings together famous theoretical models (e.g., Wickens' human information processing[9] model and Endsley's situation awareness model[10]), enriched with concepts I introduced in earlier chapters above.

[9] Wickens, C. D. (1992). Engineering psychology and human performance. Harper Collins.

[10] Endsley, M. R. (1995). Toward a theory of situation awareness in dynamic systems. *Human Factors, 37*(1), 32–64.

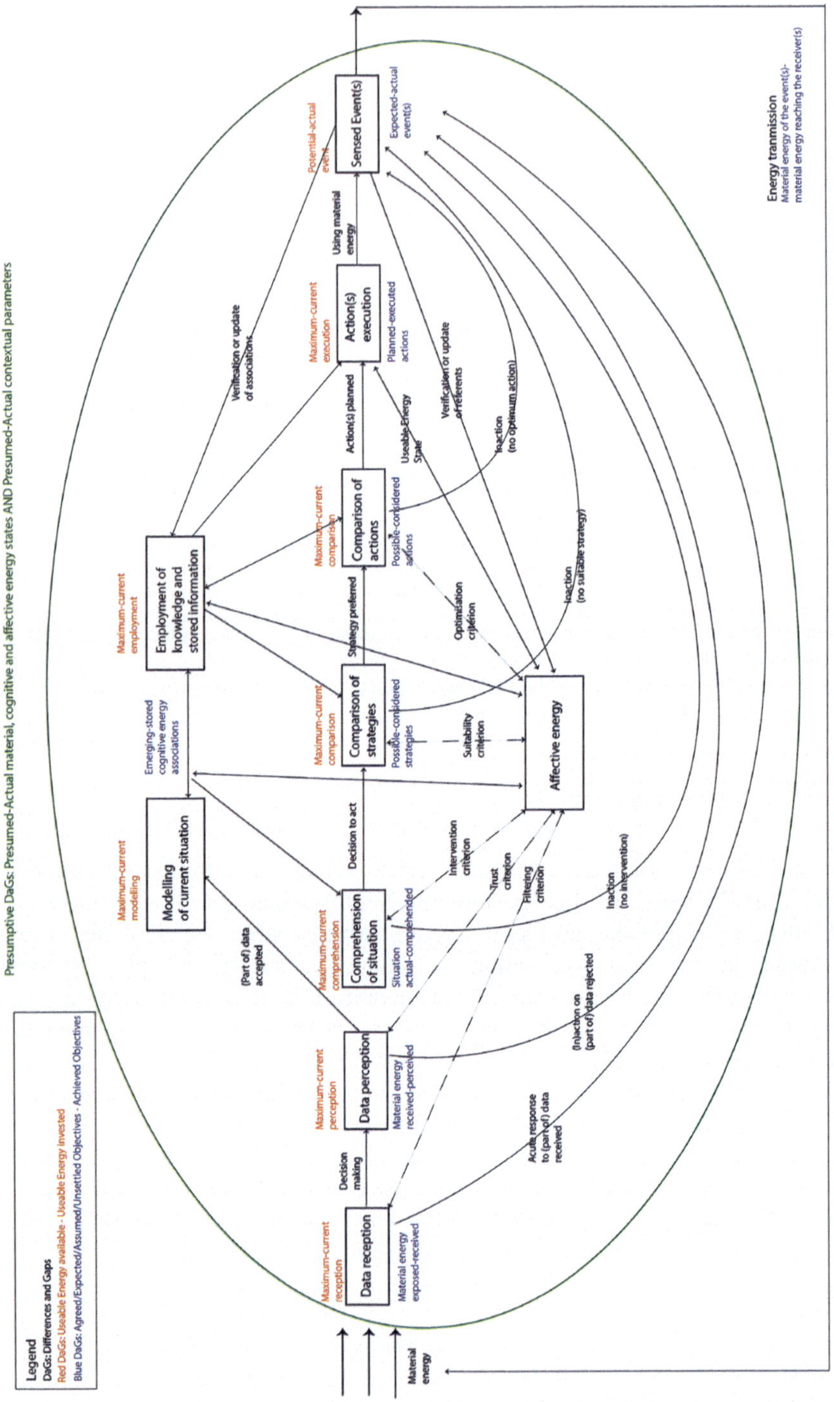

Fig. 16.2 Micro-level DaGs

Moving from left to right, in Fig. 16.2 I present various processes taking place and different interactions: the material energy received by the senses is translated into data signals travelling throughout the nervous system and translates into information through cognitive and affective energies. The sensed event(s) on the far-right side of the graph can be unrelated, contextual, or resultant (Sect. 2.3). They will modify the context through respective material energy transmission to energy recipients.

Admittedly, Fig. 16.2 is a simplification of the parallel processing that occurs in human cognition. While the model presents these processes sequentially for clarity, they mostly occur simultaneously when exposed to different energy types and sources simultaneously. Literature frequently uses the terms working/short-term memory for information processing and long-term memory for the retrieval of stored associations. However, as memories represent static entities, Fig. 16.2 employs different terms with the goal of portraying the dynamic nature of information processing.

Subject to the explanations about affective criteria I provide later in this section, the principal processes I depict in Fig. 16.2 are:

- data reception through material energy from the external environment,
- data perception that leads to the modelling of the current situation,
- situational comprehension by comparing situation models and cognitive energy associations (e.g., schemas, expectations),
- comparisons between response strategies combining different activity types (i.e., reaction, self- change, and transformation of others—Sect. 11.1) and action types (i.e., organisation, design, alteration, improvement or maintenance—Sect. 14.1), informed by cognitive energy,
- comparisons between actions, informed by cognitive energy, with the possibility to get back to the stage of comparing strategies (e.g., no action to realise the preferred strategy is feasible),
- execution of the planned action(s), informed by the cognitive energy, shaped by affective energy depending on the current usable energy, and producing the sensed event(s) though using available material energy (i.e., passive or reserved self-energy and other material unities),
- verification or update of cognitive associations and affective referents following the sensed event(s) and respected differences and gaps DaGs (i.e., comparison with agreed EADO, expected EETO, assumed IATOs, and unsettled USOs objectives), and
- material energy transmission from the sensed event(s) back to the person and other individuals and unities in the proximal environment.

In Fig. 16.2 I also present areas of gaps which naturally appear within each one of us because of the continuous exchange and transformation of energy. The outer green circle shows the broader *presumptive differences and gaps DaGs* at the macro-level (Sect. 16.2). It represents the possible mismatch between presumptions (e.g., project planning and task allocation) and reality (e.g., project execution and job performance) regarding:

- the energy state of each person involved, and,

- contextual parameters, such as the energy to be managed, comprehension and endorsement of objectives, time boundaries and environmental variability, including interactions with other humans.

The red differences and gaps DaGs correspond to the useable energy available versus the energy invested, meaning the material and cognitive energy states that are present and used per unit of time. The blue DaGs regard the objectives aimed (i.e., agreed, expected, assumed, and unsettled) and the ones achieved, including their quantity, quality, and timeliness. Of note, it would not make sense practically and theoretically to measure any of red or blue DaGs or give them numerical values when considering:

- the multitude of external and internal objectives that can exist concurrently,
- that individuals' energy levels fluctuate over time, and
- the exposures to and interactions of individuals with the variable environment.

Thus, although differences and gaps DaGs can always exist in hindsight and retrospectively (Sect. 16.1), it is hard to predict when they appear and their magnitude, especially at the micro-level. However, Fig. 16.1 can help identify external and internal areas that can be managed to minimise DaGs.

The single-spearhead solid lines in Fig. 16.2 show the expected order of processes based on theoretical models of how the brain works. The double-spearhead solid lines represent interactions that could affect the next process or lead back to a previous one. The dashed lines represent *affective criteria* corresponding to influences of affective energy that does not involve specific processes but drives material and cognitive energy (Sect. 5.3). Those criteria originate from the Energy Motivational Envelope that serves the needs and desires of the individual along with their Wilful Energising Investment (Chapter 12).

The Filtering Criterion

This is the first affective criterion that applies when we get exposed to material energy and receive the data through our sensory system. It can trigger automatic (in)actions (e.g., pulling the hand away when sensing extreme heat; ignoring someone speaking) or allow data to be processed further. Sometimes, we may have a strong initial response to data but still process it cognitively.

Neuroscience defines acute responses of the body, namely reflexes, as actions which are not processed by conscious cognition and manifest automatically when we are exposed to some form of stimuli. The startle response, for example, is a reflex associated with rapid changes to material energy (e.g., increased heart rate, larger eye pupil size). Cognitive psychology examines fast reactions to understand behaviours not driven by conscious thought.

All those are expressions of natural/innate and fundamental laws (Sect. 11.3) that heavily involve the effects of affective energy (Sect. 5.3). The latter closely relates to acute bodily responses analysed by neuroscience and non-mentally processed information examined by psychology, whereas also addresses the cases of non-responses. That neither neuroscience nor psychology has conclusively explained how a unity inherits the 'knowledge' of acute responses and how this becomes innate across many living unities (Sect. 5.2), justifies confidently the attribution to affective energy of acute responses or continuation of further processing.

The Trust Criterion

Whatever is not immediately (in)actioned, proceeds to the first cognitive stage of perception. There, the trustworthiness of data sensed (Chapter 7) will determine whether to process it further or disregard it. When data is rejected, we can choose to either take no action or seek additional information (e.g., checking once more the source or the data, cross-check with other sources). This last case denotes the restart of the cyclic process of Fig. 16.2. Also, the event of rejecting parts of or the entire dataset can also trigger further processing.

The Intervention Criterion

After processing trusted data and building our situational model, the comprehension process uses the intervention criterion. This criterion will drive the decision to (in)act upon the situation based on stored (in)action-event relationships and the current affective energy balance. The intervention criterion examines what could occur if we (in)act.

Intervening will depend on cognitive associations, current, acceptable and desired energy states, past and anticipated effects on energy, and comparisons with norms. As a reminder of Table 2.1, events can be unrelated, contextual, or resultant, meaning that an inaction can be still classified as a sensed event. Inaction means no purposeful interactions and exchange of energy to influence the unfolding situation. Inaction includes cases like when one entirely neglects the situation or postpones their engagement with it while collecting more information, securing more energy, etc.

The Suitability Criterion

If someone decides to intervene and there is more than one response strategy, their cognitive and affective energy will interplay once more to contemplate the various effects on the energy of themselves and others and direct the selection of the preferred strategy. If we cannot decide about the most suitable strategy, then we can disengage from acting, as above.

The Optimisation Criterion

This criterion examines how immaterial energy shapes the execution of the preferred option to achieve expected results (i.e., quantity, quality, and timeliness of agreed and expected objectives). It relates to how one could invest their available energy in different execution ways (e.g., maximise efficiency) and whether they would employ additional energy sources in a specific fashion (e.g., ask someone else to undertake a particular task, use a tool). Like the other baselines above, if someone perceives no current execution way can optimally achieve all the above aims, they might (in)act.

Differences and Gaps: Key Reflections and Actions

Reflections

- Differences and Gaps (DaGs) represent variations or discrepancies in performance, expectations, resources, or outcomes at both macro and micro-levels. Recognising these distinctions is critical for effective professional practice.
- Macro-level DaGs involve broader systemic differences, such as disparities in access to resources, organisational structures, or socio-cultural contexts.
- Micro-level DaGs pertain to individual-level variations, including skill sets, emotional states, or immediate task performance.
- Material, cognitive, and affective energies interact with environmental demands, shaping the manifestation and impact of DaGs.

Actions

1. Identify Macro and Micro DaGs: Analyse the differences and gaps in your professional and organisational environment. Categorise them as macro-level or micro-level and assess their origins and implications.
2. Understand Energy Interactions: Reflect on how material, cognitive, and affective energies influence DaGs. Recognise how these energies shape individual and collective performance in specific contexts.
3. Leverage Positive DaGs: View differences and gaps as opportunities for growth and innovation. Identify ways in which they can inspire creative solutions or drive systemic improvements.
4. Address Negative DaGs: Develop targeted strategies to reduce or mitigate gaps that hinder equity, performance, or collaboration. Focus on long-term solutions that align with organisational goals and values.
5. Balance Contextual Demands: Tailor your approach to DaGs based on environmental and situational demands. Consider the interplay between systemic factors and individual capacities in your decision-making.
6. Foster Open Dialogue: Encourage discussions about DaGs within your team or organisation. Use these conversations to build awareness, share insights, and co-create strategies to address gaps constructively.

By identifying, understanding, and addressing Differences and Gaps, you can enhance adaptability, equity, and innovation in your professional and organisational contexts, turning challenges into opportunities for meaningful progress.

Chapter 17
Role and Importance of DaGs

17.1 General

In Sects. 16.2 and 16.3 and in Figs. 16.1 and 16.2 I demonstrated that there are a multitude of differences and gaps DaGs we can discuss when considering one or more humans and other living beings in a specific context. If you additionally consider the interactions of an individual with other persons, contemplate that those have their own energy states and experience their own DaGs within various collections, acknowledge that each collection has its own objectives and realise the diversity and changes of contexts over time within collections exist, you can think of numerous DaGs. This chapter argues that, despite their pros and cons, DaGs are essential at both individual and collective levels.

First, it is paramount to define what types of differences and gaps DaGs are of interest and decide about the respective comparison baseline, along with identifying the opportunities and obstacles present in the particular context. Second, it is important to recall from Sect. 14.2 that a random focus on different f DaGs within a collection at different time-points and areas would not add much value.

If we want to examine differences and gaps DaGs in collections, we must detect and analyse all of them at each level of abstraction/detail. Selectivity in particular DaGs of the same collection without prior justification and a focus on random time-points of collecting DaG-relevant data and information could threaten inclusiveness, and any findings could be incomplete and inconclusive (Sect. 14.3). Excluding some DaGs would signal a narrow approach since they are all linked.

N. Karanikas, *Professional Generalism in a Hyper-specialised World*,
https://doi.org/10.1007/978-981-96-4039-3_17

17.2 DaGs in Collections

Several professionals focus on differences and gaps DaGs of observed events against expected events. When these DaGs indicate failures to achieve the planned or expected level of quantity, quality, and timeliness, we typically label them as negative and unwanted (e.g., low service quality, delayed product delivery, inadequate production volume of material items). While positive DaGs (e.g., successes, abundance) have also driven progress and civilisation, in professional practice, we often fixate on negative DaGs.

Undoubtedly, while DaGs serve as essential catalysts for innovation and adaptation, unmanaged or excessive DaGs can pose significant risks to systems and organisations. When left unaddressed, DaGs may lead to misaligned objectives, inefficiencies, and even conflict amongst stakeholders. For example, in organisational settings, skill gaps in teams cause problems with teamwork and output. Similarly, an overabundance of technological or operational DaGs may overwhelm an organisation's capacity to integrate changes, resulting in stalled projects or failed initiatives. Therefore, while DaGs are inherently valuable, their potential to destabilise systems underscores the need for careful identification, monitoring, and management to ensure they foster growth rather than dysfunction.

However, from the viewpoint of the persons involved (e.g., supervisors, workers, professional advisers) any negative differences and gaps DaGs can often be fully justified. This is not only because those individuals might have insights into the reasons behind any negative DaGs in material and immaterial energy balances that affected results and could justify substandard outputs. It is also because anyone would have their own objectives that do not necessarily align with the 'formally' agreed and expected ones (Chapter 10).

Calling negative differences and gaps DaGs 'undesirable' is not always fair or accurate. This is because, historically, negative DaGs have mobilised our human civilisation and the economy. They could be even named the heart of innovation emerging from overcoming constraints and driving adaptation and evolution. Larger negative DaGs increase research and expert consultation to bridge reality-model and expectation-outcome gaps.

The larger the negative differences and gaps DaGs, the more detrimental and potentially catastrophic the outcomes, perhaps. Conversely, the more the need to examine, cooperate, consult, debate, educate, train, and so on. Sizeable and unexpected DaGs create new fields, like complexity science,[1,2] which fuel more research, conversations, events, publications, and other artefacts.[3] Also, although positive DaGs reflect events with better quantity, quality, and timeliness than planned, the individuals involved can occasionally perceive these DaGs as negative if those persons do not personally enjoy something from the positive DaGs a collection achieved.

---

[1] Wilson, A. (2016). *Global dynamics: Approaches from complexity science*. John Wiley & Sons.

[2] Rivas, D. (2016). *Complexity science in air traffic management*. Taylor & Francis Group.

[3] Erçetin, Ş., & Potas, N. (2019). *Chaos, complexity and leadership 2017 explorations of chaos and complexity theory*. Springer International Publishing. https://doi.org/10.1007/978-3-319-89875-9.

For instance, a project team could successfully complete a project earlier and under budget, meaning a significant positive outcome in terms of time and cost. If the project manager or team members do not receive any personal rewards or recognition the expected, they might perceive the positive differences and gaps DaGs in time and cost as negative. Even if the project succeeds, the project manager and team may feel unappreciated. Also, if team members were promised bonuses or promotions that are not delivered, they might view the project's success as a missed opportunity.

Although we can flag differences and gaps DaGs as positive or negative in hindsight, the question is, 'What lessons do we get from any DaGs when explaining them through conversations with the people who (co)experienced them when acting in any active or supportive role?' In collections, it is important to learn from both successes (i.e., positive DaGs) and failures (i.e., negative DaGs)[4,5,6] while acknowledging which persons and teams harvested the benefits and who suffered any adversities of any DaG. Transferring lessons to other activity areas is essential for information sharing and self-change, but it is equally important to avoid exploiting positive DaGs by pushing us and other humans and unities to their energy state limits, such as imposing excessive demands and accelerating changes, with the possible outcome of turning previously positive DaGs into negative ones.

Thus, when inquiring about any difference and gap DaG, it is important to consider all parameters and the role of everyone in shaping them. Before addressing individual energy management problems, we should examine how others could have provided support or reduced the workload of individuals. Last, it is valuable to converse and agree about which DaGs and when they become acceptable within particular contexts and what we would do with unacceptable gaps. If a discussion is not possible, it is equally significant to acknowledge who has the authority to draw the acceptable/unacceptable line and the respective criteria.

17.3 Conditioning, Resilience, and Evolution

At the individual level, negative differences and gaps DaGs might inflict some discomfort. This can occur during the real-time execution of an activity (e.g., experiencing negative useable energy UES DaG—Fig. 16.1) or after an activity has progressed or finished (e.g., realising that the situation comprehended was far from the actual one—Fig. 16.2). Reversely, neutral, or positive DaGs might create a feeling of comfort and satisfaction.

[4] Scott, T. (2007). *Implementing an electronic medical record system: successes, failures, lessons.* Radcliffe.

[5] Onishi, Y., Voitsekhovich, O. V., & Zheleznyak, M. J. (2007). *Chernobyl—What have we learned? The successes and failures to mitigate water contamination over 20 Years.* Springer Netherlands. https://doi.org/10.1007/1-4020-5349-5.

[6] Grübler, A., & Wilson, C. (2014). *Energy technology innovation: Learning from historical successes and failures.* Cambridge University Press.

Even under similar circumstances, (dis)comfort will fluctuate across individuals and over time. As discussed in Sect. 16.2, individual differences exist because of the different energy states in each person. The variability with time occurs because of changes to the way material and immaterial energy interact within each individual and the way each individual channels and uses material and cognitive energy to meet any objectives.

Within this variability, the innate, untraceable, and continuous adaptation of a living unity to maintain or advance its overall energy state and ensure its existence defines the constructs of *conditioning* (i.e., adaptive use of energy) and *resilience* (i.e., adaptive response to energy), respectively. As I mentioned in Sect. 11.1, adaptation is a special case of self-change. It is a natural law activity (Sect. 11.3) governing how a living unity's immaterial and material energies interact and work together towards increasing efficiency of using its energy and prolonging its physical survival while exposed to varying incoming energy.

As such, conditioning and resilience are not about conscious self-changes in response to the environment by, for example, adopting behaviours and practices shared by others.[7,8,9] They are about the internal and unstoppable adaptations occurring in the time continuum. Certainly, the choice and the ways to interact with and get exposed to other unities through different activity types (Sect. 11.1) can be a choice and be driven by our affective and cognitive energies (e.g., previous experience and information about best practices and the potential outcomes).

Regardless, as soon as any interactions and exposures begin, conditioning also occurs and contributes to reshaping our energy states. For example, for someone who lacks physical strength or endurance, completing a task may seem difficult. Despite this, gradually facing this situation can make it easier to complete the task over time (e.g., on-the-job training of employees). Similarly, cognitively processing relatively unfamiliar information (e.g., new topics and concepts) can become easier with time, provided an individual is continually and incrementally exposed to it.

Also, challenging situations can lessen sensitivity over time (e.g., medical staff involved in operations, first responders in emergencies, people experiencing for long war or unsafe work conditions). Such conditioning cases driven by negative differences and gaps represent how we secure, enrich, and employ our useable energy in specific contexts (i.e., quantity, quality, and accessibility of material and cognitive energy), affectively respond to challenges and changes and, ultimately, develop resilience.

Conversely, not experiencing cases with negative differences and gaps DaGs, meaning one consistently enjoys neutral or positive DaGs, might lead to lower resilience levels in particular contexts. Of note, this can also happen because of conditioning. If we do not need to invest energy and optimise its use when dealing

---

[7] Zeff, T. (2004). *The highly sensitive person's survival guide: Essential skills for living well in an overstimulating world*. New Harbinger Publications.

[8] Lebrun, M. (2016). *Surviving school stress: Strategies for well-being in today's complex world*. Rowman & Littlefield Publishers, Incorporated.

[9] Hill, A. (2020). *Living in bonus time: Surviving cancer, finding new purpose*. InterVarsity Press.

with a situation, we will expectedly reserve our energy or redirect it to other contexts. As such, if everything seems physically, mentally, and emotionally easy across all activities, the ability to mobilise our usable energy and ensure a good overall energy under future variable conditions could degrade. This is a conditioning case too.

Someone can have enough energy available and feel comfortable to use it for completing daily activities (e.g., drive to work, attend a meeting) but may find it hard or impossible to coordinate their energies to respond to an emergency (e.g., finding and using an escape route the soonest). This can happen regardless of any 'static' value of its overall energy level, which cannot guarantee the person will mobilise their energies effectively within the particular context. Similarly, somebody else having gained a university degree in science decades ago could find it difficult to apply this knowledge over time in resolving complex problems if not having worked on and maintained updated about their scientific discipline.

However, conditioning and resilience driven by negative differences and gaps DaGs have boundaries set by innate/natural laws (Sect. 11.3). Usually, they are achieved when demands and expectations do not exceed dramatically the available useable energy and do not lead to a breaking point, which differs per person and collection. Besides, considering that material, cognitive, and affective energies influence each other, a highly negative balance in one energy type with no external and timely support could lead to the entire unity or collection underperforming, dysfunctioning, or even collapsing.

If a person gets physically fatigued while loading a truck, and there is no timely and adequate material support, whatever the cognitive energy levels (e.g., experience in the task) and the external support of its affective balance (e.g., motivation from others), they will finally collapse. Likewise, if I am heavily loaded cognitively (e.g., dealing with a complex situation for long), whatever material support (e.g., food and drinks) or affective balance boost (e.g., encouragement) I receive, they will not definitely remove the possibility of a burnout. This means that energy could be wasted in ineffective interventions.

Also, developing conditioning and resilience cannot continue forever and everywhere. The mobilisation of energy to match a particular context competes with the necessity of dealing with plenty of other conditions and their combinations, which could demand different optimisation channels and areas. The 'better' we become in some fields, the 'worse' our performance could become in other fields. You can be an expert in a very few contexts, excellent in more, better in even more, and average in much more. Also, someone deprived of one aspect could develop strengths in another, as for example, visually impaired people can develop sensory compensation.[10]

Likewise, the risks of developing high familiarity with a given context can negate the benefits of feeling 'always good' because of constant neutral or positive differences and gaps. This may cause some environmental factors to be ignored, even if things change (e.g., modified objectives, new or changed unities). For instance, if

[10] Zhang, W., & An, C. (2024). Research on multimodal interaction design patterns for visually impaired people under sensory compensation theory. In L. C. Jain et al. (Eds.), *Design studies and intelligence engineering* (pp 799–808). https://doi.org/10.3233/faia231495.

something labelled as hazardous remains unmanaged (e.g., a chemical or bullying behaviour) and leads to no visibly adverse outcome, it can become a normal part of reality, as everyone in the workplace can get conditioned to this hazard over time. Hindsight often reveals that our conditioning contributed to negative outcomes from unacceptable hazard exposures.

In literature, the term 'normalisation of deviance[11]' is used to describe situations where we gradually start accepting higher risks without fully realising it. Regardless, those deviances stem from the same innate processes that help all living beings adapt successfully to the ever-changing environment through internal changes. In long-term, conditioning and resilience together support the *evolution* of unities and their collections.[12,13,14]

Also, getting conditioned to a new normal (i.e., positive or neutral differences and gaps DaGs) might hinder a return to previous or different conditions. Someone who was born and raised in an environment with amenities and opportunities that cannot be found in other contexts will find it initially hard, if not appalling, to condition by experiencing negative DaGs until they achieve a new equilibrium level. Similarly, a person who lived in demanding physical, cognitive, and emotional conditions and experienced negative DaGs frequently, but over time they managed to create or join an environment which offers more positive or balanced DaG experiences, will probably deny denouncing their current reality.

The concepts above equally apply to human and other collections. The way muscles and connective tissues (i.e., myofascial arrangements) are organised in bodies can be compared to systems, where everything is interconnected and works together. Bodies strive to maintain balance through two processes resembling resilience and conditioning: allostasis (i.e., adapting to changes and stress) and homeostasis (i.e., keeping things stable). These concepts, which already exist in physiology and biology, can be likened to how social systems maintain resilience and reliability. Just as our bodies adjust and stabilise to stay healthy, social systems also adapt and remain reliable to function effectively.

17.4 Context and Overfocus

Despite their often-useful role, any differences and gaps at macro-levels (Sect. 16.2) or micro-levels (Sect. 16.3) can also lead to minor or major issues with outputs and their outcomes. For instance, differences in definitions of constructs, understandings

---

11 CCPS (2018). *Recognising and responding to normalisation of deviance.* Center for Chemical Process Safety, American Institute of Chemical Engineers. John Wiley & Sons, Incorporated.

12 Laszlo, E., & Goetsky, R. (Eds.). (1971). *Evolution-revolution: Patterns of development in nature society, man and knowledge* (1st ed.). Routledge. https://doi.org/10.4324/9780429325359.

13 Graziano, M. (2018). *The spaces between us: A story of neuroscience, evolution, and human nature.* Oxford University Press, Incorporated.

14 Robbins, K. (2013). *The laws of nature: Reflections on the evolution of ecosystem management law & policy.* University of Akron Press.

of mandates, needs, objectives, and expectations, and interpretations of events can generate outcomes ranging from just discomforting to catastrophic.

For instance, a lecturer's misunderstanding of the procedure and due date to post grades may not cause significant harm. This case will cause some disturbances, and colleagues will remind the lecturer of their obligations. However, miscommunication about electrical safety precautions and procedures when replacing a socket (e.g., cutting off electricity supply), misunderstandings of training content, ambiguous procedures, and any other relevant communication issue might lead to serious injuries, even a fatality. Thus, although differences between the messages transmitted, received, and internalised cannot be avoided, their impact can vary depending on the situation.

As another example, in workplace safety, the differences between how management believes workers perform their duties and how workers carry out their tasks are named as gaps between Work as Imagined (WaI) and Work as Done (WaD).[15] Such differences are unwelcome as they can be harmful and counterproductive for both the workplace and the individuals involved. Hence, any WaI-WaD differences become gaps by default regardless of their sign, magnitude, and nature. The premise is that organisations need to minimise such gaps, and, if possible, close them.

Naming differences as gaps can expand everywhere, such as expectations-results gaps, plans-reality gaps, and theory–practice gaps in various fields.[16,17,18] You can endlessly name all differences as gaps, such as the gaps between what we decide and what we do, what we sense and what we understand, what we did and what we meant to do, what we did and what the others saw, what others say and what arrives in our ears and so on.

However, labelling all differences (i.e., results of natural variability) as gaps (i.e., noticeable differences to be acted upon) could sound counterproductive. It seems to ignore there will always be variabilities and disparities (Sect. 16.1) and is rather impossible to map and 'measure' all types of differences whenever energy flows and is exchanged internally and externally to a unity or collection. Thus, in professional practice and beyond, it is crucial to acknowledge that, while closing identified gaps can be beneficial to avoid negative outcomes beyond defined thresholds, getting obsessed with detecting, analysing, and minimising all differences can compete with the natural processes of conditioning and resilience within individuals and collections and lead to negative side effects in mid- and long-term.

Consider the case of a technology company that aggressively pursues innovation by investing heavily in groundbreaking tools and systems to gain a competitive advantage. While the technological advancements promise improved efficiency and

[15] Dekker, S. (2019). *Foundations of safety science: A century of understanding accidents and disasters*. Taylor & Francis, CRC Press.

[16] Szwed, P. (2016). *Expert judgement in project management: Narrowing the theory–practice gap*. Project Management Institute, Inc.

[17] Smith, C. (2009). *Researching older people's nursing: The gap between theory and practice*. Palgrave Macmillan.

[18] Zijm, W., Klumpp, M., Clausen, U., & Ten Hompel, M. (2016). *Logistics and supply chain innovation: bridging the gap between theory and practice*. Springer.

market differentiation, the company could neglect critical cultural and organisational gaps. Employees might lack adequate training to use the new technologies effectively, and communication silos between departments can lead to misaligned objectives and resistance to change. The company may not have considered how its fast changes affect employees, who worry about losing their jobs or feeling left out. As a result, the anticipated benefits of the technological investment might not fully realised, and employee morale and productivity could suffer. This example illustrates how overfocussing on one type of DaG—technological innovation—without addressing cultural and organisational gaps can undermine overall success, highlighting the importance of a balanced approach to managing and leveraging DaGs.

Roles and Importance of DaGs: Key Reflections and Actions

Reflections

- Differences and Gaps (DaGs) are not inherently negative; they play a crucial role in driving adaptation, resilience, and innovation in professional and organisational contexts.
- DaGs in Collections: Within systems, networks, and groups, DaGs highlight discrepancies that can reveal opportunities for growth, areas of misalignment, or risks to stability.
- Conditioning and Resilience: DaGs can serve as triggers for adaptation, prompting individuals and organisations to develop new strategies, refine processes, or enhance capabilities to overcome challenges.
- Evolution and Progress: At a broader level, DaGs drive progress by fostering diversity of thought, experimentation, and creative problem-solving. Addressing these gaps thoughtfully can lead to systemic improvements.
- Context and Overfocus: Excessive focus on specific DaGs without considering the larger context can lead to inefficiencies or missed opportunities. A balanced perspective is critical to ensure efforts are aligned with broader objectives.

Actions

1. Identify DaGs in Collections: Assess how DaGs manifest within systems, networks, or groups. Look for patterns that indicate misalignments or opportunities for improvement.
2. Leverage DaGs for Resilience: View DaGs as opportunities to build resilience. Develop strategies that enhance adaptability and prepare individuals or systems to thrive in dynamic environments.
3. Promote Diversity of Thought: Recognise that DaGs often reflect diverse perspectives or approaches. Create environments that encourage the sharing of ideas and the exploration of innovative solutions.
4. Address DaGs Systematically: Avoid overfocusing on isolated gaps. Instead, integrate efforts to address DaGs into broader strategies that consider the system's overall goals and interdependencies.

5. Evaluate Outcomes Continuously: Monitor the effects of interventions designed to address DaGs. Use these insights to refine your approach and ensure sustainable progress.

By understanding the role and importance of DaGs, you can transform disparities into opportunities for growth, resilience, and innovation, fostering a more adaptive and inclusive professional environment.

Chapter 18
Performance and Evaluation

18.1 General

The constructs of performance and evaluation (P&E) hold a central role in professional contexts and for the entire society. Performance is not a self-standing concept. It is a construct used to make judgements by comparing unities between them or against standards (e.g., structured rules, cultural norms, formal and informal expectations). Those comparisons can have outcomes whose sign and magnitude we cannot deterministically predict (e.g., how the individual feels, whether they want to get closer to the standard or other unities, what persons will be seen as role models).

In the previous chapters, I have already covered several performance and evaluation aspects. Chapter 7 discussed how evaluation strategies can be subjective. In Chapter 3 and Chapter 4, I highlighted the misunderstandings and issues rising when we attribute performance characteristics to and develop respective criteria for immaterial, physically unperceivable constructs. Chapter 14 explains that data and information used for performance monitoring must align; for example, individual data cannot assess team performance. I also presented arguments and paradoxes when the above is not observed.

In Chapter 9, I connected all the performance and evaluation concepts above with the scope, approaches, and practices of exact, inexact, and hybrid sciences introduced in Chapter 8. Regarding more specific, technical aspects, Chapter 13 focussed on assessing inputs, activities, and their outputs for unities and collections. I explained how outputs from one step usually become inputs for the next.

I have discussed quantity, quality, and timeliness throughout the book, giving examples and suggestions for evaluating them. This includes the material, cognitive, and affective energy constructs (Sect. 5.3) and the definition of agreed objectives (Sect. 10.2). Last, Chapter 16 discusses the concepts of longitudinal and cross-sectional variabilities and disparities and differences, and gaps that can exist between activities and their outputs and agreed, expected and implicit objectives, as defined in Chapter 10.

N. Karanikas, *Professional Generalism in a Hyper-specialised World*,
https://doi.org/10.1007/978-981-96-4039-3_18

Through the constructs of performance and evaluation, either in their formal/structured or more informal/intuitive versions, together or separately, we identify differences and gaps, possibly explain those through variabilities and disparities (Chapter 16), attach judgements on unities and collections (Sect. 2.3) and, ultimately, mobilise humanity and our civilisation (Chapter 17).

Below, I formulate principles about performance and evaluation P&E by consolidating concepts covered in previous chapters with information from books regarding the P&E of individual unities, like humans[1,2,3,4] or collections of various unities, usually named systems.[5,6,7,8] Those books use occasionally different terminology and often focus on what unities do (a.k.a. functional requirements) and what unities or collections are (a.k.a. non-functional requirements or quality attributes).

18.2 Performance and Evaluation (P&E) Principles

Foundational Principles

FP1. Unity activities (i.e., reactions, self-changes, and transformations of others), independently or within collections [i.e., networks, groups, or (a)typical systems]:

- can be manifestations of natural, fundamental, basic or emerging laws, and
- can be driven by various objectives (i.e., agreed, expected, implicit, and unsettled), and,
- involve energy exchange (i.e., interactions and exposures), which,
- lead to some form of energy transformations that are physically perceivable through material energy (i.e., physically perceivable outputs), which,
- affect the energies of unities [i.e., physically (un)perceivable outcomes] in the proximal and distant environments.

FP2. Outcomes of outputs can trigger new unity and collection activities, including the creation and modification of objectives and fundamental or basic laws.

FP3. Outputs from activities become energy transmission sources and can be used as inputs to other activities.

---

[1] Campbell, R. D., & Bagshaw, M. (Michael). (2002). *Human performance and limitations in aviation* (3rd ed.). Blackwell Science. https://doi.org/10.1002/9780470774472.

[2] Blazevich, A. J. (2007). *Sports biomechanics: The basics: Optimising human performance.* Bloomsbury Publishing.

[3] Kramar, R., Bartram, T., & De Cieri, H. (2017). *Human resource management in Australia: Strategy, people, performance.* (5th ed.). McGraw-Hill Australia.

[4] Gawron, V. J. (2019). *Human performance and situation awareness measures* (3rd edition.). CRC Press, Taylor & Francis Group.

[5] Douglass, B. P. (2016). Agile systems engineering. Morgan Kaufmann.

[6] Griffin, P. M., Nembhard, H. B., DeFlitch, C., Bastian, N. D., Kang, H., & Muñoz, D. A. (2016). *Healthcare systems engineering.* Wiley.

[7] Nise, N. S. (2019). *Control systems engineering* (8th edition.). Wiley.

[8] Kossiakoff, A., Seymour, S. J., Flanigan, D. A., & Biemer, S. M. (2020). *Systems engineering: principles and practice* (3rd ed.). Wiley.

FP4. Performance & Evaluation, formally/structurally or not, regard all activities, outputs, and outcomes inevitably. This includes the decisions and actions related to the conception, design, manufacturing/implementation, delivery/deployment, use/maintenance and decommissioning/cancelling, and any other process related to products and services.

FP5. In their most abstract and high-level definitions:

- performance corresponds to measuring differences and gaps DaGs, and,
- evaluation corresponds to judging performance within the variabilities and disparities those DaGs were identified.

Performance Principles

PP1. The construct of performance refers to:

- unity activities and their outputs and outcomes (i.e., unity performance).
- outputs and outcomes of collections generated by their unities' activities (i.e., collective performance).

PP2. Whereas individual contributions can have significant and traceable impacts on collective performance, the latter:

- is more than just the sum of individual performances.
- cannot be fully traced to the performance of a single unity of the respective collection.

PP3. Physically perceivable unities and collections perform literally. Physically unperceivable constructs can perform only metaphorically.

PP4. The construct of performance represents the degree of meeting the metric criteria attached to objectives regarding activities, outputs, and outcomes of unities and collections, as applicable.

PP5. The metrics of objectives mainly refer to constructs that can be:

- physical and calculative—(quasi) quantitative, such as size, height, quantity, accuracy, reliability, affordability, and
- abstract and inferential—(quasi) qualitative, such as accessibility, adaptability, vulnerability, flexibility.

PP6. An ideal and complete performance concept requires:

- metrics that uniquely and exclusively correspond to each of the quantitative and qualitative aspects applicable to each of the objectives,
- units or scales that indisputably, uniquely, and exclusively correspond to each of the metrics employed,
- information about the context and conditions within which the unities and collections perform activities and generate outputs, and
- criteria that are used to evaluate performance by comparing metric results between unities or collections or against formal and informal standards.

Evaluation Principles

EP1. The construct of evaluation represents the judgement of performance or outcomes by considering the type of objectives applicable and pursued within a specific context and conditions.

EP2. When a performance concept cannot meet the requirements stated in principle PP6 above, it becomes an evaluation concept.

EP3. Evaluations from comparisons against standards are not directly and entirely valid for comparisons between unities or collections if these act in quite dissimilar contexts and under markedly different conditions.

Performance and Evaluation: Key Reflections and Actions

Reflections

- Performance and evaluation are interdependent constructs that provide insight into how individuals, teams, and systems achieve objectives. Both must be contextualised to ensure meaningful and accurate assessments.
- Performance Principles: Performance is influenced by material, cognitive, and affective energies interacting with environmental demands. Evaluating these interactions helps identify strengths, gaps, and opportunities for improvement.
- Evaluation Principles: Effective evaluation considers the context, resources, and objectives. It requires balancing qualitative and quantitative metrics to capture the full scope of performance.
- Performance and evaluation are dynamic processes that evolve with changing conditions. Periodic reassessment ensures relevance and alignment with goals.
- Focusing solely on outputs or outcomes without considering inputs and processes can lead to incomplete or misleading evaluations.

Actions

1. Contextualise Performance: Reflect on how material, cognitive, and emotional energies contribute to performance in your specific professional or organisational context. Tailor performance criteria to align with these factors.
2. Integrate Holistic Metrics: Combine qualitative and quantitative measures when evaluating performance. Ensure that evaluations account for inputs, processes, and outcomes to provide a complete picture.
3. Avoid Over-Simplification: Recognise the complexities of performance and avoid reducing evaluations to a single metric or score. Use multiple dimensions to capture nuanced insights.
4. Conduct Periodic Reassessments: Regularly review evaluation criteria and methodologies to ensure they remain relevant to evolving goals and contexts. Update them as necessary to reflect changing demands.
5. Link Evaluations to Growth: Use evaluation results to identify areas for improvement, celebrate achievements, and guide personal or organisational development strategies.

6. Promote Transparent Evaluation Practices: Foster trust by making evaluation processes clear, consistent, and inclusive. Encourage feedback from those being evaluated to enhance the fairness and accuracy of the process.

By adopting a balanced, contextualised, and dynamic approach to performance and evaluation, you can drive continuous improvement, foster trust, and achieve sustainable success in professional and organisational endeavours.

Part VI
Change Concepts

Chapter 19
Change Focus

19.1 General

In literature, change can be found with different synonyms, such as modification, alteration, improvement, and redesign. Change happens always when energy exchange occurs (Chapter 12), during which interactions and exposures (Chapter 10) result in and lead to reactions, self-change, and transformations of others (Chapter 11). Conversely, because energy exchange always occurs, there is always change. All unities, including our material and immaterial energy, and all constructs that we and other unities generate, are finite and changeable at the same time.

There are also several books dealing with the concept of 'change management', in its general application[1,2] or specific domains such as facilities[3] information services[4] projects[5] and the public sector.[6] Actually, 'change management' is a metaphorical and short expression corresponding to the deliberate and systematic effectuation on unities to influence or control the way they interact with other unities, their activity outputs, and the subsequent outcomes.

Considering the above, from a more deliberate perspective, any performance and evaluation P&E concept (Chapter 18) that results in unfavourable results or reveals opportunities not previously capitalised (i.e., it reveals differences and gaps), would expectedly lead to some form of change. Otherwise, any formal or more intuitive P&E activity would have no real aim and value.

---

[1] Cooke, R. D., & Pollitt, D. (2009). *Change management*. Emerald Group Publishing Limited.

[2] Murthy, C. S. V. (2007). *Change management*. Himalaya Pub. House Pvt. Ltd.

[3] Finch, E., & Finch, E. (2012). *Facilities change management*. Blackwell.

[4] Penfold, S., & St. Clair, G. (2013). *Change management for information services*. De Gruyter, Inc.

[5] Baca, C. (2005). *Project manager's spotlight on change management*. Harbor Light press.

[6] Baker, D. (2007). Strategic change management in public sector organisations. Chandos.

N. Karanikas, *Professional Generalism in a Hyper-specialised World*,
https://doi.org/10.1007/978-981-96-4039-3_19

In this part and chapter of the book, I cover the construct of change management as representative of an individual functioning as a change agent that influences or transforms other unities. This excludes mere reactions to incoming energy and adaptation and self-transformation of the change agent. I have already discussed those cases earlier in Chapter 11 and Chapter 17.

In change management, it is widely encouraged that before conceiving, designing, and implementing changes, we should understand and map the system. This means we should decipher how immaterial and material energy interact between human and other unities within the collections of interest. In parallel, we shall acknowledge that energy always flows and transforms (Chapter 11 and Chapter 12), resulting in inevitable differences and gaps DaGs between transmission and reception, plans and reality, drawings and products, and so on (Chapter 16).

We are all vulnerable to uncontrolled and unwelcome energy flowing and exchanged all around, but we all also need it. This does not mean we should obsessively worry about everything by trying to understand perpetually how our energy management can affect unities and interactions very far from us or deep down beneath us. Perhaps, it is ethically imperative to contemplate any indirect and butterfly effects of energy management on other unities and vice versa and decompose everything to elementary unities to understand what is happening in the microworld.

However, nobody has the necessary capability (i.e., capacity and ability) to perceive, process, and evaluate everything that has happened, is happening and could happen across all their exposures and interactions in various collections and contexts. As the saying goes, we should not miss the woods for the tree. Still, this does not mean we would abandon the tree and neglect its role in the woods.

The proposition I picture in Fig. 19.1, which is an enriched version of Fig. 10.1, largely aligns with what several books propose about direct and indirect management through lines of reporting[7,8,9] as well the concepts of micro-management and macro-management. These concepts correspond to the open and focussed sensing, respectively, and the various management types I presented in Chapter 13 and Chapter 14.

Notably, several management-related publications associate the levels which someone manages with the extent of control over resources through various governance forms (e.g., hierarchical or matrix management structures). Some publications discuss the ethical side of management and how people interact (e.g., trust and confidence between different parts of the organisation). While such approaches are valuable, this section supports them by factoring in human/unity capability and placing energy management on more pragmatic grounds.

---

[7] Schermerhorn, J., & Schermerhorn, J. (2017). *Management* (6th Asia–Pacific ed.). Wiley.

[8] Robbins, S., Bergman, R., & Coulter, M. (2018). *Management* (8th ed.). Pearson Australia.

[9] Samson, D., Donnet, T., & Daft, R. (2018). *Management* (6th Asia–Pacific ed.). Cengage Learning Australia.

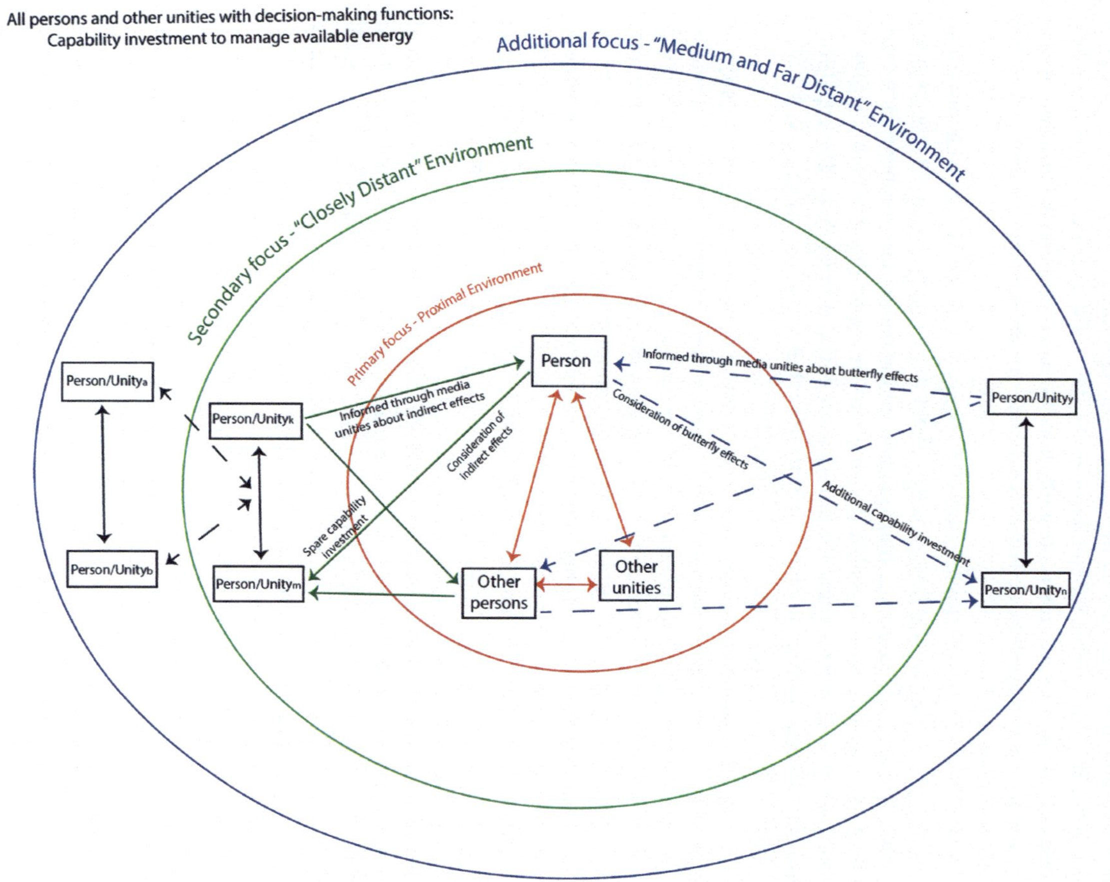

Fig. 19.1 Energy management focus

19.2 Proximal Environment

As I picture in Fig. 19.1, the proximal environment necessitates our primary focus. This is where we manage available energy through active interactions with other individuals and unities, including monitoring dormant interactions (Sect. 10.2). This is also something inevitable for any living unity. The difference lies on in the number of interactions and exposures each unity gets involved, which dictates how much energy it invests in respective activities (i.e., reaction, self-change and transformation of others—Sect. 11.1).

Ideally, because of the ripple effects of energy exchange beyond our proximal environment, we should also be concerned about the scope and focus of any changes and the influences of our energy management on the distant environment. However, the degree to which this is possible depends on our capability: the combination of usable energy UES capacity and the ability to mobilise it (Sect. 5.4). The capability construct extends from someone's UES to the whole envelope of energy: UES + energy possessed + energy trusted (Chapter 15).

In cases of a balanced energy state (i.e., energy demands $\approx$ energy supply), it is logical to expect that an individual will restrict their energy management within the proximal environment to avoid running into a negative balance, especially if this has occurred in the past, since conditions often change. If per unit of time the total energy balance is negative (Fig. 16.1), a person cannot be expected or asked to invest energy in contemplating anything additional or beyond the proximal environment. When someone suggests the opposite, then they explicitly or implicitly accept that the individual's outputs or outcomes will not meet the agreed objectives (Sect. 10.2) or expected objectives (Sect. 10.5) objectives (i.e., quantity, quality, and timeliness of outputs and outcomes).

Besides the responsibilities for own outputs and outcomes, formal and informal norms might suggest we must use some of our capability to ensure other people in the proximal environment can deliver as well. This can only happen successfully when a person has a positive sign in its total energy balance. Thus, ideally, energy management within the proximal environment is shared between what we are responsible for delivering as personal and tangible outputs and how we support others in the proximal environment to deliver. Such support must be part of the agreed and expected objectives.

Consequently, as professionals, besides directly managing their internal, possessed, and trusted energy, we are also expected to invest energy in:

- lowering or negotiating the demands imposed on others or ourselves (i.e., changes in output standards, delivery times, material energy to handle, total variability), and
- increasing the capability of ourselves and others (e.g., more physical, cognitive, or affective energies and external support).

The above becomes especially important when considering that within human collections characterised by agreed and expected objectives and being subject to continuous energy exchange and interdependencies, the outcomes of the 'outstanding' deliverables of one might clash with and be threatened by the 'substandard' outputs of others. For instance, a quality management professional might have secured very accurate and reliable equipment (i.e., outstanding deliverable by one professional), but the poorly designed and delivered training on using those (i.e., substandard deliverable by another professional) might threaten the outcome of enhancing product quality.

Indeed, while increasing others' capability and becoming energy sponsors (Sect. 12.4), we could deviate from the objectives towards delivering our own outputs. Despite seemingly odd, this could be acceptable or expected. My outstanding outputs, partially attributed to not helping others, might not even matter that much if others cannot benefit from what I generate and how I manage my energy. Conversely, over-investing in others might fully jeopardise fulfilling my own responsibilities to deliver. However, this does not mean we should aim for an equal split or any set boundaries in the distribution of energy. It depends on what responsibilities everyone has been assigned and has accepted through agreed and expected objectives.

For example, a professional in a management position has rather a few deliverables of their own to be concerned about (e.g., periodic reports, participation in meetings). Their primary focus must be the support of others to deliver agreed outcomes. Despite the above being a normative expectation of managers, it is not rare that such professionals get excessively absorbed by their own deliverables and neglect their principal responsibility for helping others deliver. On the flip side, an employee with high demands in energy management to generate outputs cannot neglect their prime responsibility for achieving agreed objectives and direct efforts to supporting others predominantly.

Within collections, we and others have different roles with different responsibilities, which jointly lead to the achievement of wider and local objectives and the delivery of respective outputs. Doers, thinkers, decision-makers, supporters, talkers, trainers, and every other role can be necessary in human collections. Each role is fully responsible and accountable for and trusted in managing different amounts and types of energy and achieving different parts or aspects of agreed objectives, expected objectives, and corresponding outputs (Chapter 15).

Ideally, we should not endorse into agreed and expected objectives when we cannot deliver them. We must not share energy with others when, because of various reasons, we have insufficient capability to deliver objectives we previously endorsed. Preferably, we should not waste time on extra tasks that distract us from our goals.

When the above do not occur, there are inescapable *energy use trade-offs*, a construct addressed by several professional contexts.[10,11,12,13] Those represent the diversion from or switching of energy management across various objectives when our capability does not suffice to deliver all corresponding outputs concurrently or within agreed criteria (i.e., expected timeframe, quantity, and quality).

People may not realise they lack the skills or experience needed. (e.g., overestimation of own capacities and abilities). Besides, they may not want to reject additional requests for reasons related to perceived or explicit pressures (e.g., family, social, organisational expectations), fear (e.g., stigmatisation, rejection, dismissal), and personal causes (e.g., perceived opportunities to self-grow and or activate dormant capabilities).

The equation is difficult to solve and there is no standard pathway to suggest, but each time we endorse agreed and expected objectives, we become responsible and accountable to achieve those unless we inform the trustees timely for any capability deficits and renegotiate some or all objectives. We should not also underestimate the role of affective energy and the fact that the total capability is something an individual experiences and not a directly measurable construct with standardised values.

The above means that, on the one hand, each of us might exercise differently our responsibilities for managing energy. On the other hand, the only way we could evaluate the total capability per person is to ask them and accommodate, influence, or direct if we are authorised, how they should manage energy. We must primarily focus on managing our own energy, how this contributes to different objectives, and how it affects humans and other unities around. You must improve and optimise your energy management before you move to influencing or enforcing how the others should manage their energy.

Assuming one is supremely confident they cannot improve their own energy management further in a given context, they could only influence, and possibly direct, how much energy other people and unities possess and are trusted to manage and in how many and what types of interactions an individual can get involved. This, of course, requires that those 'influencers' or 'directors' have been delegated with the respective authority.

For instance, court and police penalties can decrease/change possessed or trusted energy (e.g., confiscation of materials or assumed energy/monetary capital) or deprive/change active and dormant interactions through shrinking or altering the proximal environment, respectively (e.g., prison time, change of tasks). You can find similar analogies in the measures which people in different collections take in case of

[10] Dell'Ariccia, G., Martinez Peria, M. S., Igan, D. O., Awadzi, E. A., Dobler, M., & Sandri, D. (2018). *Trade-offs in bank resolution*. International Monetary Fund.

[11] Naik, V. K. (1993). *Multiprocessing: Trade-offs in computation and communication*. Springer New York. https://doi.org/10.1007/978-1-4615-3196-8.

[12] World, B. (2006). *Sustainable land management: Challenges, opportunities, and trade-offs*. World Bank Publications.

[13] Brownley, C. W. (2013). *Multi-objective decision analysis managing trade-offs and uncertainty*. Business Expert Press.

unexercised responsibility (e.g., measures employers can take when workers misbehave repeatedly; restrictions imposed by professional bodies on members who do not adhere to codes of conduct).

The cases of directing humans to invest their own energy for the benefit of a collection (e.g., community work) as compensation for past poor energy management is an intermediate influential step. Still, if the agreed goals are not met, someone may need to use the enforcement measures described above. Of note, we cannot be authorised to manage directly the energy owned by someone except for rare circumstances of direct threat (Chapter 15). Most importantly, as articulated above, before judging others' energy management, we must ensure we have done our best.

19.3 Distant Environment

If there is available capability, we can contemplate the indirect effects of energy exchange within our proximal environment on others in the distant environment. We can consider the 'closely distant' environment in Fig. 19.1 to ensure our energy management does not affect it negatively. We can also contemplate how 'closely distant' unities might influence our energy management outputs. We might receive information from this layer about negative or positive effects (e.g., news, reports). However, this does not mean we will action this information if we are consumed by managing our energy to honour the endorsed agreed and expected objectives in our proximal environment.

The sparer the capability and more the time we have, the more we can move to layers deeper than our proximal environment and outwardly. The narrower the proximal environment is and the fewer the objectives to be fulfilled are per unit of time, the more opportunities exist to consider the different layers of the distant environment and vice versa. This principle is often misused (or just 'used', subject to prevalent ethics) by some social engineering practices in different contexts, such as companies, organisations, and governance.

Indeed, 'social engineering' is not inherently negative if used to support positive development. However, social structures might often overwhelm people with demands and tasks to minimise their capabilities to look further than their proximal world and question, debate, and argue about what is imposed on them and the effects of the distant environment. More demands and tasks mean more energy and interactions to handle, a potentially negative-to-balanced capability, and perhaps an enduring concern about achieving agreed and expected objectives. This strategy works especially in cases that the humans targeted have a genuine interest in delivering and are committed and loyal to what they have consented.

In cases that no strict commitment is explicitly necessary (e.g., leisure time), the pathway to minimise opportunities of people to examine the distant environment is to bombard them with information, lock their attention into matters that stimulate positive emotions or cognitive mechanisms, usually to the direction the energy sender desires. In those cases, the 'social engineer' might increase the active interactions to the degree there is no capability available for looking deeper and further, while the 'engineered' persons enjoy their proximal environment as it aligns with their affective referents and stimulates their brains.

As such, to avoid 'being used', it is crucial for us to realise our capabilities, filter and use incoming energy towards honouring our responsibilities and caring about the proximal and 'closely distant' environments, and reflect on and adjust our referents so that we create space for thinking wider and deeper. Of course, you would wonder about our role as humans in our 'medium distant' and 'far distant' environments. You could justifiably ask whether we should be apathetic observers and not consider ripple effects.

First, it is crucial to note that the proximal and distant environments are not static constructs. From a physical perspective, family is the proximal environment when one spends with them time at home or on holidays. Whereas work in these settings becomes a distant environment physically, someone can be still thinking about work when being together with their family. Also, when someone spends time with club members, the club becomes their close environment, while their family and work become distant environments from a physical viewpoint. Yet, this does not mean that the individual does not invest energy in thinking about their family and work.

When driving a car, the co-passengers and other drivers on the road and the elements of the infrastructure and the physical environment constitute one's proximal environment. Their job and club become distant environments from a physical perspective. This does not mean that a person cannot have thoughts about their club mates and work colleagues when driving. Hence, environmental boundaries shift constantly, allowing flexible energy management to meet various needs.

Of course, there are distant environments which might never become proximal in the physical sense, like humans, communities, and physical environments we would never interact with directly. In those cases, we must be open to the information we receive about what is happening elsewhere. Indeed, we may need to adjust our energy use, considering how others might affect us or we might affect them.

The above applies to upwards and downwards directions, meaning the micro- and macro-levels relative to in which meso-level someone perceives themselves. Had we have additional capability available and are confident that we have managed our energy with successful outcomes for our proximal environment and consideration of our 'closely distant' unities and collections, we would be very welcome to invest energy in directly affecting and improving the entire world.

Second, if we would all sincerely care about effective energy management in our proximal environment and the mutual energy exchange effects within our 'closely distant' environment, then there would be a perfect situation where all humans in neighbouring environments would attend to each other, this leading to the proliferation of care to all directions. The problem, of course, is that several persons might not exercise this care and do not execute their responsibilities originating from the written and unwritten codes of each era and any collection with which they associate.

Usually, however, something other than an energy antagonist causes the above. Contrary, apart from the example of social engineering above, the norms and codes of various collections often conflict with each other. Achieving agreed and expected objectives may benefit the immediate environment but harm the distant environment or the future immediate environment.

Here is where affective energy will principally shape decisions and drive actions. Affective energy will inform which side, what environment, and which persons and unities to accommodate. Admittedly, we cannot work for two masters; we cannot satisfy two or more conflicting parties, unless we do not fulfil our objectives completely for either of those. In such conflicting and competing environments, if you wish to exercise your responsibilities entirely, you need to choose a side and, ideally, inform the others.

Change Focus: Key Reflections and Actions

Reflections

- Energy Management in Proximal Environments: Focus on managing your commitments and energy where you interact directly. This ensures stability and effectiveness within your immediate context.
- Adaptive Energy Allocation: Recognise that your proximal environment shifts with your roles and contexts. Adapt your focus as these environments change—whether moving between family, work, or community.
- Ripple Effects: While it is important to be aware of how your actions affect distant environments, prioritise sustainable, actionable steps aligned with your capability.
- Balancing Influence and Ethics: Understand the ethical implications of extending your influence. Act responsibly within areas you can directly affect and avoid overreaching into distant contexts without sufficient knowledge or control.
- Sustainability of Efforts: Attempting to manage everything simultaneously dilutes focus and effectiveness. True professionalism involves knowing your limits and expanding influence gradually and sustainably.

Actions

1. Prioritise Immediate Interactions: Use tools like priority matrices to identify and manage the most critical factors in your immediate environment. Address these with clarity and purpose.
2. Evaluate Resource Allocation: Regularly review how you distribute your time and energy. Ensure your focus aligns with personal, organisational, or professional objectives.
3. and Prepare for Ripple Effects: Maintain awareness of how local actions influence distant systems. Develop mechanisms to evaluate these impacts periodically and adjust accordingly.
4. Embrace Systems Thinking: Analyse your environment holistically. Use systems-thinking methods to understand interconnections and foster balanced decision-making.
5. Foster Adaptability: Change is dynamic. Cultivate a habit of reflection and flexibility, reassessing priorities and strategies as environments and circumstances evolve.

This integrated approach encourages professionals to focus energy where it is most impactful, aligning immediate responsibilities with broader, long-term goals. By doing so, you create a stable base from which to expand your influence effectively and ethically.

Chapter 20
Change Subjects

20.1 General

As I argued in Chapter 16, differences and gaps DaGs in most contexts carry negative connotations; it is not positive to experience gaps. On this line of thinking, there are several publications focussing more on explanations of negative than positive DaGs. Such publications argue that we do not fail to perform our activities and realise our responsibilities in a rando fashion. Instead, systemic factors external to us create and breed variabilities and disparities that affect our performance systematically[1,2] leading to DaGs.

Poor work environments, inadequate training, and incompetent and authoritative managers can be examples of systemic and systematic effects of variabilities and disparities, as applicable. These could threaten our energy states and overwhelm our internal defences, leading individuals and teams to underperform and, consequently, create differences and gaps.

Perspectives like the ones above suggest that we should not focus on changing the low-hanging fruits, black swans, or black sheep, meaning the humans who try their best to manage the energies available internally and externally. Instead, we should first fix the system, or more broadly any collection type (Chapter 10) within which humans function. This is the Good Individual—Bad System Concept (GIBSC).

The fundamental assumption is that individuals are most of the times energy sponsors (i.e., they use their energy for the benefit of others), and systems are occasionally energy antagonists (i.e., they use their energy to discomfort, even harm others) (Sect. 12.4). Therefore, the Good Individual—Bad System Concept (GIBSC) can sound appealing from an individual perspective, but uncomfortable from a system perspective. However, a narrow interpretation of GIBSC hides several contradictions.

[1] Shorrock, S. T., & Williams, C. (2017). *Human factors and ergonomics in practice: Improving system performance and human well-being in the real world*. CRC Press Taylor & Francis Group.

[2] Berlin C. & Adams C. (2017). *Production ergonomics: Designing work systems to support optimal human performance*. Ubiquity Press. https://doi.org/10.5334/bbe.

N. Karanikas, *Professional Generalism in a Hyper-specialised World*,
https://doi.org/10.1007/978-981-96-4039-3_20

20.2 Systems Versus Individuals

The Good Individual—Bad System Concept (GIBSC) primarily views humans as unities and the system as the environment. Thus, it implies we are not part of the system. If we were, any so-called systemic effects should include the outputs and outcomes of our interactions with the rest of the system unities. If we are part of a system, we should bear some responsibility and accountability for the systemic effects that influence our performance. This is a fact that relevant published positions do not touch explicitly.

Hence, a first paradox. Whereas, referring to a system, GIBSC sees humans predominantly as energy recipients and the environment as the hostile energy transmitter. The good humans and the rival system/environment, briefly speaking. Another paradox becomes evident when you look at the system that needs to be improved and wonder what is to be fixed.

If you want to fix a system, you must introduce, modify, suspend, or cancel its unities or their activities and interactions. Socio-technical system unities include other humans, technology (e.g., infrastructure, equipment, tools), products of unity activities (e.g., training, procedures, rules, records, documents, instructions), and the unities in the physical environment (e.g., wind, sun, flora and fauna, ground).

Changing others contradicts a central principle of GIBSC that individuals are not the problem and are always affected by negative external factors. As stated in Chapter 15, we have no authority over the energy contained in, possessed by, and trusted in other humans. Thus, any reference to changing other individuals can be only metaphorically accepted when used with the meaning of influence via energy transmission. Attempting to change other humans in the hostile system is not allowed by GIBSC, unless somebody views those individuals (e.g., colleagues, line managers, senior managers) as non-humans or humans isolated from any external factor. That would be incompatible with the world's constant change and the energy flow.

Then, if you want to fix technology, it means you must improve the processes through which technological artefacts are designed, manufactured, transported, installed, maintained, tested, etc. The problem is that all the above processes are human-constructed and human-dependent. Hence, if you want to improve those, it will mean again changing the humans involved in the lifecycle of technology unities. Once more, GIBSC does not allow this, and it is, therefore, not considered. The same applies to other human-generated artefacts like rules, standards, and common practices.

Hence, the only set of unities remaining to be changed is the physical environment. However, considering that we cannot fix the physical environment dramatically, we would rely on the ability of humans to protect themselves and others from adverse environmental conditions through various means. This would direct back to humans, who, according to GIBSC, should not be the change target. Therefore, there is nothing remaining to change, deliberate influence, or transform. Complicity is an area that deals with this phenomenon,[3] although it seems focussing more on negatives rather than positives.

Thus, if you accept GIBSC devoutly, every investigation and inquiry that targets to uncovering causes, finding explanations, and affording interpretations with the goal to improve, is carried in vain. Your performance and evaluation programmes are pointless and wasteful; although someone is always responsible and accountable, GIBSC prevents to address them.

The point is not whether we or any other entities should change. It is about the need that we maintain consistent language and strategies when discussing unities, collections, and environments, since their definition is arbitrary. We are unities within systems and systems themselves. The physical environment is a system that includes us as unities, and it is a unity if approached from a universal angle. We cannot isolate unities from their systems and systems from their unities. We cannot claim we underperform because of systemic factors only.

This is because we are parts of our collections and systems. In parallel, we are systems ourselves in which constantly immaterial and material energy interact. The message is that *humans are collective unities and unitised collections* at the same time. As I argued in Chapter 15, collective and individual responsibility and accountability do not cancel each other. In human collections, we all play a role in both successes and failures.

20.3 Systemic Versus Random

Another area GIBSC considers is whether the interplay between immaterial and material energy occurring within humans results from systemic or random factors. If systemic, it means there are some recurring or underlying pathogens (i.e., harmful exposures and interactions) that can be identified, and which should be eliminated. If random, GIBSC rarely recommends an action, although the logical change would be to guard the humans and other vulnerable unities against adversities that cannot be anticipated easily and could happen just once. As this implies the need to 'change' humans, it is not that acceptable by GIBSC (Sect. 20.2).

Deliberating about the systemic-random dipole does not matter much. That is because the concepts of randomly and systemically are immaterial constructs; these do not exist in absolute terms and physically. What could be labelled as systemic within a particular timeframe can be easily tagged as random in a far wider timeframe or system. A reoccurring technical failure of ones' device is systemic for the individual. However, if only a few customers experience this failure, the manufacturer may view it as a random occurrence.

Any cases of underperforming humans can be locally systemic but broadly random and vice versa. While it is possible for a worker to underperform consistently in their role, this could not be a systemic occurrence when looking at all employees and

[3] Mellema, G. (2016). *Complicity and moral accountability*. University of Notre Dame Press.

roles in the company. Conversely, each of several staff members could underperform occasionally, thus randomly, but the organisation could become concerned because of those plenty, locally random events of underperformance.

Also, humans often use the constructs of systemic and random to justify whether they will invest energy in supporting other humans from a cost–benefit perspective. When a small number of humans require assistance, this viewpoint almost treats them as insignificant parts of a system. For instance, when a disease is local (i.e., low prevalence and incidence rates), from a mere cost–benefit perspective fed by the construct of randomness, there would be little urgency to develop drugs to fight the disease. The decision could be different if the problem would become systemic, meaning the disease developing in many unities, the 'wider' system.

Similarly, several use frequency statistics to identify trends of problems in organisations and then justify whether to proceed with further investigations and improvements. This is fair considering the finite pool of resources, the investment of which needs to be prioritised. However, it also implies that bettering the conditions for only a few is not worthwhile.

You would wonder whether the above is ethical, but this is not the correct question to ask. There is no energy to cure everyone and rectify every problem per unit of time. Therefore, when it would be (un)ethical depends on how we view our role within the different collections we are part of and how we understand our influences on others.

We cannot control and command the material and immaterial energy and their interactions within other unities for ever. Maybe such control is superficially and temporarily possible, subject to the prevalent ethics (Chapter 1) and what is acceptable by a community at each time-point. However, those who tried did not thrive. Human history offers abundant examples of accidents attributed to overconfidence in controlling systems, overturned regimes who were controlling their citizens, and breakdowns of highly reliable technical systems that were controlling material energy flow and interactions.

It is only the energy available to us and each unity we possess we can manage, convert, diffuse, etc., and decide how much and what for to exchange. It is the responsibility of each of us to manage the energy and unities trusted in us. Thinking in terms 'systems versus unities' and 'systemic versus random' can be helpful, but be aware of their limitations.

Change Subjects: Key Reflections and Actions

Reflections

- Interconnected Systems and Individuals: Recognise that individuals and systems are inseparable. People contribute to, and are influenced by, the systems they inhabit.
- The Systemic-Random Spectrum: Issues classified as systemic or random are often perspectives shaped by scale and timeframe. What appears systemic at one level may seem random at another, affecting problem-solving and resource allocation.

- Limits of Control: Complete control over systems is unattainable due to their complexity. Professionals should focus on influence rather than overreaching for command.
- Ethical Considerations: Balancing systemic improvements with individual care requires ethical reflection. Professionals should prioritise actions that align with their sphere of influence while considering broader ripple effects.
- Energy Management: Effective change requires understanding the flow of material and immaterial energy within systems and allocating resources where they are most impactful.

Actions

1. Balance Systemic and Individual Efforts: Identify opportunities for systemic improvement while supporting individual growth and adaptation. Use tools like stakeholder analyses to map influences and roles.
2. Adopt a Systems Perspective: Apply systems-thinking methodologies to assess systemic barriers and identify opportunities for meaningful interventions.
3. Prepare for Uncertainty: Build resilience within your team or organisation to adapt to unpredictable, random elements. Develop contingency plans and foster a culture of adaptability.
4. Leverage Tools and Frameworks: Use methods like scenario planning and feedback loops to integrate systemic insights and proactively address random influences.
5. Reflect and Learn: Treat change initiatives as opportunities for learning. Regularly review outcomes, failures, and lessons to inform future strategies.

This integrated approach aligns systemic and individual responsibilities, enabling professionals to navigate change thoughtfully and effectively. By prioritising reflection and adaptable action, you can foster sustainable, ethical, and impactful transformations.

Chapter 21
Change Implementation

21.1 General

Having contemplated and possibly decided about the focus of change (Chapter 19) and the proper change subjects (Chapter 20) does not guarantee that a change will go ahead. Extending the concepts I presented in Sect. 16.3 to collections, there must be a decision by individuals or their collections (e.g., teams, groups, departments, organisations) whether to intervene (i.e., intervention criterion), which option is the most suitable (i.e., the suitability criterion) and how to operationalise the preferred option (i.e., optimisation criterion).

After processing trusted data, the intervention baseline interacts with the comprehension process to inform whether to act based on what could occur if we or our collection (in)act. If we do not act, the intervention baseline will stop future interactions and will not affect the expected result, because no one will contribute any energy. Inaction can mean ignoring a case completely or postponing further engagement with the situation. The intervention criterion examines whether the intervention is acceptable to the change agent(s) and others.

Importantly, considering solely the numbers of individuals or collections to identify minorities and majorities for the goal of pursuing a change might be insufficient. From the perspective of energy, it could be useful for you to consider not only the numbers of unities but also their useable energy state. This includes the energy possessed and entrusted in people, and the influence and power they have over the energies of others.

Therefore, a majority transcends mere headcount. *Majority for the purpose of change* is the combined index of:

- the energy state levels in the proximal environment that are directly and collectively managed by specific individuals or their collections (i.e., *total energy power*),
- the energy state levels in the distant environment that are indirectly and collectively influenced by specific individuals or their collections (i.e., *total energy influence*),

N. Karanikas, *Professional Generalism in a Hyper-specialised World*,
https://doi.org/10.1007/978-981-96-4039-3_21

Table 21.1 Change Intervention Typology: whether to implement a change

Change agent's perspective	Acceptable by the majority to intervene		Unacceptable by the majority to intervene	
	Acceptable by a minority to intervene	Unacceptable by a minority to intervene	Acceptable by a minority to intervene	Unacceptable by a minority to intervene
Acceptable to intervene	Harmonised accord	Excused accord	Excused discord	Isolative discord
Unacceptable to intervene	Isolative discord	Excused discord	Excused accord	Harmonised accord

Note Under the presumption of tendency of humans to conform with the majority

- the collective authority of specific individuals or their collections to manage the energy states of others in the proximal and distant environments (i.e., *total energy authority*).

Of note, literature often combines the constructs of energy power, influence, and authority under the umbrella term 'power'.[1,2,3] In the rest of this chapter, I define majority as over 50% of the combined index value above for each specific context. This is an arbitrary threshold I use for the combined index of total energy power, influence, and authority for the sake of explaining this chapter's concepts. In reality, the complex nature of these three components means different contexts might require different thresholds in determining what constitutes a majority.

21.2 Intervention, Suitability, and Optimisation

In Table 21.1 I present the typology of cases of acceptability and unacceptability of change interventions from the perspectives of others and the change agents. We all belong to many groups with differing opinions on interventions. The accord/discord categories in Table 21.1 assume we tend to conform with the majority[4], as I defined it in the section above. The particular typology also shows how individuals and collections can use majorities and minorities as excuses for inaction or to isolate themselves by choosing not to act against expectations.

If the change agents decide to intervene, then they would consider which change option and alternative to pursue based on projected option–outcome pairs. This could

[1] Paul, T. V., Wirtz, J. J., & Fortmann, M. (2004). *Balance of power: Theory and practice in the twenty-first century*. Stanford University Press.

[2] Chang, E. C. C., Kayser, M. A., & Linzer, D. A. (2010). *Electoral systems and the balance of consumer-producer Power*. Cambridge University Press.

[3] Kaufman, S., Little, R., & Wohlforth, W. (2007). Balance of power in world history. Palgrave Macmillan. https://doi.org/10.1057/9780230591684.

[4] Sunstein, C. (2019). *Conformity: The power of social influences*. New York University Press.

differ from what version of change majorities and minorities would support. The typology of intervention suitability in Table 21.2 follows the logic of the intervention decision above.

Last, the optimisation criterion will inform the manner the preferred change option will be executed with the aim to achieve the agreed or expected objectives and outcomes under, usually, the least energy investment and higher efficiency axiom (Chapter 5). It makes sense for people and groups to save energy when they have options. However, what seems efficient for the change agent(s) could look inefficient from the perspective of other individuals or collections. Hence, in line with the typology of change decision and suitability presented above, in Table 21.3 I propose the optimisation typology.

Table 21.2 Change Suitability Typology: what sort of change to pursue

Change agent's perspective	Change option acceptable by the majority		Change option unacceptable by the majority	
	Change option acceptable by a minority	Change option unacceptable by a minority	Change option acceptable by a minority	Change option unacceptable by a minority
Acceptable change option	Harmonised accord	Excused accord	Excused discord	Isolative discord
Unacceptable change option	Isolative discord	Excused discord	Excused accord	Harmonised accord

Note Under the presumption of tendency of humans to conform with the majority

Table 21.3 Change Optimisation Typology: how to implement the change selected

Change agent's perspective	Change pathway acceptable by the majority		Change pathway unacceptable by the majority	
	Change pathway acceptable by a minority	Change pathway unacceptable by a minority	Change pathway acceptable by a minority	Change pathway unacceptable by a minority
Acceptable change pathway	Harmonised accord	Excused accord	Excused discord	Isolative discord
Unacceptable change pathway	Isolative discord	Excused discord	Excused accord	Harmonised accord

Note Under the presumption of tendency of humans to conform with the majority

21.3 Conformity and Radicalisation

The categories I presented in Table 21.1 (i.e., whether to proceed with the change), Table 21.2 (i.e., what change option to pursue) and Table 21.3 (i.e., how to implement the change) are not mutually dependent or exclusive and are not subject to deterministic relationships. For example, someone can decide an intervention of 'Isolative discord' type (i.e., proceed with a change while almost everyone opposes it), move to an option possibly yielding outcomes of 'Harmonised accord' type (i.e., consider a change that almost everyone would accept) and adopt an implementation path of 'Excused accord' type (i.e., follow a change method the majority accepts).

Hence, assuming conformity as the prevalent norm, different combinations of the categories of those three typologies could signal different levels of conformity from the perspectives of majority and minority, different levels of radicalisation from the perspective of the change agent or, in general, any individual or collection deviating from any (in)formal norms. Under this lens, the constructs of majority and minority conformity and radicalisation could apply concurrently and complementarily to each other per unit of time and change agent. For instance, high conformity with the majority in a specific context would also mean low-to-average minority conformity and low radicalisation.

To illustrate the above, in Tables 21.4, 21.5, and 21.6 I present conceptual scales of the majority conformity, minority conformity, and radicalisation spectrums, correspondingly. Real change is not always as linear as these scales suggest. While those scales are not supported by theoretical justifications, I introduce them only as vehicles for facilitating the understanding of the positions and concepts I unfold in this section.

Table 21.4 Majority conformity spectrum

Intervention	Suitability															
	Harmonised accord (HA)				Excused accord (EA)				Excused discord (ED)				Isolative discord (ID)			
	Optimisation															
	HA	EA	ED	ID	HA	EA	ED	ID	HA	EA	ED	ID	HA	EA	ED	ID
Harmonised accord (HA)	9	8	7	6	8	7	6	5	7	6	5	4	6	5	4	3
Excused accord (EA)	8	7	6	5	7	6	5	4	6	5	4	3	5	4	3	2
Excused discord (ED)	7	6	5	4	6	5	4	3	5	4	3	2	4	3	2	1
Isolative discord (ID)	6	5	4	3	5	4	3	2	4	3	2	1	3	2	1	0

Table 21.5 Minority conformity spectrum

Intervention	Suitability															
	Harmonised accord (HA)				Excused accord (EA)				Excused discord (ED)				Isolative discord (ID)			
	Optimisation															
	HA	EA	ED	ID	HA	EA	ED	ID	HA	EA	ED	ID	HA	EA	ED	ID
Harmonised accord (HA)	0	1	1	0	1	3	2	1	1	2	3	1	0	1	1	0
Excused accord (EA)	1	3	2	1	3	5	4	3	2	4	4	2	1	3	2	1
Excused discord (ED)	1	2	3	1	2	4	4	2	3	4	5	3	1	2	3	1
Isolative discord (ID)	0	1	1	0	1	3	2	1	1	2	3	1	0	1	1	0

Table 21.6 Radicalisation spectrum

Intervention	Suitability															
	Harmonised accord (HA)				Excused accord (EA)				Excused discord (ED)				Isolative discord (ID)			
	Optimisation															
	HA	EA	ED	ID	HA	EA	ED	ID	HA	EA	ED	ID	HA	EA	ED	ID
Harmonised accord (HA)	0	1	2	3	1	2	3	4	2	3	4	5	3	4	5	6
Excused accord (EA)	1	2	3	4	2	3	4	5	3	4	5	6	4	5	6	7
Excused discord (ED)	2	3	4	5	3	4	5	6	4	5	6	7	5	6	7	8
Isolative discord (ID)	3	4	5	6	4	5	6	7	5	6	7	8	6	7	8	9

From the perspective of majority conformity, the more the accord with the majority, the stronger the conformity. Hence, in Table 21.4 I adopt an arbitrary 0–9 scale with the maximum level 9 assigned to cases of Harmonisation Accord (HA) across all three variables (i.e., intervention, suitability, and optimisation) and the minimum level 0 in the case of Isolated Discord (ID) across the three variables. In the rest of the cases, the scale follows a decreasing scale pattern from harmonisation to discord across the variables.

Minority conformity gets a value of 0 in the cases of extreme accord and extreme discord (Table 21.5). It is hard to debate the existence of a minority when everyone is either completely unified or completely independent in their focus. This means that the concept of minority applies wherever there is no Excused Accord (EA) or Excused Discord (ED) in at least one of the three variables of intervention, suitability, and optimisation.

Thus, minority conformity primarily floats in the regions of Excused Accord (EA) or Excused Discord (ED) as the individual or collection of interest can agree with part of the majority views while maintaining different positions elsewhere. Thus, minority conformity gets its maximum value 5 when having 3 EAs or EDs and its lowest value 0 when there is no EA or ED.

Contrary, from the viewpoint of radicalisation, the more disagreement there is with the majority or minority, the more radical the individual becomes. Hence, in Table 21.6 I also adopt an arbitrary 0–9 scale with the maximum level 9 assigned to cases of Isolated Discord (ID) across all three variables (i.e., intervention, suitability, and optimisation) and the minimum level 0 in the case of Harmonisation Accord (HA) across the three variables. In the rest of the cases, the scale follows an increasing value pattern, from harmonisation to discord across the variables.

It is, therefore, interesting to observe the cross-sections of the intervention, suitability, and optimisation categories from the lenses of each construct. For instance, if someone considers the case of Excused Accord (Intervention)—Excused Discord (Suitability)—Isolated Discord (Optimisation), they could label it as:

- 'considerably low majority conformity' to proceed with a change (i.e., level 3 in the scale of 0–9),
- 'lower than average minority conformity' (i.e., level 2 in the scale 0–5) regarding the type of change, and
- 'considerably high radicalisation' (i.e., level 6 in the scale 0–9) for the method of implementing change.

Although these scales are conceptual and not mean to introduce any measurements, they demonstrate how possible differences and gaps DaGs from norms and prevalent practices can be seen from different view angles, this time at the collective level and not within the individual as covered in Chapter 16. The typologies and scales above are useful for managing stakeholders[5,6,7] and can help plan and implement changes that involve or affect various individuals and groups.

If you prefer a moderate approach, your changes will float in the centre of the scales by satisfying majorities, minorities, and self/change agents in different aspects of intervention, suitability, and optimisation. For example, a construction project could:

- secure the agreement of most sponsors and affected communities to proceed (harmonised accord HA—intervention), then,

---

[5] Wasieleski, D. M. (2017). *Stakeholder management*. Emerald Publishing Limited.

[6] Dahl Rendtorff, J., & Bonnafous-Boucher, M. (2023). *Encyclopedia of stakeholder management*. Edward Elgar Publishing.

[7] Freeman, R. E. (2010). *Strategic management: A stakeholder approach*. Cambridge University Press.

- adopt the project features suggested by a minority (e.g., expert group) but not endorsed by the majority (excused accord EA—suitability), and,
- execute the project based on techniques and practices the construction company has developed although those have not been widely tested in other projects or accepted by the industry (isolated discord ID—optimisation).

In the fictitious case above, the professionals acting as change agents would achieve 4/9 (44.45%) majority conformity, 1/5 (20%) minor conformity, and 5/9 (55.6%) radicalisation. To keep the minority more engaged and interested, professionals could, for instance, opt for excused discord in optimisation, leading to 3/9 (33.3%) majority conformity, 3/5 (60%) minority conformity, and 4/9 (44.45%) in radicalisation.

This example illustrates again the trade-offs and relativeness when evaluating changes. You should always consider the context of change before deciding how much you want to conform or radicalise. Each change variable (i.e., intervention, suitability, optimisation) can have different stakeholders that contribute to majority or minority groups. For instance, the decision to intervene can include the change targets and the ones having authority over the resources. The change suitability aspects could involve subject matter experts and representatives of various groups of the change targets, and change optimisation could include professional bodies, regulators, and technical specialists.

Change Implementation: Key Reflections and Actions

Reflections

- Redefining Majority Influence: The concept of the majority in change management transcends numbers. It involves assessing stakeholders based on energy power (resource management), influence (possible effects), and authority (formal decision-making roles). This broader perspective aids in identifying true drivers of change.
- Decisions in Implementation: Change implementation revolves around three core decisions:
- Intervention: Whether to initiate change.
- Suitability: What type of change is most appropriate.
- Optimisation: How to execute the chosen change effectively.
- These decisions require navigating the perspectives of both majority and minority stakeholders to maintain balance and ensure inclusivity.
- Balancing Conformity and Radicalisation: Success lies in strategic combinations of conformity and radicalisation across intervention, suitability, and optimisation. This approach fosters innovation while respecting the existing system and stakeholders.
- Ethical Considerations in Change: Change implementation is often fraught with ethical dilemmas. Professionals must weigh majority conformity against minority interests, ensuring equity and sustainable outcomes without succumbing to oversimplistic resistance-versus-acceptance models.

Actions

1. Map Stakeholder Influence: Create detailed maps of stakeholder energy power, influence, and authority. Use this information to strategise intervention points and engage effectively with key players.
2. Tailor Change Decisions: Break down decisions into intervention, suitability, and optimisation. Analyse each component independently, adjusting approaches based on stakeholder dynamics and contextual requirements.
3. Adopt a Mixed Approach: Combine majority conformity with strategic radicalisation to introduce innovation while maintaining stakeholder alignment. Use conceptual frameworks to evaluate when and where to deviate from norms.

This integrated approach to change implementation bridges the gap between planning and execution. By navigating stakeholder dynamics thoughtfully and balancing innovation with established norms, professionals can foster sustainable and impactful transformations.

Connecting the Dots

Understanding our systems, groups, and networks, within and beyond professional contexts, is a lifelong journey at conscious and subconscious levels. We all analyse past events and present circumstances to make choices and prepare for the immediate, short-term, and long-term future. Making sense of *own world* at each time-point is an inescapable, natural, and unstoppable process. This enables us to dive deeper into our disciplines and describe and analyse phenomena in more detail through own skilful lens. We can then explain, evaluate, offer, review, and adjust solutions based on our gained knowledge and expertise.

However, it is also important that any professional journey includes making sense of *the world*. This book can support you in that as it covers broad but highly important concepts. Regularly using these concepts will help you see how they connect and create a better, more complete worldview. Developing and maintaining *Professional Generalism* is a purposeful path where you should diligently invest time and energy in searching, identifying, processing, and glueing what you know, or you think you know, with what others know or claim they know, and how all those can come together and underpin your professional choices and activities.

It is important for you to understand how your expertise fits into the bigger picture and how it affects others. You should harness the energy, material and immaterial, of yourself, and other persons and unities in the most unbiased manner possible. Certainly, embracing the concepts and principles I included in this book also requires an open mind and an open heart, as many of the statements in the book may not be perceived as mainstream. This is one of this book's strength, yet considerable opposition persists, even with our promotion of tolerance and diverse viewpoints, especially recently.

It is imperative that you comprehend that your expertise might not be enough or even proper to gain insights and implement changes and solutions. During this journey, you can acknowledge and respect the many versions of the world that exist for each one you interact with directly and indirectly. The best compliment you can offer to others as a professional is 'I am looking forward to learning from you'.

N. Karanikas, *Professional Generalism in a Hyper-specialised World*,
https://doi.org/10.1007/978-981-96-4039-3

Other people's views of the world can agree with, add to, disagree with, or simply exist alongside our own. Professional Generalism allows you to view matters from different perspectives, bringing new insights to your work. It gives you the opportunity to expand your horizons and challenge your comfort zone. However, Professional Generalism should not become an obsession or a concern. It does not have to take a very specific, systematic, and structured form, like the rigour and rigidness we sometimes seek in our professions.

Instead, take any chance you can get to evaluate your professional position in relation to others. It is about realising what you and others have discovered, how you and others believe things could relate to and connect with each other, what more is necessary, what is missing, etc. This would be a purposeful break from daily professional duties that often demand technical expertise. By investing time in supra-disciplinary personal development and growth, you can discover new possibilities. Those could benefit you as a professional generalist and everyone around.

Professional Generalism Practice Guidance

This section offers discipline-agnostic guidance, drawing on this book's Professional Generalism concepts. The guidance can apply to any professional activity and any development stage of products or services. It can support your professional plans, decision, deeds, and judgments, and in general, when you decide and act.

Of note, the phases and items I list below do not apply universally and always in all professional contexts. You can use them at any level of abstraction or detail of unities and collections and their inputs, processes, outputs, and outcomes. Therefore, this guidance is not a compliance checklist.

Not actioning any of its items does not indicate you are not 'generalist' enough. Still, the more you consider the phases and the items below when circumstances allow and resources are available, the more your professional practice will 'make sense' to others involved and affected directly and indirectly, and the more inclusive and holistic your practice will become over time.

Phase-agnostic principle: Sense respectfully, process critically, embrace contextually

Activity	Key actions	Book chapter
Phase A: Preparation		
Acknowledge, identify or revisit underlying ethics that will define the scope of your practice and the overall expectations from self and others and about any resultant actions	• Move beyond absolutist ethical positions and actively seek ways to reconcile different ethical perspectives in your professional practice based on the context • Challenge your assumptions about objectivity by actively seeking diverse perspectives and acknowledging the limitations of your viewpoints • Examine how you allocate resources and support • Ensure your approach to building capabilities promotes equity rather than reinforcing existing advantages • Regularly re-examine your professional ethical principles in light of changing contexts, while maintaining core principles of fairness and effectiveness	Chapter 1
Scope your practice and actions	• Focus on understanding and directing the flow of energy (material, cognitive, and affective) within your sphere of influence—this means shifting from 'How do I manage these people?' to 'How do I best allocate and direct available energy to achieve our objectives?' • Develop your capability for both open and focussed sensing—do not let your focus on specific targets blind you to broader environmental changes • Recognise when you are defaulting to either purely analytical or purely synthetic processing, and consciously consider whether the situation's urgency and environmental conditions warrant a different approach • Remember that abstract constructs like safety, quality, or performance cannot be directly managed—only the energy directed towards achieving these outcomes can be managed—focus on concrete actions and energy allocation rather than abstract goals	Chapter 13

(continued)

(continued)

Activity	Key actions	Book chapter
Endorse, modify, or create definitions that link and frame the physically perceivable and unperceivable elements within and outside the scope of your practice	• Seek explicit definitions in professional communications—do not always assume a shared understanding of terms and concepts • Use clear definitions when designing and implementing solutions but be ready to employ appropriate metaphors when explaining concepts to different audiences, while remaining mindful of different cultural contexts • When engaging in debates about definitions, do not just criticise—contribute constructively by offering clear alternatives and supporting arguments • When working with abstract concepts, explicitly clarify their intended meaning within the specific context	Chapter 2
Employ, modify or create classifications to simplify the scope of your practice and actions, if and as necessary	• Before using any classification system or label, pause and reflect on whether you are using it as a tool for understanding and improvement, or unconsciously using it to create barriers and judgments • Identify and question the mental models, frameworks, and 'truths' you take for granted in your work. Consider how these might limit your perspective or decision-making • While metaphors and simplifications are valuable communication tools, explicitly acknowledge their limitations and the complexity they might be masking • Create spaces where different perspectives and approaches are valued, remembering that your professional 'truths' are constructs that may not hold the same meaning or value for others	Chapter 3
Phase B: Identification		

(continued)

(continued)

Activity	Key actions	Book chapter
Identify and define current and new types of collections and current and new objectives of individuals/unities and collections	• Explicitly define boundaries and level of focus—do not assume everyone shares the same perspective on where a collection/system begins and ends • Look beyond formal, agreed-upon objectives—identify and consider expected and assumed objectives that might influence behaviours and decisions—be particularly mindful of unspoken assumptions that could impact collaboration or create misalignments in expectations • Recognise that objectives transform as they move through the organisation- create mechanisms to verify relative alignment and understanding • Challenge default categorisations of organisational arrangements—assess whether it is about a true system, a network or a group so that you can better manage interactions and expectations	Chapter 10
Identify and define roles of individuals/unities in their collections and their proximal and distant environments	• Actively seek clarifications about expectations, provide feedback on challenges, and share ideas about resource management before issues arise • Consciously evaluate how you manage not just your own resources, but also those trusted in you by others, and consider how your actions affect those who receive energy through your management decisions • Embrace your dual role as both a 'responsibility reminder' and an 'accountability guardian' in your professional practice • Help others understand their responsibilities when they may be unaware, and hold others accountable when they knowingly mismanage resources • Acknowledge that while you cannot monitor all potential impacts of your energy management, you can build trust through consistent adherence to established (in)formal codes and open communication about challenges—make it a practice to review regularly and understand the codes governing your professional responsibilities	Chapter 15

(continued)

(continued)

Activity	Key actions	Book chapter
Identify the current and anticipated needs and desires any objectives fulfil for each individual/unity	• Look for opportunities to become an 'energy sponsor' by purposefully investing your resources—whether material, cognitive, or emotional—to benefit others without expecting immediate returns • Remember that what appears antagonistic in the short term might have positive long-term intentions, and what seems beneficial today could have hidden future costs • When making professional decisions, consciously weigh how your energy investments will affect both your immediate professional circle and the broader ecosystem of stakeholders in your distant environment • Rather than focussing solely on short-term outcomes in your proximal environment, consciously assess how your actions might affect those in your distant environment and over extended timeframes	Chapter 12
Identify activities of each individual/unity that lead to achieving objectives	• Challenge yourself to distinguish between automatic reactions and adaptations and conscious transformations in your professional practice • Respect the stochastic nature of human interactions and avoid applying purely deterministic models when dealing with human behaviour • Embrace the complexity of both material and immaterial energy exchanges in your approach to change management • Ensure you understand both your own energy state and that of those you aim to influence and obtain their informed consent for any transformation process • When implementing changes that affect others, invest the necessary energy in understanding the complete picture—including both observable and unobservable aspects	Chapter 11

(continued)

(continued)

Activity	Key actions	Book chapter
Identify the types of energies and their interactions currently/would be involved in the activities identified above	• Treat all three forms of energy—material (physical), cognitive (mental), and affective (emotional)—as an interconnected system that requires balanced attention and management • Make conscious decisions about when to deploy energy, ensure you maintain adequate reserves and consider creating an 'energy budget' that helps you track and optimise energy allocations into activated (currently in use), passive (protective), and reserved • Anticipate how decisions and interactions will affect future energy states • Acknowledge that energy states influence and are influenced by others in the environment	Chapter 5
Identify and consult with concepts and empirical evidence from relevant scientific fields	• Recognise and transcend disciplinary boundaries—challenge yourself to move beyond your primary field's concepts and methods • Critically evaluate whether any numerical measurement is appropriate and meaningful • Integrate multiple analytical perspectives—deliberately combine insights from different scientific approaches • Be explicit about the limitations of whatever analytical approach you are using in your professional practice	Chapter 8
Phase C: Criteria and Sources		
Identify, modify, and create metrics based on energy types and parameters and other constructs, and adopt, modify, and develop respective performance and evaluation criteria	• Before attempting to measure performance, ensure you are dealing with physically perceivable elements. If you cannot physically perceive it, shift your focus to evaluation rather than measurement • When assessing collective performance, resist the urge to trace it back to individual contributions—instead, develop metrics that genuinely capture group-level outcomes • Build complete performance frameworks by establishing three essential elements: unique metrics that correspond to your objectives, clear units/scales for measurement, and well-defined contextual conditions • When comparing performance across different contexts or conditions, pause before making direct comparisons—first verify whether the contexts are similar enough to make such comparisons valid	Chapter 18

(continued)

(continued)

Activity	Key actions	Book chapter
Identify and acknowledge advantages and limitations of performance and evaluation choices	• Break down the artificial hierarchy between scientific approaches in your professional practice—actively seek to understand and apply insights from multiple scientific domains when addressing complex problems • Foster collaborations between professionals from different scientific backgrounds • Look beyond linear thinking and basic statistical approaches when dealing with social and organisational phenomena • Integrate different types of scientific knowledge in your professional practice—use this integrated understanding to develop more effective and sustainable solutions	Chapter 9
Acknowledge and differentiate knowledge and information sources available for implementing, assessing, and evaluating the practice	• Recognise that communications are stories carrying versions of truth—ensure you acknowledge the limitations of your perspective rather than presenting it as absolute truth • Actively distinguish between what constitutes stored information versus experiential knowledge • In high-stakes situations, strive to minimise story gaps by gathering multiple perspectives and sources of information, while accepting that some gaps will always exist • Transform critical information into knowledge by creating opportunities for direct experience—move beyond just reading and discussing to actually practising and experiencing key concepts	Chapter 6
Acknowledge and improve the trustworthiness of sources used	• Avoid the common trap of blindly accepting something just because it comes from a trusted source or because it has been repeated many times • Challenge your automatic trust responses in professional settings by recognising when you are making assumptions based solely on source reputation. Evaluate the actual content, especially for critical decisions • When dealing with intangible concepts, recognise the limitations of measurement and validation • Do not dismiss industry practices just because they lack theoretical validation, nor reject academic insights just because they have not been extensively tested in practice	Chapter 7
Phase D: Analysis and Action		

(continued)

(continued)

Activity	Key actions	Book chapter
Establish and maintain management consistency	• Before implementing changes, ensure that your information gathering matches the scale of your intended interventions—if you plan to make organisation-wide changes, make sure you are gathering data at the organisational level—if you are focussing on individual unities, ensure you have unity-specific data • Regularly audit your management practices to identify misalignments between how you monitor (sensing), analyse (processing), and respond to situations (actions) • When planning major changes, consider not just the theoretical feasibility but also the practical energy requirements—physical, cognitive, and emotional—needed for implementation at all levels • Examine whether you are applying double standards to different organisational levels, particularly regarding how deviations are handled. If you allow yourself to make intuitive decisions, consider whether it is fair to require purely analytical approaches from others	Chapter 14
Identify, measure, and anticipate variabilities and disparities (VaDs) and gaps and differences (DaGs)	• Rather than attempting to eliminate all DaGs in performance, recognise them as natural and sometimes beneficial aspects of professional life—focus on understanding and managing VaDs rather than aiming for perfect consistency • Actively monitor your material, cognitive, and affective energy states to better understand when you are best positioned for different types of activities—from simple reactions to transformative actions • When developing support mechanisms in professional environments, ensure they can adapt to both individual differences and temporal variations in needs • Avoid one-size-fits-all solutions. Instead, create adaptable resources that can serve different energy states and requirements • Move beyond simple cause and effect assumptions about performance and energy states—recognise that, while energy states influence our capabilities, they do not definitively determine outcomes	Chapter 16

(continued)

(continued)

Activity	Key actions	Book chapter
Interpret and contextualise DaGs based on VaDs	• When analysing DaGs in your professional environment, resist selective focus. Examine all types of DaGs at each level to ensure comprehensive understanding and effective solutions • Recognise that negative differences and gaps are not inherently harmful—actively engage with them as opportunities for growth and innovation while ensuring appropriate support systems are in place to prevent system collapse • When evaluating DaGs, always consider both individual and collective perspectives—engage with everyone involved to understand how different stakeholders experience and are affected by these gaps • Foster environments that balance challenge and support—create conditions where people can experience and learn from manageable negative DaGs while receiving adequate support to develop resilience, avoiding both the extremes of constant comfort and overwhelming difficulty	Chapter 17
(In)act on your analysis results	• Focus first on delivering your direct responsibilities and supporting those with whom you interact directly—only expand your focus to more distant environments when you have genuinely positive capability • When accepting new responsibilities or objectives, carefully evaluate whether you have the capability to deliver them without compromising existing commitments—be prepared to decline or renegotiate when your capability assessment indicates overreach • Recognise when your environments shift (e.g., from work to family) and consciously realign your energy management to match the needs and expectations of your current proximal environment—be present where you are • Before attempting to influence or enforce how others manage their energy, ensure you have optimised your own energy management—your credibility in affecting others starts with demonstrating effective self-management	Chapter 19

(continued)

(continued)

Activity	Key actions	Book chapter
	• When planning change initiatives, acknowledge that people are both agents and subjects of change—they are simultaneously part of the system and systems themselves • Move beyond binary classifications of problems as either systematic or random—instead, examine issues through multiple perspectives and timeframes to develop more comprehensive change strategies • Rather than attempting to command and control all aspects of change, focus on understanding and working with the natural dynamics of energy exchange within your systems • When allocating resources for change initiatives, carefully consider the ethical implications of prioritising systemic versus localised issues—develop approaches that balance practical constraints with the responsibility to address both broader and individual needs	Chapter 20
	• Before implementing any change, assess the complete landscape of influence by looking beyond simple numerical majorities—map out who holds direct power, indirect influence, and formal authority in your change context • Break down your change implementation decisions into three distinct components—whether to intervene, what option to pursue, and how to execute—and evaluate each component separately to develop a more nuanced implementation strategy • Do not feel constrained to maintain the same level of conformity or innovation across all aspects of your change initiative—strategically mix different approaches to intervention, suitability, and optimisation based on your specific context and stakeholders • When planning change implementation, actively consider the trade-offs between majority conformity, minority interests, and innovation needs—aim to find a balance that serves the change objectives while maintaining necessary stakeholder support	Chapter 21

The manufacturer's authorised representative in the EU is Springer Nature Customer Service Centre GmbH, Europaplatz 3, 69115 Heidelberg, Germany. If you have any concerns regarding our products, please contact ProductSafety@springernature.com

Printed and bound by CPI Group (UK) Ltd, Croydon, CR0 4YY
01/10/2026
02225942-0001